The Taoist Body

The Taoist Body

Kristofer Schipper

Translated by
Karen C. Duval

Foreword by
Norman Girardot

UNIVERSITY OF CALIFORNIA PRESS

Berkeley / Los Angeles / London

First published in 1982 as *Le corps taoïste* by Librairie Arthème Fayard, Paris

University of California Press
Berkeley and Los Angeles, California

University of California Press
London, England

Copyright © 1993 by The Regents of the University of California

Library of Congress Cataloging-in-Publication Data
Schipper, Kristofer Marinus.
    [Corps taoïste. English]
    The Taoist body / Kristofer Schipper ; foreword by Norman
Girardot.
        p.   cm.
    Translation of: Le corps taoïste.
    Includes bibliographical references and index.
    ISBN 0-520-08224-9 (alk. paper)
    1. Taoism.   I. Title.
    BL1920.S2813   1993
    299'.514—dc20   93-28999
                                                         CIP

Printed in the United States of America

    3 4 5 6 7 8 9

Contents

Foreword

Kristofer Schipper and the Resurrection of the Taoist Body

The Way that is sagely within and kingly without has fallen into darkness and is no longer clearly perceived, has become shrouded and no longer shines forth. . . . The scholars of later ages have unfortunately never perceived the purity of Heaven and earth, the great body of the ancients, and "the art of the Way" in time comes to be rent and torn apart by the world.

Chuang Tzu

It is ironic that the rediscovery, if not the full resuscitation, of the Taoist body—the "great body of the ancients" which was the cosmic corporeality of heaven, earth, and humankind—has come about through the work of a scholar of this later age. This turn of events is particularly surprising when it is recalled that in this later age, this dark modern era, the original country of the Tao has officially renounced its ancient ways in favor of an alien dialectic. In this sense, the "art of the Tao"—which depended on the primordial visions of such ancient Chinese wayfarers as Lao Tzu and Chuang Tzu and the later revelations of the "Celestial Masters"—has surely been rent and torn apart by the world. It was, after all, the Chinese Cultural Revolution that sought to obliterate every remnant of the "superstitious" past.

Having fallen into an extreme darkness within the land of its birth, as well as having been largely maligned by Christian missionaries and almost wholly ignored by traditional Chinese dynastic historians and Western scholars, the ancient way of the Taoist religion has, nevertheless, continued—albeit shrouded, dispirited, and germinal—at the margins of the contemporary Chinese world. Hidden amidst the everyday ways of Chinese people peripheral to both the People's Central Kingdom and the modern industrial world of the Chinese diaspora, the insular corporation of the Taoist religion has started to reveal itself publicly to the whole world just when it seemed that it had totally expired. The special, though perhaps fitting, curiosity of this unexpected occurrence is that the public manifestation of the Taoist religion in the modern world is due to the fortuitous discoveries of Kristofer Schipper, a young Dutch scholar trained in Paris who had been working and living on the island of Taiwan in the 1960s.

While acknowledging the importance of Japanese scholarship and pioneering French scholars like Henri Maspero, Max Kaltenmark, and Rolf Stein, it may be said that the actual study of the Taoist religion, as distinct from the scholarly fetish for the "philosophical Taoism" of Lao Tzu and Chuang Tzu, is almost entirely an accomplishment of the latter half of the twentieth century and stems in large measure from Kristofer Schipper's findings in Taiwan in the sixties. For this reason, it is worthwhile recounting some of the story of Schipper's initial involvement with, and public unveiling of, the living Taoist religion. It is, moreover, a story that provides some of the essential background for appreciating the empathetic quality, authoritative nature, and synthetic breadth of Schipper's *The Taoist Body*. Indeed, it may be said that *The Taoist Body,* most of all, represents the cumulative digest of Schipper's more than twenty years of experience with, and reflection on, the Taoist vision of life.

A number of semi-popular works on the Taoist religion that are written from the standpoint of Western scholarship have appeared in recent years (notably, Isabelle Robinet's *Méditation taoïste,* 1979, and John Lagerwey's *Taoist Ritual in Chinese Society and History,* 1987; there are, of course, several important Japanese introductory works by Yoshioka Yoshitoyo and Kubo Noritada), but they have been focused on particular aspects of the tradition and, either directly or indirectly, are indebted to the interest in Taoist studies stimulated by Schipper's original experiences in Taiwan and his ongoing work in Paris. It is in this sense that Schipper's *The Taoist Body* is still the only work in any language that can be considered a general guide to the actual practice, sociological significance, and symbolic meaning of the Taoist liturgical tradition.

To start at the beginning, it may simply be said that the earliest phases of Kristofer Schipper's scholarly career in Paris were conventionally focused and respectably distinguished. Thus, after an initial concern with Oriental art, he turned in 1958 to the study of the history of Chinese religions under the tutelage of Max Kaltenmark and Rolf Stein, two great exponents of the French sinological passion for technical precision and interpretive breadth (primarily from the sociological perspective of Marcel Granet and *L'Année Sociologique*). During this same period at the Ecole Pratique des Hautes Etudes, he was also influenced by a number of brilliant French scholars in related fields—especially Paul Demieville in Buddhology, Jacques Gernet in Chinese history, André Leroi-Gourhan in ethnology, and Roger Bastide in the general history of religions.

It was, however, only after Schipper's dutiful completion of his Ecole Pratique diploma (which resulted in a significant work of textual analysis devoted to the *Han Wu-ti nei-chuan,* a Taoist novella of unknown authorship dating to the end of the Six Dynasties period) that the real turning point in his sinological destiny came about. It was, therefore, in 1962 that he decided, following the advice of Rolf Stein, to step outside the confines of the Parisian libraries and embark, as a member of the Ecole française d'Extrême-Orient, upon a period of ethnographic fieldwork on popular religion in Taiwan.

After several discouraging years on Taiwan, while associated with the Academia Sinica near Taipei (the official Chinese academic establishment on Taiwan) and while studying the popular marionette theater (which had, he was quick to learn, profound affinities with Taoist ritual), Schipper decided to forsake official academic prerogatives and the formal procedures of ethnographic observation in order to conduct his studies of popular tradition while living within, and as a part of, the "real country" of the common people.

This decision was partially due to his frustrations with the inability of Chinese intellectuals at the Academia Sinica to take their own popular traditions seriously—even to know or to admit that such traditional folk forms as the marionette theater continued in contemporary Taiwan. But equally important for his resolve to go underground were the problems he had in playing the role of the ethnographic observer whose very presence, research apparatus, and methods of bartered information tended to influence the phenomenon under investigation. In fact, it was this "destruction du terrain," which he observed while studying the marionette theater, that directly prompted Schipper's decision to leave his official life as a research scholar in Taipei and go to the south of Taiwan to live, as the Taoist saying goes, "hidden among the people."

In the spring of 1964, after having established himself on the south side of the island and not having any particular scholarly agenda in mind, Schipper was invited by a Chinese friend to an important Taoist community ritual (generically a *chiao* ritual, an offering and banquet, or more specifically in this case, a *wen-chiao,* enacted in a multi-year cycle for the prevention of epidemics and the renewal of this regional group of confederated communities) performed over a period of several days in a temple somewhat to the north of the city of Tainan. It was this chance occurrence that was the formative moment in Schipper's career and, as proved to be the case, a significant threshold event in the scholarly understanding of the Taoist religion.

Other Westerners had observed various public celebrations associated with this kind of ritual—as, for example, is seen in the work of J. J. M. de Groot, an earlier Dutch scholar who described, at the turn of the century, what he called the "Wuist" or quasi-shamanistic rituals of South China (see vol. 6 of de Groot's *The Religious System of China;* and John Lagerwey's comments in his *Taoist Ritual in Chinese Society and History,* pp. ix–x). But no outsider until Kristofer Schipper, it seems, had witnessed, accurately described, or sympathetically appreciated the private "pure" rites of the Taoist priests (or "masters"/"adepts"/"teachers" of the Tao—i.e., *tao-shih*) that took place within a temple sanctuary.

Alternately fascinated and bored by the intricate and lengthy ritual spectacle that unfolded before him, Schipper initially reacted in a way that was in keeping with the prevailing consensus of academic scholarship at that time. While realizing the inadequacies of his formal scholarly training for appreciating what he was seeing in the field, he could not help but feel that the performance manifested only a hopelessly degenerate modern version of the "true" Taoist tradition that claimed the hoary ancestry of the mystical philosophy of Lao Tzu and the later revelations of the first Celestial Master, Chang Tao-ling. How, he asked himself, could any authentic aspect of the ancient lineage of Lao Tzu and Chang Tao-ling be preserved in such an unlikely place in the last half of the twentieth century?

The first hint toward an answer to Schipper's bemusement came when, during a pause in the ritual proceedings, he was able to peruse one of the celebrant priests' ritual manuscripts and was astonished to discover that it was a liturgical text transcribed in the early nineteenth century. It was, moreover, a manuscript that clearly reproduced canonical texts found in the ancient Taoist scriptural corpus known as the *Tao Tsang* (a compendium of over one thousand works from various historical periods, over half of which are liturgical texts).

What was incredible about this discovery was that the Taiwanese priest's calligraphic manuscript could not have been directly copied from the *Tao Tsang* itself since the printed edition of the Taoist scriptures was only available on Taiwan after 1949 (i.e., a copy of the 1926 Commercial Press edition published in Shanghai that had been deposited at the Academia Sinica). From the time of its fourth and last official Ming dynasty printing in 1445 until its photoreproduction in 1926, the *Tao Tsang* was, aside from its existence in a very few mainland Taoist monasteries, largely an unknown and inaccessible work. In nineteenth-century pre-revolutionary China, it was certainly not available to the married Taoist clergy of the Celestial Masters tradition living in villages and towns throughout the countryside.

As was verified by Schipper's Taoist master, the liturgical manuscripts used in the rituals had not been copied from a printed edition of the Taoist canon, but depended upon a living tradition of textual transmission kept within a priest's family lineage. As a general rule, it was only at the time of a new ordination that a family's ritual texts were recopied and passed on to the next generation. These manuscripts were, moreover, the exclusive and secret property of the ordained priest whose lengthy apprenticeship gave him the ability to decipher the text's highly technical esoteric terminology.

Schipper's initial insights into the contemporary practice of religious Taoism, along with his preliminary verification that the priest's hand-copied manuscripts actually replicated the ancient printed texts of the *Tao Tsang,* led to the realization that the age-old "Way of the Celestial Masters," ultimately dating back to the revelations of Chang Tao-ling in A.D. 142, was still a coherent living tradition within this obscure community in modern-day Taiwan. Given the vicissitudes of Chinese history, especially with respect to the fortunes of traditional Chinese religion in the modern period, this continuity was, to say the least, truly remarkable.

Perceiving that these latter-day Taiwanese priests possessed the key to understanding the technical vocabulary of the canonical texts he had previously struggled with in Paris, and having developed an empathy for popular Chinese tradition so often spurned by Western sinological scholarship and contemporary Chinese intellectuals, Schipper decided that a real understanding of Taoism would require his own initiation into the esoteric lore of the tradition. He would no longer just study Taoism, he would undertake the path to becoming a Taoist priest.

Here it needs to be mentioned that, while Schipper's initial encounter with Taoist ritual was largely happenstance, his ability to recognize the significance of what he had found and to take advantage of this unique opportunity for understanding the religion of the people from the inside was not a matter of pure chance. His earlier scholarly training and linguistic facility had obviously prepared him to capitalize on these discoveries, but even more important was his self-found respect for the popular tradition and his integration into the daily life of the common people.

It was, then, in the autumn of 1964, after having been adopted into the family of the priest who had been the chief celebrant of the *chiao* he had witnessed in the spring, that Kristofer Schipper started his formal apprenticeship as a *tao-shih*. In the years that followed, this young Dutchman, who had previously trained in Paris with some of the greatest European adepts of sinological lore, became the first Westerner to learn the secret oral tradition and ritual methods of the Taoist masters.

Learning the ways of a Taoist priest was, as Schipper discovered, essentially in keeping with the *Lao Tzu's* ancient description of the sage who is "concerned with the belly, not with the eyes." His training, in other words, was not directly concerned with the intellectual decipherment and understanding of the Taoist scriptures, but was centered on the practical mastery of performing liturgical forms. Knowing the rhythmic ways of the Tao in the human world was, in this sense, a theatrical and musical craft that involved the gradual tuning of his body to a complicated system of physical movements, gestures, sounds, and words. Most of all, as Schipper says, the Master never tried to "explain the meaning" of what they were doing.

Thus, it was in the spirit of the Yellow Emperor's method of learning to perform the "music of heaven" (see the *Chuang Tzu,* chap. 14) that

Schipper, at first, played a small gong in his Master's ritual orchestra and helped in the preparation of the temporary sacred area that was constructed for each major liturgy. He eventually graduated to the flute, to the role of acolyte in charge of incense, and finally to the position of cantor. The culmination of his training, and a verification of his embodiment of the ritual ways of the Tao, came in 1968 when he was officially ordained as a Taoist priest by Chang En-pu, the sixty-third Celestial Master in direct descent from Chang Tao-ling. After four years of intense practice, Kristofer Schipper had become the first Western master of the sequestered liturgical arts of the Way.

There is perhaps something strangely appropriate in the fact that it took an educated stranger from Europe to rediscover and immerse himself in a tradition that had become almost totally alien to contemporary Chinese intellectuals. The Taoist tradition's affinity for a kind of ambiguous peripherality as related to all forms of the official world—which includes traditional Chinese imperial bureaucrats, PRC party officials, and KMT politicians, as well as Confucian scholars, Christian missionaries, and modern-day sinologists—is nothing new. Indeed, one of Schipper's most important observations is that it is the ironic genius of the Taoist religion to serve essentially as the "official" legitimation of the "non-official" world of the people of the land, those who were traditionally the flesh and blood of the "real country" of China.

This is, then, the story of Kristofer Schipper's discovery of the hidden heart of the Taoist body. It is not, however, a brief for Schipper's own Taoist hagiography since, as he tells us, a full apprenticeship as a *tao-shih* should properly involve some twenty years of training. But even more significant is that, while becoming a Taoist priest, Schipper never renounced his Western scholarly heritage. Though the esoteric side of the tradition would seem to contradict the demands of open scholarly inquiry, it needs to be understood that Schipper's ordination was not a matter of converting to some concealed set of dogmatic beliefs or of swearing an oath of total secrecy.

The Taoist priestly office primarily involves the learning of ritual forms, the inner truth of which can only be known by and through each person's own body (which is, in fact, the meditative side of the liturgical art). There is no required faith in a collection of intellectual propositions or creedal "secrets" and, therefore, no necessary conflict of interest between Schipper's priestly status and his scholarly profession. It is in this way that Schipper's public revelations about Taoist revelation and ritual can abide by the strict canons of scholarship while not violating the trust of the Taoist tradition. It is, finally, the very nature of the Tao in the world to be open to multiple explanations and interpretations—as long as they are based on a precise knowledge of the actual performance of authentic ritual forms and scriptural formulas.

Schipper's scholarship has, in fact, always been respectful of the highest critical standards and of its privileged access to the living tradition. From the time of his ordination and his provisional report on his findings in 1968 (at the first international conference on Taoism in Italy), until the present, he has avoided hasty generalizations about his experience on Taiwan. After his return to Paris to take up a position at the Ecole Pratique in 1970, he was therefore preoccupied with producing, in cooperation with a growing international group of scholars, the crucial philological and historiographical tools for working with the printed Taoist canon.

This kind of critical research by Schipper and others is an ongoing enterprise, but inasmuch as it is addressed primarily to other sinological specialists, there needs to be a sharing, and a provisional synthesis, of the fruits of this work with a broader public. It was, then, some fourteen years after his ordination in Taiwan, and twelve years of technical scholarship in Paris, that Schipper published *Le corps taoïste* (Paris, 1982) as his first general discussion of the Taoist liturgical tradition for "le grand public."

As with all popular "explanations," *The Taoist Body* represents a provisional introductory appraisal of an exceedingly rich tradition that up until the past few decades had been the least understood, and most commonly ignored and maligned, of all the major religions of the world. There are, as Schipper himself indicates, still many historical lacunae in our understanding of the tradition, as well as ongoing problems of emphasis and interpretation. Granting all of this, *The Taoist Body* stands as a milestone in the history of Taoist studies and was duly awarded the prestigious Prix Julien in recognition of its significance within the overall field of Chinese scholarship. For the "grand public," it is surely the essential first step toward understanding the actual nature and significance of the Taoist vision as it relates to the liturgical tradition and the mystical philosophy of Lao Tzu and Chuang Tzu.

As a brilliantly provocative summation of Schipper's experiences in Taiwan and Paris and the growing scholarly recognition of Taoism's role throughout Chinese history, *The Taoist Body* has important implications, not only for a revised understanding of Chinese civilization, but also for the general history of world religions and the comparative phenomenology of religious experience and ritual. It is a work, therefore, that deserves the broadest possible international and interdisciplinary audience. In this sense, the appearance of an English version is an especially welcome event.

More so than has been fathomed in endless ethereal adumbrations of the *Lao Tzu,* the embodied Taoist religion—the "real" national religion of the Chinese people—has, as John Lagerwey rightly suggests, "much to teach us about what it is to be, or rather, become human." One of the silent lessons of both the *Lao Tzu* and Lord Lao, and the whole corpus of Taoist revelation and ritual, is, after all, simply the way to recover a common humanity amidst everyday life. It is this "teaching without words" to which Kristofer Schipper's *The Taoist Body* so powerfully speaks.

Bibliographic Note: For biographical details I have relied on Schipper's unpublished "Exposé de titres et travaux" which was prepared in 1983. I am indebted to Professor Schipper for providing me with a copy of this valuable account of his scholarly career.

Although there are no comprehensive histories of either the general study of Chinese tradition or the specialized analysis of Taoism, the following works can be recommended for setting out some of the sinological context for Schipper's Taoist scholarship: on nineteenth-century European scholarship, see Désiré Marceron's *Bibliographie du taoïsme* (Paris, 1898); for more up-to-date and reliable discussions, see T. H. Barrett's "Taoism: History of Study," pp. 329–332 in volume 14 of *The Encyclopedia of Religion* (New York, 1987), and his introduction to the English translation of Henri Maspero's writings on Taoism (titled *Taoism and Chinese Religion,* Amherst, 1981); concerning modern Japanese scholarship, see Sakai Tadao and Noguchi Tetsuro's "Taoist Studies in Japan," in *Facets of Taoism,* edited by Holmes Welch and Anna Seidel (New Haven, 1979), pp. 269–287; on the controversial and scandalous side of contemporary Taoist scholarship, see Michel Strickmann's "History, Anthropology, and Chinese Religion," in the *Harvard Journal of Asiatic Studies* 40(1980), pp. 201–248; and, in relation to the overall history of the study of Chinese religions, see the article, "Chinese Religion: History of Study," pp. 312–323 in volume 3 of *The Encyclopedia of Religion* (New York, 1987).

Concerning the fitful reappearance of the Taoist religion in post-

Maoist China, and the modest revival of mainland Chinese scholarship, see Jan Yun-hua's "The Religious Situation and the Studies of Buddhism and Taoism in China: An Incomplete and Imbalanced Picture," *Journal of Chinese Religions* 12(1984):37–64; and Barbara Hendrischke's "Chinese Research into Daoism after the Cultural Revolution," *Asiatische Studien/Etudes asiatiques* 38(1984):125–142.

Author's Note

Taoism still lives, be it in the face of many adversities. It has remained part of the daily life of the Chinese people and has no clearly defined profile. In order to explore it, we must take into account all its components, those concerning the physical body as well as those related to the social body. In other words, we should consider not only the techniques of Tending Life and the Way of the Immortals, but also Taoist liturgy, mythology, and mysticism. All these aspects, which may sometimes strike us as discrepant, are closely related in Taoism.

This is a book about Taoism in general. Such a vast and little-known topic is difficult to grasp in its entirety, and I am aware of the hazards of my undertaking. The attempt is motivated by the present state of the understanding of China in the West. Much has been written on the official history, on the emperor and the mandarins of yore, on the revolutionary republics of our times. But there is also the unofficial side of China, which has been much less publicized: the society of the ordinary people, the regional and local cultures, the temples and networks. This side of China—which represents the vast majority of its citizens—is not just that of the "ignorant and superstitious peasant masses," as official propaganda wants us to believe. Popular society has deeply rooted traditions of belief and worship which are strong and ardent enough to have survived the most violent of persecutions. Popular Taoism keeps its holy mountains, its festivals, its theater and, above all, its literary treasure house, of which the *Taoist Canon* is the most important example. Chinese popular religion can thus be considered as the counter-weight of China's official culture and ideologies.

The sources of this book are twofold: first, Taoist literature as it has been preserved in the *Taoist Canon* and elsewhere; and second, the fieldwork I did as research fellow of the Ecole française d'Extrême-Orient from 1962 to 1970 in the city of Tainan (Taiwan) and its surrounding villages. As much as possible, I have tried to express in this book the ideas of my Taoist masters of those years, instead of my own.

Since then, it has again become possible to do research on Taoism on the Chinese mainland. I have thus had the opportunity to test my findings on Taiwan against the circumstances there. Of course, one is struck by the considerable differences, but on closer scrutiny, these can be shown to be mainly of a material nature: there were once a thousand temples in Peking; today only a few are left. In many, if not all, respects the religion has essentially remained the same. I therefore do think that the information in this book is, with the exception of local variations, valid for China in general.

I am indebted to many persons who helped with the English edition. First of all to Professor Norman Girardot of Lehigh University, for the interest he has shown in my work, for the steps he undertook to have it published in the United States, and for his most kind introduction. Special thanks go the Mrs. Karen Duval, who made the first English version of the text; to Pamela MacFarland and Frits Staal, who helped with the revisions; to the editors and staff of the University of California Press at Los Angeles for their help and great patience in the production of the book, and especially to Nomi Isak Kleinmuntz for the painstaking job of copyediting. My warmest thanks to all.

K. S.

1

Taoism

Chuang Tzu tells about a conversation among four Taoists:

Who can think of nothingness as his head, of life as his spine, of death as his buttocks? Who knows that life and death, consciousness and unconsciousness are all one body? He shall be my friend! The four looked at each other and laughed. They felt no opposition in their hearts and thus they became friends.[1]

A little further on, the same book tells us about three other friends who talk among themselves:

Who can join with others without "joining with others?"[2] Who can do something with others without "doing something with others?" Who can go up to heaven [make himself one with nature], wander in the mists [of mystery], dance in the Infinite, become oblivious of life, forever, without end? The three looked at each other and laughed. They felt no opposition in their hearts and thus they became friends.[3]

These texts come from the oldest part of the book of the philosopher Chuang Tzu (the *Chuang-tzu*), itself one of the most ancient Taoist texts which has come down to us. They tell us about a certain relationship between the physical body, the cosmic body, and the social body, that of the "friends in the Tao." Even today, Taoist masters call each other "friends" when they address one another. Never very numerous, these priests of the true religious and philosophical traditions of China are nowadays few indeed. As to their traditions, they are comparable, to a certain degree, to the ancient mystery religions of Greece and the

1

Hellenistic world, which vanished at the end of the age of Antiquity. Today, Taoism is threatened with a similar fate and its disappearance, which may be near at hand, will leave our knowledge of the religion of ancient China quite incomplete.

Not that great efforts have been made to understand China's religion up to now! In the course of its history, China has known and assimilated all the major creeds of the world: Buddhism, Islam, Judaism, Christianity, and even Hinduism, which was introduced through the intermediary of Tantric Buddhism. All these religions have had their moment of glory, have been in fashion for longer or shorter periods, before being slowly absorbed into the Middle Kingdom, which integrated them into its own culture, though not without first introducing profound modifications. In scholarly works these religions of foreign origin occupy a prominent position. There are, for instance, countless studies on the history of Buddhism or the history of the Jesuits in China. In contrast, very little is made of the religion that preceded them and that has survived them all: Taoism, the religion of the Chinese themselves. And yet, to understand the history and the fate of the other beliefs, one must always refer to Taoism, for it was mainly under its influence, direct or indirect, that the foreign creeds were transformed. To cite but one famous example, Indian Buddhism was changed into that radically different form of Chinese Buddhism called Ch'an (better known under its Japanese name of Zen).

The Notion of Religion

The widespread ignorance concerning Taoism can by no means be imputed to the nature of Chinese religion as such: until the persecutions that descended on it a century ago and which still go on, it was alive, visible, and accessible in daily life. Taoism moreover, which can be seen as the most elevated expression of Chinese popular religion, possesses a rich and vast literature comprising more than a thousand works, covering all aspects of its traditions. Rather, this loss of interest on the part of Western scholars is due, I think, to the difficulty in understanding Chinese religion. The very notion of religion as we define it in the West is an obstacle, and a great number of observers have fallen into the trap of failing to see that in a society so dissimilar from ours the religious system must also be very different.

In everyday life, religious activity had no particular name or status, since—as the French sinologist Marcel Granet was fond of pointing out—in China, religion was formerly not distinguished from social activity in general.[4] Even its most distinguished representatives, the Taoist masters, were generally integrated in lay society and enjoyed no special status. In modern times and in imitation of Western culture and its concept of religion as something setting humanity apart from nature, the authorities have applied themselves to the task of classifying and dividing the people, trying in vain to convince the ordinary peasant that he was either a Confucian, a Buddhist, a Taoist, or, more recently still— in keeping with the party line—simply "superstitious." In fact, none of this really applies and certainly no ordinary person would call himself a Taoist, since this designation always implies an initiation into the Mysteries, and consequently is even now reserved for the masters, the local sages.

Traditionally, no special term existed to express religious activity. In order to translate our word *religion,* modern Chinese usage has coined the term *tsung-chiao,* literally "sectarian doctrine." This may be correct for Islam or Catholicism, but when this term is used for the Chinese popular religion and its highest expression, Taoism—that is to say, a religion which considers itself to be the true bond among all beings without any doctrinal creed, profession of faith, or dogmatism—it can only create misunderstandings.

The Tao

One may say that it is the absence of definition that constitutes the fundamental characteristic of Chinese religion. Whether other cultures have conceived a notion analogous to the Tao, I do not know, but in China, from the times of antiquity on, this notion has always been fundamental.[5] By definition, the Tao is indefinable and can be apprehended only in its infinitely multiple aspects. A principle at once transcendent and immanent, the Tao is unnameable, ineffable, yet present in all things. It is far more than a mere "principle." The first meaning of the character *tao* is "way": something underlying the change and transformation of all beings, the spontaneous process regulating the natural cycle of the universe. It is in this process, along this *way,* that the world as we see it, the creation of which we are an integral part, finds its unity.

But we should be careful not to extend this notion of unity to the Tao itself. The Tao may make whole, but is not itself the Whole. It gives birth to the One, it can be the One, and then it can again split this unity into fragments, divide it. "The Tao gave birth to the One, the One to the Two; the Two produced the Three and the Three the Ten Thousand Beings," says the *Tao-te ching*.[6] This generative action of the Tao is called its "power," *te,* a word which is also often translated as "virtue." But *virtue* comes from the Latin *virtus* and the root *vir,* meaning "male," whereas the Tao's action, its creative power, is on the contrary feminine.

The Tao is flux, transformation, process ("way") of alternation, and principle of cyclical time: "Nameless, it is the origin of Heaven and Earth; named, it is the Mother of the Ten Thousand Beings" (*Tao-te ching,* chap. 1).

The absence of any definition is not only characteristic of Taoist philosophy, but also of the practice of Taoism, and of its very existence in the world. For almost two thousand years now, the people have lived in communities organized around the local temples, observing festivals and holding ceremonies that correspond to the liturgical structures of Taoism, and calling on its masters without, however, professing the "Taoist religion" in a conscious way. As a religious and liturgical institution, Taoism, the social body of the local communities, has never had any true governing authority, nor canonical doctrines, nor dogma involving a confessional choice.

Nor in the course of its long history has Taoism ever known any internecine strife or any serious rivalry among its several branches, for nothing is further from the spirit of the Tao than cabals and factions. On the contrary, Taoism tends to absorb and harmonize all its currents in order to overcome its contradictions and outlast the vicissitudes of the world. It succeeds in this not by adhering to any formula or doctrine, but by modeling itself on the Tao and its effect in the reality closest to us, in our own physical bodies. "The tao is not far off; it is here in my body," say the sages.

The priority given to the human body over social and cultural systems may be seen in the predominance of the internal world over the external world and in the refusal to seek the absolute in our mind. Taoism is always rooted in the concrete, indeed the physical, and is at the same time universal and commonplace. These are the main reasons Taoism resists the Western mind. For still other reasons, of a more circumstantial nature, it remains difficult to access.

The History of Taoism

It is hard to say what the origin of Taoism is. In the vast number of Taoist texts, historical data are lacking. The *Tao-te ching*, the fundamental book which dominates the entire tradition of the Mysteries, contains no dates and mentions no proper names, nothing that would tie it to history.

As for the supposed author, Lao Tzu, the "Old Master" (or the "Old Child"),[7] he belongs primarily to legend and secondarily to theology; historiography has never managed to confer on him a more ordinary reality.[8] In any case, one should distinguish the Old Master, who is said to have lived in the sixth and fifth centuries B.C., from the book that bears his name, the *Lao-tzu* (better known as the *Tao-te ching* [The Book of the Way and its Virtue]), as this book supposedy did not obtain its present form until the third century B.C.

The ahistorical nature of the *Tao-te ching* is shared by almost all the texts that make up the *Taoist Canon*. The latter, which comprises some fifteen hundred works and is representative of Taoist literature throughout the centuries, abounds in works that carry no signature, no date, nor any proper name. It is as if, to their authors, linear history made no sense at all and as if individual authorship was considered contrary to the nature of things. Furthermore, Chinese official historiography, though exact and abundant, is virtually silent on the subject of Taoism, which stands apart from, or even in opposition to, the cult of the state and its ideology. Indeed, the annalists prefer to ignore Taoism as much as possible. Therefore, the dynastic annals do not reflect its importance in the life of the nation.

Nevertheless, one would like to know more about the history of Taoism. However, no serious study yet exists on the history of Taoism through the ages. My purpose will therefore be to consider only the problem of its historical dimension in light of its destruction in recent times, and not to write a chronicle which would necessarily be incomplete.

Taoism originated in ancient China at the times of the first emergence of philosophical thinking and of the general inquiry into the nature of humanity and the meaning of life. The first great thinkers, Confucius (born in 551 B.C.) and Mo Ti (fifth century B.C.), were concerned with moral philosophy, but not with individual freedom and destiny. The aristocratic religion, that of the feudal class, considered the human being only in terms of his social role, codified in rituals which themselves expressed the entire feudal order. This order seems to have envisioned an afterlife only for the nobles, the great ancestors. As a Confucian work has it: the "rites do not extend to the common people," and, thus, ordinary people went anonymously to the Yellow Springs in the underworld.

For the religion of the common people, from antiquity up until the present, I often make use of the term *shamanism*. To some specialists, this term may seem inadequate, and even inappropriate, to describe a sociocultural phenomenon of such great scope, so rich, so sophisticated and poetic, as Chinese popular religion. Indeed, if we had to limit ourselves to the information furnished by classical literature, we would be ignorant of practically everything concerning the religion of the people. But Chinese shamanism has survived until today, admittedly as a poor relation of the higher religion of Taoism, but with sufficient vitality to be reckoned with. It should be seen, I think, as being the *substratum* of Taoism; it is at certain times its rival and, in modern China, its inseparable complement. In every period Taoism has been defined in relation to shamanism. And so we too must take this Chinese shamanism as our point of departure.[9]

But let us first return to Taoism itself. In tombs of the third century B.C., we find the first examples of a beautiful object made of bronze, sometimes inlaid with gold, and whose relationship to Taoism seems undeniable: an incense burner in the shape of a miniature mountain (*po-shan lu*). On the mountain, we see a decoration representing trees, wild animals, and curious figures with elongated heads: the Taoist Immortals. The mountain, wide at the top, narrows toward the bottom to form a round basin representing a sea. In fact, it is a kind of upside-down mountain in the shape of a mushroom rising from the waters. It represents the land of immortality, either Mount K'un-lun, dwelling place of the Queen Mother of the West—the great goddess of the setting sun and of death, who offers initiates invited to her banquets peaches that confer Long Life—or else the island of the rising sun, in the sea of the East, home of the Immortals.

The first chapter of the book of Chuang tzu tells us of these lands:

On the distant mountain of Ku-yeh[10] live divine beings. Their skin is cool like frosted snow and they are delicate and shy like virgins. They eat no cereals, only breathe wind and drink dew. They mount clouds of *ch'i* and ride winged dragons to wander beyond the Four Seas [the limits of the world]. By concentrating their minds, they can protect all beings from the plague and ripen the crops. . . . These men! What power [*te*]! They embrace the Ten Thousand Beings, making them into a single one. The men of this world may beg them to bring order but why would they tire themselves with the concerns of this world? These men! Nothing can hurt them: were the waters to flood even to the sky, they would not perish; were it to become so hot as to melt stone and burn the land and mountains, they would not even feel warm.[11]

The *po-shan lu* incense burner may well have been used as an aid to ecstatic meditation.[12] Sitting in front of it and looking at the coils of smoke coming out of the holes (the grottoes) in the moutain-shaped cover, one could mentally reach those wondrous lands and become like the Immortals mentioned above: light, shy, doing good without acting or interfering, so absorbed in the universe that they gather all of creation into themselves. The great deluge and the great heat wave are apocalyptic themes; only the real Being, the True, the Pure will survive. We also find here a mention of the abstinence from grains, which is a characteristic aspect of Taoist dietetics. The simple mention suffices to call up the vast range of practices for "tending life" in the search for immortality.

The Taoist diet does not conform to what people generally eat. This—as well as the practice of meditation and physical exercises—allows one to recognize, even today, initiates within society. They are often spoken of as hermits; indeed, withdrawal "to the mountains and the valleys" is an image and a frequent theme in Taoist literature. However, this does not necessarily correspond to an observed rule, for as we shall see further on, initiation into the "mountain" can include many other realities. One need not leave the world of men nor attempt to set oneself apart from others. One follows others, for that is the price of freedom.

The initiates of ancient Taoism, as presented by Chuang Tzu, are—in addition to the "Old Master"—interesting characters, such as "Gourd," "Toothless," and "Inspired Madman." Confucius too is described as an initiate, but as one who still has much to learn. The Awakening of the Yellow Emperor, the great ancestor of Chinese civilization, to the Tao constitutes a major maieutic theme.

What came to be called *Taoism*—the term did not yet exist in the Chuang Tzu's times—must have constituted a higher, initiatory dimension of the religion of the people. As is still the case today, traditions *existed,* whereas Taoists *knew* (that they did not know).

In Taoism, the rites and myths of popular shamanism become Mystery cults and give rise to liturgy and theology. Chuang Tzu uses the ancient myths only to reach beyond them. He shows that no mythological hero, no legendary animal knows the freedom of those who "mount on the regulating Principle of the universe, ride the transformations of the Six [cosmic] Energies to go off and wander in the Unending."[13]

Towards the beginning of the first empire (221 B.C.), these cosmological visions of the Tao were associated with the "Way of the Yellow Emperor and the Old Master" (*Huang-lao chih Tao*).[14] This school appears then to have been a Mystery religion with a wide following that has inspired many thinkers.

During the following Han dynasty (206 B.C. to A.D. 221) the tombs contained objects related to the quest for immortality; shrouds were decorated with images representing the flight of the body towards the lands of bliss. Contracts inscribed on funerary vases guaranteed a home in the next world. The texts of such contracts carried with them a symbol, that is, an inscription made up of sibylline signs. This corresponded to a "password," which identified the initiate at the gates of paradise. Such symbols were called *fu,* a word whose etymological meaning is similar to the Greek word *tessera.*

In addition, the tombs contained objects related to alchemical research, also known to us through texts. By transforming cinnabar *(tan)* into mercury, Chinese alchemy sought to reproduce the cyclical alternation of *yin* and *yang* and to integrate the adept into this cosmological model. The fortunes of alchemy varied over the course of Taoism's history, but the theory of transmuting cinnabar became a fundamental part of Taoist discourse.

The same situation prevailed in medical science. Not all the doctors were Taoists, but the quest for immortality certainly influenced medical research, and contributed especially to its theoretical systematization as found in the classic *Simple Questions of the Yellow Emperor,* the oldest manual to have come down to us.[15]

Under the first rulers of the Han dynasty, the Way of the Yellow Emperor and Lao Tzu were introduced to the court. But this situation was profoundly changed under Emperor Wu (140–86 B.C.), when Confucianism was established as the state ideology, excluding all other systems. A strange fate for this ancient philosophy, mainstay of the feudal order, to become the doctrine of imperial absolutism, the moral philosophy of the central administration! With this, a deep gulf opened which, despite noticeable variations, was to remain constant throughout Chinese history. On the one hand, there was the state and its administration, the official country, claiming the "Confucian" tradition for its own; on the other was the real country, the local structures being expressed in regional and unofficial forms of religion. It was then that Taoism consciously assumed its own identity and received its present name.[16]

Relegated to the opposition, Taoism remained out of official favor—even though it was to enjoy imperial patronage from time to time—and became the basis for the liturgical organization of the "country." Local leaders, the elders who headed the villages, and sometimes even the chiefs of non-Chinese minorities, found in Taoist initiation and worship the consecration that legitimized their power, outside the imperial administration and sometimes in opposition to it.

Such a situation carried within it the ferment of revolt, and as early as the first century B.C., Taoist-inspired messianic and millenarian movements appeared in the hope of establishing the reign of Great Peace (*T'ai-p'ing*). The Great Peace was believed to have existed before civilization and to be destined to reappear one day on earth. The state fought these movements, while certain politicians tried to exploit the messianic expectations of the masses.[17] The great millenarian revolt of the Yellow Turbans, in A.D. 182, was so widespread that the Han dynasty was left drained and exhausted by its efforts to repress it. The fall of the Han empire, comparable to that of the Roman empire, allowed the local Taoist organizations, which had been obscured by the official mantle, to surface: certain regions possessed true autonomous theocratic structures; the communes were administered by ordained masters, guarantors of freedom within the area and equal partners with the heads of neighboring communities. It was a democracy in some way comparable to that of ancient Greece.

Part of what was then China—the richest and most developed western provinces—was organized into local units, all claiming allegiance to the same movement, that of the "Heavenly Masters." The movement originated in the revelation which Lao Tzu (who had "come again" in A.D. 142) made to the Taoist, Chang (Tao-) Ling, the first "Heavenly Master." This revelation marked the beginning of a new era, fortunate for the elect, disastrous for those who would continue to follow the old customs and practices in spite of the new covenant. Chang Ling became

Zhang Daoling - 'Heavenly Master'

the prophet of this revelation as heir to the new heavenly mandate, and thus "Heavenly Master." Historians tend to identify the birth of organized Taoism with this movement of the Heavenly Masters, but in fact the situation is more complicated. Although primary sources are scarce, there is enough evidence to show that before Chang Ling there were many earlier organized religious groups that were seen as Taoist, both by the groups themselves and by others. The prophecy of a new era was not unknown in these earlier movements. The fact that Lao Tzu is presented as "come again" (*hsin-ch'u*) shows the idea of a continuity with the religion of the Old Master of earlier times. It is true, however, that the appearance of the popular organization of the Heavenly Masters does mark a turning point in the social history of China. Their tradition has lasted to this day,[18] and with it the Taoist liturgy of local communities. Despite important changes, this tradition remained through the centuries the superstructure of local cults, the written and initiatory expression of a shamanistic, popular religion, of which it is both the antagonist and the supporter; even when Taoism opposes itself to shamanism, it always strives to complement it.

We find the Heavenly Masters and the "dignitaries of the Tao" in today's liturgy. Let me simply point out here the remarkable continuity of these structures which were able to survive while our ancient religions disappeared with the emergence of the great universal religions of salvation.

China came to know these proselytizing foreign religions, as well. The decline of the imperial order and, more important, the conquest of Northern China by non-Chinese tribes from Central Asia, introduced into China a guest who had waited at its gates for a long time: Buddhism. At first, it was considered a junior relative of Taoism and even presented itself as such. The first Buddhist books translated in China responded to Taoist preoccupations, for they concern breathing techniques and medicine.[19] But the movement soon broadened and in so doing established its autonomy with respect to the indigenous religion.

On its own, or under the barbarian sword, China discovered a new world, an intellectual tradition very different from and in some respects superior to its own. The impact was great and the prolific output of Buddhist literature (translations and Chinese apocrypha) over time gave rise to the flowering of a Taoist literature of revelation: hundreds of works dictated by the "Tao" rival texts spoken by the "Buddha." In the early days, however, the influence of Buddhism remained formal.[20]

Taoism was able to assert its position as the national religion, especially in South China, which had remained Chinese since 317 when the North passed under foreign rule. The clash between the liturgical organization of the Heavenly Masters—brought from North China by the refugees—and the local traditions—which preserved the ancient Taoist mysteries of the Han of South China—was the source of a new current which perfectly embodied the spirit of the Middle Kingdom before its downfall. Known as the school of Mao shan, it originated in the divine revelations made to a family of Southern notables in the second half of the fourth century.[21] They communicated through a medium (shamanism is never far away), and the visions and the sessions of inspired writings crystallized into pages and pages of the most beautiful ecstatic literature. True tokens of the gods, the medium's manuscripts ensured the initiate salvation in the cataclysms to come. Mao shan literature would thus gradually develop into a real movement and a new orthodoxy.

The religious organization did not change: it remained that of the Heavenly Masters. The liturgical ritual, however, did change. New hymns and then elements of the Buddhist rite, namely circumambulation and, in particular, the psalmody of the holy books, were incorporated into the service. For the Taoists, this psalmody of the scriptures was considered most beneficial, inasmuch as it reproduced the original sounds of the spontaneous writing of the heavens, which itself was the origin of the *fu* symbols, those "passwords" in the form of talismans. The *fu* were originally tokens (tesserae) for messengers and envoys. These were also called "sacred jewels" (*ling-pao*).[22] Thus, texts recited in the Buddhist manner retain this symbolic quality by appearing as *Sacred Jewels,* signs of initiation turned into words. They rarely contain any doctrinal discourse and are hardly ever used in preaching, which is virtually unknown in Taoism. The *Books of Sacred Jewels* multiplied just as fast as the ecstatic writings of Mao shan, and together, in the fifth century, they made up an impressive corpus. A dynasty adopted them, a Taoist patriarch[23] collated them: the first *Taoist Canon* was born (the Chinese response to Buddhism), and canonical Taoism became for a brief period an official institution.

One can bring the Mysteries under state control, but one has then to reckon with the profound hopes for salvation that arise in counterpoint. Lao Tzu had appeared to Chang Ling, thus he would perhaps not be long in coming again. His coming would be preceded by deluge and conflagration. Non-initiates and "bad men" would all die. When he did return, Lao Tzu would establish the kingdom of Great Peace.

Certain popular texts of the fifth century describe the apocalypse in highly colorful images and prophesy the coming of the Messiah in the near future. He would come to reign over the Pure, the Very Pure, the elect of his Kingdom.

This ardent waiting is part of the Chinese soteriological tradition. It was to influence Buddhism profoundly and, inevitably, to have political repercussions as well. During this period of successive short-lived dynasties, from the Chin to the Sui, the emperors sought more than ever to cultivate the image of Redeemer of the People, sovereign savior of the Great Peace. Efforts were made to turn Taoism into a national religion and an ideology of reunification, to refine it and make it official. The founders of the T'ang dynasty (618–907) went so far as to take advantage of the messianic expectations of the masses and tried once again to take over Taoism to make it into a state cult.[24]

Despite these maneuvers, state control of Taoism remained incomplete and provisional. The ancient Mysteries would never become a religion of universal salvation.[25] The basic organization remained firmly rooted in local structures, and the masters, whose duties had become hereditary, were not tied to any central administration. Attempts to reform Taoism into a church were not carried out. Taoism, united in its diversity (the Tao is not the One), firmly maintained its base in the countryside and preserved its exclusive and initiatory character. Thus, the great dynasty of the T'ang, though officially Taoist, stands out as the high point of Buddhism in China.

Buddhism is truly a universal and all-embracing faith. Removed from society, it generally remained close to the state. Able to attract the charity of its faithful, the gifts of the lay believers became the inalienable property of the Buddha. The church thus accumulated capital, invested it for profit, but never spent it except to build magnificent sanctuaries: pagodas several hundred feet high filled with statues of gold, silver, jade, and precious stones! The church weighed heavily on the economic and political life of the nation. Restrictive measures, indeed persecutions of the church, which must be viewed as measures of economic rehabilitation, became inevitable.[26] They occurred regularly with a varying degree of severity, even as the emperors, their wives, and the entire ruling class themselves remained fervent Buddhists.

In the high level transactions that characterized relations between the state and Buddhism, Taoism had no great role to play: it was no match for these mighty institutions[27] and confined itself to the country. From the eighth century on, the rituals of the Mysteries and the liturgy of the Heavenly Masters were associated with local festivals. The gods of the people became Taoist saints and vice versa.

Far from the capitals, Taoism then found an ally: Confucianism, the doctrine of the literati. Ever since the fall of the Han, the rural clans had preserved its classical and scientific tradition. Not in opposition with this tradition, Taoism even assimilated it and became its guardian. At the end of the sixth century, the *Taoist Canon* adopted all the ancient philosophers, including those of Confucianism, in an effort to represent the national stand against Buddhism. The reunification under the T'ang signifies the end of Confucianism's exile. But the two currents of thought continued to accommodate and influence each other. This had a profound effect on the evolution of Taoism whose traditional mythological cosmology was gradually replaced by the abstract one of the *Book of Changes,* the *I-ching*. At the same time, the literati became interested in the arts of longevity and took up alchemy. During the whole second half of the T'ang and up to the ninth century, Confucianism and Taoism coexisted and together prepared the great renaissance of the Sung (960–1279). They also took on Buddhism together. The great proscription of 842–845, whose true motivations were economic, took place at their instigation. This outright persecution of Buddhism was a real blow to the church, already weakened from within by corruption and decadence. The great period of Buddhism in China was coming to a close.[28]

But a reaction to the internal weaknesses had been brewing within Buddhism itself for a long time already. Opposed to luxury, ceremonies, and parasitism, a new current of thought was preaching the return to simplicity, intuition, and nature. This was *Ch'an* (Zen), typically Chinese, practical, concrete, and above all Taoist. Ch'an thought, at odds with the scholasticism of the Buddhism of the Great Vehicle, borrowed from Taoist mysticism its shattering of concepts, its teaching without words, and its spontaneity. Its simplicity and its proximity to the masses would allow it to survive when the Buddhist high church itself collapsed. Alongside a rediscovered Confucianism and basic Taoism, Ch'an became the third component of this reawakening which marks the beginning of modern China.

If, thanks to the work of Paul Demiéville, we acknowledge Taoism's important contribution to Ch'an, the same cannot be said for Confucianism, or "Neo-Confucianism," which under the last dynasties became the official ideology of the Chinese state, the only system of thought to be accepted at the state examinations which provided access to public service. But it must be stressed that the first philosophers of the Confucian renewal were either Taoist masters or had close ties to their circle.[29] Even the great Chu Hsi (1130–1200), principal architect of the new orthodoxy, wrote commentaries on the sacred books of Taoism.

At the dawn of modern China, Taoism, which more than ever had become the religion of the people, presented itself as the root from which the new branches of Confucianism and Buddhism had developed; it was the oldest of the "Three Doctrines," *san-chiao,* the common source. We are constantly reminded that, according to the legends, Confucius was the disciple and Buddha the reincarnation of Lao Tzu. The term *Three Doctrines* (often translated as "Three Religions") in fact corresponded to that form of Taoism which proposed itself as the representative of Chinese culture. For, clearly, the other two partners refused responsibility for this ecumenism and sought instead to set themselves apart. Indeed, considering how much the ideas of the three had become convergent, it is surprising that their institutional interpenetration remained so slight. It seems thus incorrect to view "the modern popular religion" as a syncretism of the three religions. In reality what we have here is Taoism asserting itself, as it had done in the past, as the *national religion.*

It had been granted this role more than once in the face of external aggression. The Sung governments sought in Taoism an ideological and nationalist support against the Tibetans and Mongols to whom they would eventually yield the whole empire, step by step. During these struggles, and especially under the Mongol occupation, Taoism served as a movement for cultural reawakening and passive resistance. It sought successfully to impose itself on the foreigners and to sinicize them. In 1222 the master Ch'iu Ch'ang-ch'un defended Taoism before Genghis Khan as the national religion and put himself forth as the representative of the Chinese people: "If the conqueror respects Taoism, the Chinese will submit." Ch'iu won this daring bet and was installed by Genghis as head of the religious Chinese, including the Buddhists.[30] This success, which conferred on Taoism a power unknown to it before, soon became detrimental.

The encroachment upon Buddhist and Confucian domains provoked their vengeance and resulted in the first serious proscription of Taoism. In 1282 Taoist books, except for the *Tao-te ching,* were burned. The loss was irremediable, and even Taoism's spirit seemed broken. National resistance was led henceforward by the sects (the "Secret Societies") which often shared the theology and practices of Taoism, but which now became separate organizations. They worked hard for national restoration against the Mongols and eventually brought Chu Yüan-chang, the founder of the Ming dynasty (1368–1644), to power.

Henceforth, Taoism was comprised of two main schools which complemented each other without rivalry: that of the Heavenly Masters, passed on hereditarily since the Han,[31] and that of Ch'iu Ch'ang-ch'un, Genghis Khan's teacher. The latter school was called the school of Total Perfection (Ch'üan-chen). It was based on the Buddhist model, in monastic communities. As to the Heavenly Masters, they remained at the head of the liturgical organization. Installed on the Mountain of the Dragon and the Tiger (in the province of Kiangsi) since the T'ang period (eighth century), they became the "Taoist popes"—a derisive term bestowed on them by Western missionaries. This liturgical tradition of Taoism remained profoundly rooted in the communities of the people. The temples and their property belonged to them and never fell under the jurisdiction of the initiating Masters. More than ever Taoism was identified with popular religion; it represented the underlying tradition, the culture, and the institutions of the true country.

There has been a remarkable continuity in the practice of the Tao, for despite the transformations of more than two thousand years of history, it remained the typical and coherent expression of the Chinese religion, of its *she-hui* ("the congregation of the Earth God"), that is, the society vis-à-vis the state. Its liturgy provided the context within which the politico-religious structures of non-official China were formed. Taoist thought perpetuated this notion of autonomy and liberty.

It is thus legitimate to consider Taoism as a whole and to link the classic works (the book of Chuang Tzu and the *Tao-te ching*), as do the Taoists themselves, to the search for immortality ("to nourish the vital principle") and to liturgy (the social body).

The deep relation that exists between these three major components of the Taoist tradition obliges us to present them here in this book in an order contrary to that usually adopted, and to proceed counter to the chronology that the history of the texts would suggest. The works of the mystics are among the most ancient documents to have come down to us, but they also, in fact, represent the culmination of the Taoist system. They must be restored to this rightful position. Conversely, shamanism, which we know fully only thanks to the data of contemporary ethnography, actually corresponds to an archaic level which, from an objective point of view, is to be placed among the antecedents of Taoism.

The Destruction of Taoism

The destruction of Taoism coincides with the progressive decline of the Chinese culture over the last centuries. One of the main factors of this decline is Western influence.

When, in the sixteenth century, the Jesuit missionaries in China were faced with the historic choice to ally themselves either with religion against the state or with the state against religion, they chose the second alternative. Christianity entered the sphere of the imperial court and placed itself under the protection of the government. Back home, in Europe, the missionaries glorified the official imperial ideology and the image of Confucius as *Sinarum Philosophus* ("the only one"), while minimizing the religious role of the state cult. Thus China had no religion for the missionaries, and it was they who introduced into Chinese the term *mi-sin,* literally "deviant belief," to describe Taoism. Matteo Ricci, the most influential among the early missionaries, sought to confer on Confucianism the image of an agnostic doctrine or moral wisdom, a philosophy that had already recognized the existence of the Supreme Being and that lacked only the revelation of the Gospel.

This way of seeing things was very successful and, despite the quarrel over the rites and the campaign against deism inside the Roman Catholic church, these ideas gained ground and were accepted not only by the other missions, but also by European intellectuals and even, at a later stage, by the Chinese officials. In the long run, the result of all this has been that Republican China after 1912 has had two Christian presidents and that the introduction of Marxism was, without a doubt, much facilitated.

In seventeenth- and eighteenth-century France, even the opponents of the church adopted the ideas of Ricci. For lack of other sources of information? Perhaps. But one must also recognize that the thinkers of the enlightenment discovered in China the country of their dreams: a nation without religion, led by sages, which put intelligence into power and placed culture at the service of the empire, all thanks to the institution of official examinations which provided access to public service. If, in the eighteenth century, China had not existed as a model for the West, it would have had to be invented.

This continuing love affair between the intellectuals in the West and a certain image of China is amazing; it is bound to become a source of astonishment for future historians. The uncritical approval of official

China—at the expense of its popular culture—by Western minds ready to acknowledge Christian or pseudo-Christian virtues in China continues to be expressed by a sinophilia whose excessive nature betrays the existence of deep misunderstandings: a people without religion. . . . This opinion held by the missionaries, revised and simplified by our intellectuals, and still current today, shows how poorly we know China. As I have indicated, it did not necessarily displease the Chinese officialdom, who found powerful allies in the missionaries to combat the local communal structures and their Taoist liturgy, which the officials held responsible for the ailments of the country.

With the end of the Ming dynasty, the split between the bureaucracy and religion (the real country) became greater than ever. The revolts of the sects—which like their close relative Taoism, had their base in the countryside—provoked the fall of the Ming (whom they had earlier carried to power) and brought on the foreign domination of the Manchus (the Ch'ing dynasty, 1644–1912). The Manchus oppressed the Chinese and sought to suppress their religion. The class of the literati and bureaucrats, while suffering discrimination like the rest during this period, blamed religion for the ruin of the national dynasty and sought to regain power by advocating a return to the Confucian orthodoxy of the Han. This was the beginning of *Han-hsüeh,* "national studies" (a term we in the West translate as Chinese Studies or Sinology!), which returned the Classics to favor and rejected Taoism entirely.

Historical and philological studies, undertaken due to this national reawakening of the literati, almost completely ignored religious literature. When, during the eighteenth century, the great imperial library was constituted and the *texti recepti* of all the ancient writings were collated, Taoist books were virtually excluded. At the beginning of the present century, the *Taoist Canon,* long forgotten, survived only in one complete copy.[32]

An alliance was drawn up—a marriage of reason more than one of love—between the officials and Western Christianity. Together they fought the T'ai-p'ing rebellion (1851–1864), that pitiful religious war led by a novice who had become the Chinese Christ and who retained of the ancient ideal only the name, Great Peace. Indeed, the first great destruction of the Taoist sanctuaries was inflicted by the T'ai-p'ings in the name of Christian truth to combat "superstition." Hundreds of magnificent architectural complexes—among them the Mountain of the Dragon and the Tiger, the thirteenth-century residence of the Heavenly Master—were entirely devastated. No one at that time, except some among the working classes, considered restoring these prestigious monuments, which were as old as the gothic cathedrals of Europe— and this at a time when Viollet-le-Duc was undertaking the restoration of the Notre-Dame cathedral in Paris!

This destruction was followed by so many others that it would be tedious to enumerate them. Let me say simply that each time there was a turning point, each time China passed through a stage towards its modern destiny, the old religion was persecuted. The reformers of 1885 tried to confiscate all the surviving or reconstructed temples to turn them into public buildings, schools, and hospitals, often a function they already served on a voluntary and religious basis. The Republic of 1912 continued this program. A spontaneous upsurge for a national renais- sance in 1917, officially termed the "Fourth May Movement," fur- nished the occasion for the confiscation by the state of all property of popular religious associations, thereby condemning most temples to ruin. A Christian warlord had all the sanctuaries in South China, how- ever small, destroyed. In the 1920s, the "New Life" movement drafted students to go out on Sundays to destroy the statues and furnishings of the temples outside the capitals of Nanking and Peking. And so it went. By the time the Communists took power, only a few great Buddhist and Taoist monasteries remained. The monks and nuns were then ex- pelled. A few of the most prestigious monasteries and temples were designated historical monuments; the rest were left to fall into neglect. During the land reform all sanctuaries that did not belong to other religions were placed under the authority of the newly founded official Taoist Association (Chung-kuo Tao-chiao hsieh-hui). But this body was unable to fulfill its task as keeper of holy places, for almost all re- maining popular temples (about three hundred in Peking, where a cen- tury before there had been almost a thousand, and around fifty of the original two hundred in Shanghai) were requisitioned as army barracks or government offices, or else taken over by factories and workshops. Most festivals, all acts of worship, and even the burning of incense— which is one of the oldest forms of Taoist practice—were marked as "superstitious" and therefore forbidden.

The Cultural Revolution (1964–1974) completed the destruction. What for the Jesuits in the sixteenth century had been only a pious vow finally seemed realized: the ancient Chinese religion—like the ancient religions of Greece and Rome—had virtually ceased to exist, and the world was none the wiser. [33]

And yet, as the following chapters will show, Taoism is not dead. It survives, poor and maligned, but also astonishingly vivacious, in the peasant communities of Taiwan, in the fishing villages of Hong Kong, and on the Chinese mainland where it has increasingly surfaced during the last few years. In the coastal provinces of Canton and Fukien the newly acquired economic prosperity finds its expression in the restoration of the temples. In Fukien they are being rebuilt in granite "so that they will not burn again." The festivals and pilgrimages are also coming back. In the cities, wherever the local political structures so allow, branches of the Taoist Association are set up. Careful but stubborn attempts are being made by this Association to retrieve the holy places which, according to the 1952 cadastre, belong to Taoism. Often the places of worship have been hopelessly destroyed, but in these cases, there are certain possibilities for monetary compensation, which can be used for the training of the descendants of the traditional Taoist families. Everywhere in China the manuscripts which survived the Cultural Revolution are being collected and recopied. For the time being, however, the liturgical lay associations, as well as the celebration of the age-old rituals of the Heavenly Master, remain forbidden.

On the surface, there appears to be little left of Taoism. The Masters are much less openly active and vocal than the Buddhists or the Roman Catholics, let alone the Muslims. Taoism never did have any strong organization. However, it is present in today's China in manifold and sometimes quite unexpected ways. One of the major forms of its revival is to be found in the present widespread enthusiasm for the health and longevity practices that go under the name of *ch'i-kung* (spelled *qigong* in modern Chinese transcription), exercises of the vital breath or energy. The *ch'i-kung* masters may well *officially* minimize any relation between their art and Taoism; however, the numerous publications—books as well as periodicals—published on the subject of *ch'i-kung* in China devote a great amount of space to Taoism, its history, and its sacred books. The same holds true for the practice of Chinese medicine and for Chinese arts and sciences in general: one only has to scratch the surface in order to find living Taoism. Thus Taoism remains present, today as in former times, in the daily life of the people and maintains its highest goal: Long Life.

2

Everyday Religion

The Temples

Before modern iconoclasm held sway, religion was in evidence everywhere in China: each house had its altar, each district and village its temple. They were numerous and easy to spot, for as a rule, the local temple was the most beautiful building, the pride of the area. Except in the capital, official buildings could not rival religious architecture in beauty or wealth. In old as well as recent guidebooks, most of the monuments noted as worthy of interest are temples.

To whom did they belong? Only a small number were erected by the government in connection with the official religion of China, that is, the imperial sacrifices and the cult of Confucius. The state ideology certainly had a religious aspect, with its offerings and prayers, but its services never had a mass following, something that was actively discouraged.

Though more numerous than the Confucianist altars and shrines, Buddhist sanctuaries were still in minority. By and large, they consisted of monastic establishments, of varying importance, where from four or five up to several thousand Buddhist monks gathered.[1]

On the whole, the majority of temples were—and, where they still exist, continue to be—part of Taoism, the religion of the people. They were always built by an association or a local community. In the cities, they were often the work of a merchants' or artisans' guild, or even that of the inhabitants of a given district. In the countryside, they were erected by all the members of a village community or regional association. Management of the common property—buildings, land, furnishings, and revenue—was strictly egalitarian.

On the local level, the large temples (*ta-miao,* sacred places for a whole region, maintained by an alliance of village communities) are distinguished from the small temples (*hsiao-miao,* local sanctuaries). In provincial cities and towns 150 years ago, there was an average of one temple for every 100 homes (400 people).[2] Large or small, they were always built with care, if not wealth and splendor.

The architecture of the temples was based on two models, one metaphorical, the other cosmological. Metaphorically, the temple is the residence of an official—that is, it imitates the architecture of administrative residences (palaces, prefectures, and so forth). From this architecture it borrows the characteristics corresponding to the privileges of rank: a curved roof ending in a swallow-tailed point, red pillars and doors, statues of lions at the entrances, a bell and drum suspended on either side of the door, and so on. Temples are thus often "palaces" or "residences."

This bureaucratic metaphor extends only to the external appearance, however. Above all, the temples are made in the cosmological image of the worlds. They are laid out so that the principal door opens toward the south; on either side of the door, one often finds the images of the Green Dragon and the White Tiger, emblems of the east and the west. Inside, under the roof, a central dome is sometimes set up in the image of the celestial vault, while the base of the temple is squared in the image of the Earth. Outside, the roof imitates a sacred mountain, the paradise of the Immortals whose summit reaches up to the heavens. The figurines that decorate the roof depict legendary figures and heroes of sacred myths. At the top of the roof, two earthenware dragons confront each other over a flaming pearl located in the center. This pearl represents the radiant energy (*ch'i*) that emanates from the incense burner placed in the temple.

The roof of the temple is meant to be the highest of all the surrounding buildings, for the sanctuary is to dominate and ensure the geological equilibrium of the area.[3] The decor is often very elaborate and expensive; frescoes, sculpted beams decorated with painted pictures, richly adorned niches, finely sculpted panels covered with gold leaf, and so on. For the price of a single village temple, one can easily have built ten mission churches.[4] But let us recall that this temple is the fruit of a joint effort to which each family makes its minimal obligatory contribution. Individual gifts are made for certain architectural features: sculpted pillars, carved windows, and furniture. The donors' names are then inscribed on them.

Sometimes villages that form a religious unit have no temple. Their inhabitants nevertheless gather together for the celebration of the most important community festivals and sacrifices of the liturgical year: the New Year, the offerings to the Earth God (T'u-ti) in the spring and the autumn, the ritual for the salvation of the orphan souls on the fifteenth day of the seventh moon, and so on.

Members of such communities share possession of the incense burner, *hsiang-lu,* each family taking its turn for a year and then passing it on. It is up to the family in charge of the incense burner to organize the year's festivities, and for this period they receive the title of "master of the incense burner," while the other families are called "servants of the incense burner." If the community later decides to build a sanctuary, the incense burner will occupy the central place in it as symbol of the community and emblem of the social body.[5]

Furthermore, the offering of incense in the burner is the essential element of worship. Indeed, although the sanctuaries are dedicated to gods, or rather to patron saints, the presence of the latter in the form of an image or a statue is not essential. One finds temples without statues, where the presence of the patron saints is simply indicated by an inscription in black characters on a band of red paper stuck on the wall behind the incense burner. Moreover, worship in a temple is not reserved exclusively for the saint or gods to whom it is dedicated. The *miao* is a place open to all beings, divine and human. A community as well as truly communal house, it is a place for casual and formal meetings. The elders go there daily to discuss village affairs. Grandmothers, the family delegates in religious matters, go there every day with offerings of incense and to fill the lamps with oil. Music and theater associations, along with clubs for boxing, reading, chess, charity, pilgrimages, automatic writing, medical research, kite flying, and cultural associations of all kinds create their headquarters in the temple, and find here as well a place of worship for their particular patron saint.

In the absence of any clergy to lead them in special worship, the inhabitants, the masters of the place, often concern themselves very little with the idenity of the main deity. In any case, homage is paid first to Heaven, then to Earth, and lastly to the tutelary god or patron saint, who, if necessary, may always be replaced by another member of the celestial bureaucracy.

What counts above all else in the communal house is the incense burner. This object is truly the emblem of social unity and on it are engraved the name of the community and the date of its foundation. Temples and communities are affiliated with each other by the rite of the division of the incense (*fen-hsiang*). This consists of collecting ashes, each time a new group is formed, from the incense burner in the "ancestral temple" (*tsu-miao*) where the worship originated and placing these ashes in a new burner, which will belong to the new community. This division expresses the tie between the two communities—a tie of economic and cultural exchange—and the duty of mutual aid.

The reasons behind the affiliation differ according to the nature of the groups. Thus, for instance, Chinese emigrants in Southeast Asia carried with them an incense burner filled with ashes from the temple of their place of origin, whereas in China the temples of the guilds were affiliated with the sanctuaries of their craft's patron saints. Whatever the reason behind the affiliation, the institution of the division of the incense reveals one thing of supreme importance to our understanding of traditional China: before the present period, the society was made up of countless communities, all linked together by a very dense network of alliances. This network of religious and liturgical organizations, whose economic and cultural importance was paramount, maintained itself almost entirely outside the control of the state.

While the temples define the community spatially, the festivals give it an identity in time.

The Calendar

The cycle of days and seasons, of centuries and ages, of the cosmic rhythm, is the working of the Tao. Hence the sacred nature of the calendar. More than a simple means of counting the days, it is a divine revelation whose disclosure remained until recently the prerogative of the Son of Heaven, the emperor of China. Drawn up in secret, the new calendar was made public each year at the New Year by the court astrologers. Printed copies were sent to all administrative county seats. On the local level, the imperial calendar was used as the country almanac, called *t'ung-shu,* Universal Book.

Even today the traditional almanac remains the most widespread book in China. Hung on a nail next to the domestic altar,[6] it occupies a central position in every household, for despite the official abrogation in 1912 of the Chinese calendar and its replacement by the Gregorian system, the peasants continue to use the traditional almanac to plan their work in the fields.

The Chinese calendar is based both on the cycle of the sun (*yang*) and that of the moon (*yin*). The former is marked by the solstices and the equinoxes, and divides the year into twenty-four periods called "energy nodes" (*chieh-ch'i*). Each of these periods has a name corresponding to the change in the weather. "Great Heat," "Small Cold," "Awakening of the Insects," and anyone who has lived in the old regions of China, in the Great Plain for example, knows how well these names correspond to the weather at any given moment.

As for the lunar reckoning, it divides the year into twelve lunar months, each beginning with the new moon, so that the fifteenth day corresponds to the full moon. These lunar months consist of twenty-nine or thirty days. In order to make the lunar and solar years coincide, additional months are inserted at irregular intervals.

The calendar also takes into account the movement of the stars, the Five Planets and the Twenty-eight Palaces (*hsiu.*) Some stellar conjunctions are considered lucky, others unlucky. A whole series of interdicts has been developed according to an elaborate system of correspondence: on such and such a day, one should neither have one's hair cut nor make any business deals; on another day, field work is forbidden and moving furniture in the house is ill-advised. These interdictions remain especially important for the big events of life: marriage, funerals, voyages.

Finally, there is the system for counting days—as well as years—in cycles of sixty. The numbering is carried out by combining two series, one of ten units and one of twelve, called, respectively, Celestial Trunks and Terrestrial Branches. The two series are even, and each sign from the series of ten Trunks is thus combined with six signs (always the same) from the series of twelve Branches. Combining the two series gives a cycle of sixty signs, which is used for counting days or years in periods of sixty units. This system allows for a great many mathematical combinations and games. As happens with the planets and the palaces, here the elements of the reckoning are paired with a large number of other categories having to do with spatial ordering or human existence.

All of the elements that enter into the composition of the calendar make it extremely elaborate and complex. Therefore, in traditional China, no one day resembled any other. The "energy nodes," as well as all the other aspects of the reckoning, with their play of correspondences, gave time a much more tangible substance and reality than is the case for us. Time surrounded the individual closely, influencing his decisions and actions at every moment. The rhythm of time is felt more strongly still in the cycle of festivals.

Festivals

Few of the festivals are tied to the solar cycle; the winter solstice is celebrated and sometimes, secondarily, the vernal equinox. The energy node called *ch'ing-ming*, "clear and shinning," which marks the arrival of spring, falls 105 days after the winter solstice. An important festival celebrates this occasion, and, like the other festivals of the solar calendar, it centers around the family. It marks the renewal of spring as well as the renewal of the hearth fire. One or two days before the date of *ch'ing-ming*, the old fire is put out and only cold dishes are eaten. On the day of the festival the new fire is lit. Families then go to the graves of their ancestors, situated in the mountains or in uncultivated land. They clean up the tombs (in some regions where double burials are practiced, they rearrange the bones which have been placed in urns), and there consume leftovers from the previous day's cold meals, wrapped in rice pancakes and fried: the famous "spring rolls" of our Chinese restaurants. *Ch'ing-ming* is a rather unique festival, but is still observed everywhere in China.[7]

By and large though, the festivals belong to the lunar calendar and are generally celebrated by the community as a whole. But each has its own characteristics, its own foods, rituals, and legends.[8] Those common to all regions in China occur on fixed days and periods. Thus, Chinese New Year begins on the first day of the first lunar month and ends on the fifteenth day, while the festival of Universal Salvation (*p'u-tu*) occurs on the fifteenth day of the seventh month. The latter is dedicated to those who died a violent or accidental death, the "orphan souls" and other demons towards whom a collective responsibility is felt.

It is for these deprived souls that vast amounts of food are laid out, which is later eaten by the whole community together with neighboring groups invited to the feast. Villages take turns during the first half of the seventh month inviting each other to come "eat the Universal Salvation." Current governments have tried to reduce this "waste," first by allowing only one day for the festival (in this case the fifteenth), then by prohibiting it altogether.

The New Year and the festival of Universal Salvation divide the year into equal six-month periods, one devoted to Heaven, the other to Earth. A rather similar division is found in each month, in which four days are set apart: the first and fifteenth days are dedicated to Heaven, the second and sixteenth to the Earth (offerings are made to the Earth God and, on an individual basis, to the orphan souls). The days devoted to the Earth begin with the second day of the second month, the last one being the sixteenth day of the twelfth month. Then the preparation for the New Year begins.

The arrival of the New Year is thus first felt in the middle of the twelfth month, at the last offering made to the Earth and at the family banquet that celebrates it. On the twenty-fourth day of the twelfth month, the gods return to the sky. This is the day when people in every family send off the Hearth (Kitchen) God, an inspector from Heaven whose task it is to oversee the behavior of family members. At the end of each year, he is supposed to return to Heaven to make a report on which the family's fortunes in the coming year depend. According to tradition, on that day he is to be offered a New Year cake made of sweetened glutinous rice whose consistency will make his teeth stick together, so that his report will be difficult to understand.

Affairs of the ending year—employment contracts, debts, marriages, the year's business—must be renewed or settled: it is the great expiration date. To permit people to fulfill all these duties, the last day of the year is considered, by definition, a lucky one on which to conclude an undertaking.

Once the old year has been seen out, people prepare for the new one. Everyone buys or makes new clothes. The house is cleaned. The inscriptions on red paper that frame the doors are replaced.[9] New Year's Eve is an especially important event; it is the time when all family members are supposed to gather together. In modern times this has resulted in very heavy train travel: everyone goes home to "pass the year" (*kuo-*

nien). At nightfall everyone's door is closed and locked. Offerings are made to the ancestors, and after midnight, to the gods (the Kitchen God, for example) who are supposed to have returned. On this occasion the ancestors are offered bowls of rice in which are stuck red paper flowers, an offering meant to show that at the end of this year the food reserves are not used up, that, on the contrary, the household is still prosperous. With this one exception, nothing from the old year should pass into the new.

After the offerings are made to the ancestors, the family sits down to feast. A charcoal burning stove, *lu*—the same word as for incense burner—is placed under the table, surrounded by a string of coins. The family members gathered around the table thus surround this stove, which symbolizes the virtues of family unity on which their prosperity depends.

Before dawn, at a moment favored by the calendar, the doors of the houses are opened. After setting off whole strings of firecrackers, the family heads in a lucky direction to go to the communal temple and greet the returning tutelary gods. At dawn on the first day of the year, the children—all dressed up in their new clothes—bow down before their parents, who give them a small sum of money (*ya-sui ch'ien*) wrapped in red paper, a sort of birthday present, for on that day everyone grows a year older.

The first day of the year, and generally the following five days, are holidays for everyone—the only ones during the whole year. New Year's Day provides an occasion to test one's luck for the rest of the year because on that day it is lawful to gamble. The second day of the year is traditionally the time when the women go home to their parents. The ninth day (nine is the *yang* number par excellence) is the anniversary of the God of Heaven, chief of the pantheon. His title is August Imperial Jade Sovereign, Yü-huang shang-ti, but normally he is just called Mr. Heaven (T'ien-kung).

The cycle of the New Year ends on the fifteenth day at the full moon with the Lantern Festival, more officially named the festival of the First Principle (*shang-yuan*) or the Night of the (First) Principle (*yüan-hsiao*). It is a true community festival. The streets are illuminated with paper lanterns, popular works of art recalling the emblematic animal of the year,[10] votive lamps, lamps inscribed with riddles, and so forth. Families take walks to admire these street illuminations. Young girls from good families also go out on that night. And this is how many love stories begin, if one is to believe the Chinese classical theater.[11]

After the New Year cycle, which lasts a whole month, the festivals of the lunar calendar take place at fairly close intervals. They are also of varying importance. Based on the model of the New Year, the "First of the First" (or the "Ruling") moon, the festivals tend to fall on double dates. The "Second of the Second," when an offering is made to the Earth God, patron saint of small localities, is a modest festival, appropriate to the deity in question. The "Third of the Third" is already more important, but varies from region to region.[12]

In contrast, the "Fifth of the Fifth" is an important date accompanied by a mysterious festival. It marks the beginning of the hot season, when epidemics and drought threaten. Jousts on dragon-boats (often responsible for drownings) are believed to counter the drought, while different forms of exorcism ward off illness.

The "Seventh of the Seventh" is a benevolent, romantic festival. Autumn being the season of marriages—many resulting from the spring engagements—the festival celebrates the impossible marriage of two stars situated on either side of the Milky Way. The Herdsman and the Weaver—as these stars are called in legend—meet only once a year, on that night. Beneath the night sky, young girls throw cosmetics and other beauty products onto the roofs for their sister the Weaver and then, to prove their readiness for marriage, engage in contests of skill, such as threading a needle by moonlight.

And so it goes: the "Ninth of the Ninth," when *yang* has reached its apogee, marks the beginning of the rise of *yin*; now all prepare for immortality by climbing mountains to drink there the wine of longevity, like the blessed Immortals. The "Fifteenth of the Eighth," the autumn moon festival, known as the loveliest of all, already marks the coming of *yin,* and consequently, the period of the year when the forces of water are particularly strong.

For many people the celebration consists mainly of eating moon cakes (*yüeh-ping*), but in the villages, in front of the communal temple, the children enjoy a remarkable game. Seated in a circle, they each hold in their hand a small stick of lighted incense obtained from the adults. In the middle of the circle, one or several of them crouch and bury their faces in their arms. The children in the circles chant: "Mother Frog! Mother Frog! Here is the fifteenth of the eighth, come out!" After a moment, the children crouching in the center fall into a trance. They begin to hop and croak like frogs. Other aquatic animals, fish and shrimp, may also manifest themselves through the children, who become damp and cold like the creatures who possess them. Then, without any danger, the incense sticks can be put out by pressing the glowing ends into the children's skin. As soon as a child gets up from the ground, he comes out of the trance, but before this happens, the adults are careful to ask Mother Frog about the coming rains of autumn.

In addition to the universally celebrated festivals, there are community festivals which vary from place to place. These celebrations—the "anniversaries" of local gods and saints—are mostly related to regional religious networks. The alliances formed through the division of the incense play an important role here, which results in numerous pilgrimages. It is generally held that, on the anniversary of his or her birthday, the divine essence of any god or saint is more present. In other words, it is the day when the deity is nearest, the most present in the community, and when an assembly, with processions, is organized at his or her temple (*miao-hui*).

The statue of the god—that is to say, the god himself—is paraded through the streets and roads of the district. The god is accompanied by an impressive cortege. First come his servants, frequently represented by giant marionettes. One most often sees the pair of policemen friends, called White Impermanence (Pai Wu-ch'ang) and Black Impermanence (Hei Wu-ch'ang).[13] The white one is long and skinny and rewards good behavior. The black one is small and fat and punishes wrongdoing.

Behind these divine satellites comes the sedan chair of the god, carried by the young men of the community. They often fall into a trance which causes the litter to sway, sometimes violently. This motion is taken to be inspired by the divine presence who thereby expresses his satisfaction.

Finally, musicians, children disguised as the deity's servants (a sign that they have been given in adoption to him), flower-decked floats, tableaus, all join the procession. At the end of the cortege, the faithful who have called on the god and have thus contracted a debt to him take up their places, each holding a little stick of incense.[14]

In addition to the seasonal festivals and anniversaries of epiphanies, commemorated by assemblies in the temple, there are the "great assemblies" (*ta-hui*) or "great offerings" (*ta-chiao*). These are held at greater intervals and are sometimes linked to cycles of three, five, twelve, or even twenty-four or sixty years. In most places, a great assembly occurs at least once a generation for the reconstruction of the temple after a periodic restoration. These very important celebrations are the expression of a larger community, regional or even interregional. They sometimes last several days and require lengthy preparations. It is for these great assemblies, above all, that the Taoist masters are called on.[15] The great assemblies may occasionally take place in the course of an epidemic or drought to combat these calamities. The investiture of a new Taoist master from the region is also celebrated by a great assembly.

The "anniversary" assemblies, as well as the regional great assemblies, almost necessarily include theatrical representations—for theater, whatever the style, is always tied to religion. The plays enact stories concerning the presence of gods or divine powers in this world. Among the major characters, we find the gods and saints of the Taoist pantheon. The play is more than just a show: as with the children's game of Mother Frog or with solemn processions, it is a manifestation of the divine in the world, an epiphany.

Traditionally, theater in China has had virtually no existence outside religious celebrations, communal or familial. Moreover, the representations have been largely ritual in character. The play chosen for the occasion cannot begin until after the performance of a number of solemn, stereotyped scenes such as the Feast of the Gods in Heaven, the Theft of the Elixir of Immortality, the Birth of the Divine Child (the God of Music), and the Descent of Grace to Earth, to name a few.

These ritual playlets are performed before the ordinary theater, which has itself never been completely without ritual. In its totality, theater expresses what may be said to be the most fundamental dimension of the festive celebration as a whole: *the festival of the people with their gods,*[16] the communion of all beings.

Food

The passage of time marked by the festivals is also expressed by the gathering of different kinds of groups. The great passage of the New Year is a purely family affair. In the festivals of the Earth God, only the members of the district that he oversees have the right to participate. The festival of Universal Salvation enacts the alliance among villages, whereas the temple assemblies are organized on the level of communities of worship joined by the division of the incense.[17]

To each moment of the cycle corresponds a definition of unity as well as a particular prophylaxis, and both are expressed through food. A special food is associated with each seasonal festival: with the New

Year it is rice cake; with *ch'ing-ming*, spring rolls; with the Fifth of the Fifth, steamed dumplings of glutinous rice, packed in bamboo leaves (*ts'ung-tzu*); with the Fifteenth of the Eighth, moon cakes. These foods are appetizing, but also necessary at the appointed time.

More important than the traditional customs which pertain to folklore, the cycle of festivals is really part of the alimentary cycle. All the festivals provide the occasion to eat a lot, and to consume rich food. The offerings—meats and wines—are shared among the participants at the banquets which, according to the social definition of the celebration, may be familial, communal, or regional.

The universally accepted rule is that, outside of feast days, meals are frugal and mainly—if not exclusively—based on cereals. Everyday meals are taken in order of seniority. The elderly people take theirs before the others, then the younger men, and finally the women and children. Ordinary days, however, are no less sacred than feast days. Each person must observe the unwritten rules of sobriety, and the whole community, neighborhood, or village will severely criticize the person who feasts on an ordinary day. Many families also observe a periodic vegetarian feast every three, five, ten, or fifteen days. The frequent festivals, at least every ten or fifteen days, allow the people to alternate and to enhance their frugal diet with rich foods.

Far from being occasions for waste, as many recent governments have maintained, the festivals ensure harmony and equilibrium on both the nutritional and the social levels. Festivals provide a salutary rhythm to everyday life.

3

Divinity

Leafing through the eighteen volumes of *Researches into Chinese Superstitions* by Father Henri Doré S. J.,[1] one cannot help but exclaim: "What a lot of gods!" At first glance it seems that the Chinese have gods for every aspect of human life and for every taste. Farmers, boatmen, actors, drunkards, literati, prisoners, merchants, wells, hearths, privies, each has a divine patron. Doré lived in China at the beginning of this century and his interest in the indigenous culture led him to collect Chinese religious pictures brought to him by his converts, who also became his informers concerning the meaning of the pictures as well as of religious life as a whole. It seems unlikely, however, that he ever met, let alone questioned, a true Taoist master.

Doré published the pictures he had collected, having had them copied in a dry, academic style, which removed from the originals—now extremely rare—all their joyful, naive beauty. The explanations given by the Chinese converts—which were often perfectly inept—were recorded, together with a commentary in which terms such as *superstition, vain observances,* and *harmful and useless beliefs* occur over and over. But what stands out the most in Henri Doré's monumental work is the disjointed, incoherent aspect of his "researches." As his investigations proceeded, the author sought information not only in the converts' remarks, but also in literary sources. The latter, however, were rarely drawn from religious literature. Doré did not consult Taoist books, trusting rather the anecdotal, fictionalized writings of cultured bureaucrats, a bit like a historian of European medieval religion choosing to draw his information exclusively from sources like the *Canterbury Tales*.

In Doré's version—and let me emphasize that, since its publication in 1911, his work has been accepted as authoritative in this field—the Chinese religion is thus presented as a vast jumble of absurd beliefs and rituals. For Doré (spiritual heir of Descartes as well as of Saint Ignatius) to acknowledge that Chinese religion had a certain logic, that it might have its own theology, that in it a certain Reason might be found, was tantamount to admitting that it could claim a certain portion of truth and that, like the religion of ancient Greece as seen by the scholastics, it might contain a particle of divine illumination. Consequently, no attempt was made to relate the facts to each other, to detect an under-lying coherence, to observe the social, real-life dimension of the body of worship, the religious worship, the religious organization, and the liturgy. Not surprisingly, no evaluation of doctrine or theology was ever attempted.

At the bottom of this missed opportunity lies, once more, a misun-derstanding. Our word *religion* has no equivalent in Chinese. The same obviously holds true for the notion of divinity. In translating the Bible, the missionaries adopted the word *shen* to mean "god," but this was a rather unfortunate translation. The Chinese "gods"—we shall see that it is really a question of patron saints—are not called simply *shen* but *shen-ming,* which literally means "radiance of the celestial soul," thus referring to a divine and supernatural force. For *shen* means "soul," not in the Christian sense of the word, but as one of the many souls with which human beings are endowed. Chinese ontology recognizes several spiritual principles that together make up the human person: a human is a complex being, a composite of diverse essences. This notion is grounded in cosmology.

Cosmology

One can understand the nature of transcendence only by referring to the Great Beginning—as do all the ancient texts which treat this question. These cosmological theories are common to all of China, and belong to its basic philosophy. Developed in antiquity in the Book of Changes (*I-ching*),[2] these theories assumed their current form in the first centuries B.C. This cosmology is a scholarly, abstract elaboration of the creation myths, which the Confucian thinkers rejected and obscured.[3] The situation of Taoism is more complex: its mysteries preserve important elements of ancient mythology but have also contributed in a decisive way to cosmological science and to the general theory of energies (*ch'i*) and correspondences fundamental to all Chinese thought.

Cosmological and theological concepts place at the beginning of Heaven and Earth *Primordial Chaos,* called *hun-tun*:[4] a sphere or matrix that holds within itself the whole universe, but in a diffuse, undifferentiated and potential state. Those are the *ch'i,* the "breaths" or pure energy-matter which have not yet emerged from chaos, from dark confusion. This primeval matrix is subject nonetheless to the influence of the Tao, to its action of cyclical time. At a given point, the matrix comes to maturity, breaks up, and frees the *ch'i* (breaths, energies) contained within, which then escape and separate. The light, transparent *ch'i* rise and form heaven; the heavy, opaque ones sink, forming Earth. Thus, having established the polarity of Heaven and Earth, the *ch'i* join and unite in the Center, which constitutes a third fundamental modality.

The Three complete each other, forming composite entities, the "Ten Thousand Beings." The process of creation manifests itself in a constant, arithmetic series of divisions, into increasingly complex categories. The *ch'i* diversify, as numerous as the stars in the heavens: the Five Planets, the Twenty-Eight Palaces, the Thirty-Six Celestial Stars and the Seventy-Two Terrestrial Stars—the latter two totaling One Hundred and Eight—and so on.[5]

In this creation, the human being occupies no special position, except that of the most complex conglomerate, incorporating all the differentiated energies of the universe, which, according to an ancient Taoist ritual formula used in consecrating the body, gives him:

Five viscera and six receptacles,
seven directors and nine palaces,
skin and veins,
muscles, bone, marrow, and brains,
nine openings to watch and protect,
twelve abodes for the gods,
on the left three *hun* [celestial spirits],
on the right the seven *p'o* [terrestrial spirits],
three levels of the body,
with eight effulgences each,
making up twenty-four gods,
one thousand two hundred projections,

twelve thousand vibrations,
three hundred sixty articulations,
and eighty-four thousand pores.[6]

But this complex concentration is short-lived, as the Tao pursues its
action through the flux of cyclical time. The two fundamental phases of
the Tao's action are *yin* and *yang,* graphically the north- and south-
facing slopes, the shady side and the sunny side of the mountain. *Yin*
and *yang* serve to designate cold and hot, moon and sun, soft and hard,
feminine and masculine, death and life. Their complementary opposition exists in everything and their alternation is the first law of Chinese
cosmology: when *yin* reaches its apex, it changes into *yang,* and vice-
versa.[7]

This movement of transformation is ceaseless, spontaneous, moving
through phases which, like the phenomena themselves, participate in
more and more elaborate cycles. Between Water and Fire—the two elements that represent *yin* and *yang* at their apogee[8]—Wood and Metal
represent two intermediary phases. The Earth represents a fifth element
that makes possible the joining of the preceding four. These, then, are
the Five Phases, or as they are more commonly called, the Five Elements: Metal, Wood, Water, Fire, and Earth. Everyone in China knows
the correspondences of these five phases in the spatio-temporal continuum of the Tao: Wood corresponds to Spring, Fire to Summer, Metal
to Autumn, Water to Winter. The third lunar month of each season—
there are twelve lunar months to a year—falls under the sign of the
Earth, the intermediary and central phase. Here, the Earth is the Center, whereas the four other phases correspond to the Four Winds. In
the human body, the Five Elements are represented by the Five Viscera
(lungs, liver, kidneys, heart, and spleen). This classificatory model applies to all the categories: the Five Planets, the Five Flavors, the Five
Colors, and so forth.[9]

Like *yin* and *yang,* the Five Phases are found in everything and their
alternation is the second physical law. The Phases lead from one to the
other: Water produces Wood; Wood, Fire; Fire, Earth; Earth, Metal;
Metal, Water. Opposite this productive cycle stands the destructive cycle: Water versus Fire; Fire versus Metal; Metal versus Wood; Wood
versus Earth; Earth versus Water.

For the moment, let us abandon this excursion into the systems of
classification and correspondence, and return to our point of departure:
the *ch'i*. The multiplicity of *ch'i* making up the human being is expressed
by a certain number of "souls" which correspond to the *essences* of the

ch'i (energies). Among them, *shen,* referred to above, constitutes the purest of the celestial energies. *Shen* is a regulating element, which is also called *hun,* "cloud soul." In opposition to these heavenly spirits stands the soul corresponding to the terrestrial *ch'i,* called *ching.* From a physiological point of view, *ching* designates bone marrow and sperm or menstrual blood. *Ching* resides in the kidneys, *shen* in the heart (the organ of thought).

Analogous to *ching,* and in opposition to *hun,* the *p'o* ("bone souls") are souls of the solid part of the body, in particular the skeleton. The *p'o*—seven in number—are often considered to be fiendish by nature, that is, they are *kuei,* diabolical spirits. The *kuei* are in opposition with the *shen* in daily life the way a demon is to a god.

	cosmological	physiological	theological
higher	*shen*	*hun*	*shen*
lower	*ching*	*p'o*	*kuei*

Each human thus has god-souls and demon-souls, which differ from the great gods of the pantheon only in their relative strength. The *hun* fill the role of director-spirits. Enjoying freedom of movement, they leave the body during sleep or trance. It is assumed that they go to Heaven at specific times to report on a person's activities; but they are just and accuse their host only in the case of a serious sin. This controlling function is common to all the gods.

The *p'o,* on the contrary, deliberately aim to destroy us. They are the spirits of the skeleton, that which is heaviest in the human body, most earthbound. This close tie to the earth makes it difficult for them to tolerate the authority of the higher spirits. They try by every means to free themselves in order to rejoin their natural environment—to enable the skeleton to return to earth. It is, therefore, the job of the director-spirits (*shen, hun*) to dominate, discipline, and contain them.

Given a human being's many souls, how does one arrive at the notion of god? Of course, *shen,* which is a celestial *ch'i,* already has a transcendent side. But the living, after a life here below, do not become gods; if all goes well, they may become ancestors, which is not the same thing. Death and life are but the two phases of a cycle, an alternation analogous to that of *yin* and *yang.* Now, the number of *shen* in the universe is immutable, and these *shen* are constantly recycled. If a person reaches the natural term of his life, that is, the end of his phase or his revolution in the cycle, then everything is in order. His higher souls— his *shen*—go to make up an ancestor, whereas his bones—his *p'o*—are buried according to the science of Chinese geology[10] so that their power may be mastered and be beneficial to his offspring. The souls of the dead are the treasure of the living: each family possesses in the *hun* and *p'o* souls of its ancestors a certain number of vital spirits which consti- tute a sort of *charisma familiaris*.

In addition to worshiping at the tombs of their ancestors, the fami- lies also keep little tablets on the family altar to represent their ances- tors. These are little wooden stelae made at the time of burial. The tablet is consecrated in the same way a statue would be, by the *ch'i*: the members of the family of the deceased breathe on a writing brush dipped in blood or in red ink. This "animated" brush is then used to dot the tablet in various spots which correspond to the different parts of the body. The person (usually a Taoist master) who performs this ritual marking, pronounces a formula: "I mark your eyes and your eyes see, I mark your heart and your heart beats," and so on.

In this way, the tablet is consecrated and becomes an object of wor- ship on the family altar. The ancestor's spirit, present in the tablet, is constantly informed of family events, especially on important days. The ancestors play the role of benefactors, but also that of judges; their dissatisfaction can cause great trouble.[11]

As mentioned earlier, only those who die a natural death, at the end of a reasonably long life, are considered potential ancestors. Those who die prematurely, by accident or suicide, can never become ancestors; neither their casket nor their tablet can enter the family house. These dead are not correct spirits (*cheng-hun*), but become wandering, disin- herited souls (*ku-hun*). The vital forces of a person who has not fulfilled his destiny leave the normal cycle and are "left over." The cycle has been interrupted and the souls can no longer reenter it; they can neither pass on to the world of the dead nor be reabsorbed into the family matrix. They must remain in a place where their unexpected vitality condemns them to a miserable life, as exiles in the world of the living.

These orphan souls are full of resentment towards a society that they, rightly or wrongly, feel has deprived them of their natural destiny. In addition to their desire for vengeance, there is also the fact that, unless divine or religious intervention takes place, the only way for them to escape their wretched condition is to find a substitute. Therefore, they devote themselves to leading others to their deaths: they draw the stroller toward the river's edge, or cause automobile accidents on the very site of their own accidental death.[12]

The threat posed by the orphan souls is assumed by every community as both a collective and individual responsibility. Referred to euphemistically as "the good little brothers," the orphan souls are the object of constant attention. At every feast "our little brothers" are the first to be served with dishes and wines at a table set up at the entrance to the house. Sacrificial paper money is also burned as an offering to them.[13] The festival of the seventh moon is almost entirely dedicated to the orphan souls. During the rites of Universal Salvation, Buddhist priests and Taoist masters join together to retrieve and nourish the orphan souls and to reintegrate them into the cycle of births and deaths.

The Gods

Ordinary people thus have no need for their souls to be saved, given that true salvation occurs in the natural course of things. As we have seen, the aid of the gods results in a debt to be repaid and expiated. If all goes well, a person owes nothing to the gods, nor will he become a god himself. Indeed, the pantheon's origin lies in the extraordinary, in the accidental.

As I said before, the notion of divinity would seem to correspond perfectly to the concept of *shen,* that celestial soul, so why could the gods and the saints not simply be virtuous men and women deified upon their death? Some people in China actually think that way: the Confucians. They practice a kind of euhemerism which conceives divinity as the apotheosis of heroes who died for a just cause. But in Taoism, men and women, even exemplary ones, are not worshiped merely for their virtues.

The divine Lord Kuan, for example, a model of loyalty and courage, the incarnation of the chivalric spirit, protector of the Manchu dynasty and patron of merchants, was a hero of the period of the Three Kingdoms (220–265). He is depicted on horseback holding a halberd, or seated holding the classic *Annals of Springs and Autumns* in one hand and, with the other, stroking the long black beard of his noble red face. Captured by an enemy ruse, the valorous warrior was executed by the cowardly King of Wu, a rival kingdom. But, as the *Romance of the Three*

Kingdoms—one of the most popular books of China—tells it, "the souls of the noble Kuan did not disperse into the air." Instead, at the banquet the king gave in honor of Lu Meng, who had captured Kuan, the hero's spirit returned and took possession of its enemy, forcing him to speak as if he were Lord Kuan himself. Behold! Out of the mouth of Lu Meng, at the very moment the latter is to be granted a fief, comes a long series of insults directed at the king. His outrageous tirade ended, Lu Meng falls down dead. Lord Kuan has avenged himself. It was because of this demon power that he became the object of worship in the first place.

Another example is lovely Ma-tsu, the Mother-ancestor, patron of sailors and travellers, protectress of women and children. She was the daughter of a poor fisherman from Mei-chou island, off Fukien on the eastern coast of China. A precocious child, interested only in saintly things, she stayed at home to recite holy books instead of playing with the other girls. For many hours she would remain perfectly still, her eyes closed, her face shining in ecstatic meditation, while her higher souls (*hun*) left her body and roamed through Heaven and Earth. One day during a fierce storm, her souls came to the aid of her father and brothers, lost on the high seas, their boats about to capsize. As they were going down, they saw a tall white figure approach on the water and take the ropes of the boats to pull them to safety. But at the very moment, the young saint's mother saw her daughter once again lost in a trance and, being irritated, shook her out of it. In that instant Ma-tsu's concentration wavered; her souls let go of the ropes of her father's boat so that only her two brothers were saved. On their return, the brothers recounted their adventure and Ma-tsu's mother recognized her mistake. When she was old enough to be married, Mat-su took a vow of chastity. She died a few years later.

Though shorter, the legends of the lesser divinities are no less edifying. Mr. Kuo, a local god of Fukien province, a perfect servant and model of devotion to his master, used his own legs as kindling to boil water for the morning tea one day when there was no firewood in the house. An equally dramatic legend concerns Hsieh and Fan, also known as White Impermanence and Black Impermanence, the two divine satellites we met in connection with anniversary processions. Originally, they were two policemen who were friends and always worked as a team. When it began to rain one day, the big one said to the little one: "Wait here for me under this bridge that passes over the dried up stream while I run home and fetch an umbrella." Alas, once home, he became absorbed in a hundred tasks and did not return immediately to his friend. The little one, true to his word, waited under the bridge until the rising waters carried him off and he drowned. When the big one finally returned, he was so disconsolate at the death of his loyal friend that he hung himself on the nearest tree. Thus, the little one has a black face, the color that symbolizes water, and the big one's tongue sticks out to recall his death by hanging.

The God of the Hearth is supposed to have been a man who committed suicide by leaping into a kitchen fire; and the Earth God, a brave servant who died of the cold in order to protect his mistress.[14] In popular legends, none of the gods has died of natural causes; they have all either been executed, or have committed suicide, or died virgins—a terrible fate. Thus, by definition, they are all *ku-hun*, orphan souls. Normally, among the *ku-hun*, virgins who—like Ma-tsu—died young without fulfilling their female destiny are especially feared, for they have their maternal power intact and ready to avenge themselves. And according to the normal scheme of things, Lord Kuan or Mr. Kuo ought to have become fearsome demons.

What then is the difference between a demon and god? Honestly speaking, there is no ontological distinction between them, only a difference of spiritual power. If Mr. Kuo had been an ordinary man, his violent death would have made of him a common demon, one of many. But his moral strength, the determination and the intensity of his devotion as a perfect servant, enabled him to transcend his humble position. The spiritual power of his souls was no longer that of a simple person who died a violent death, but that of a god.

The case of Ma-tsu is even clearer. To be sure, she died a virgin, but her inner strength, developed by years of spiritual exercises, had become formidable. Her mana was not merely human, and even less demonic, but divine. Such a force, however, is not necessarily beneficent. Lord Kuan killed many men during his life and after his death used his homicidal power to accomplish his vengeance. His worship is therefore primarily of a propitiatory nature: one must appease the avenging spirit before channelling its forces towards more positive ends.

Spiritual Power

The strength that makes one a god lies within each being. Transcendence is not the result of a spirit separated from matter, an external divine force given to the world, but a spiritualization of *ch'i*, of energy-matter itself. Cosmology teaches us there is nothing that is not "matter" and that matter cannot be distinguished from its substance, its energy.

At the birth of the universe there was a diversification of *ch'i*-energies (the more subtle ones rising to form Heaven, the heavier ones making up the Earth), but this composite whole was not immutable; it was, and is, constantly changing. The whole cosmic body turns and changes, conforming to the process of the Tao. The third law of Chinese physics (which one could also call the first law of its metaphysics) states that every body that goes through a prolonged and repeated cyclical action is transmuted and purified. This is true even of the most humble and inert organisms and objects; trees, stones, and long-lived animals like the tortoise or the stork can become spontaneously spiritual by the simple action of the cycle of the seasons and the years. All creatures of exceptionally advanced age can manifest their power and thus influence their environment. For this reason, people worship sacred trees whose vital forces have been deified. Tied round with strips of red cloth, an incense burner at its base, such a tree becomes the protecting spirit of a village or region. The tree's body is identified with the social body of the district: if the branches of the sacred tree are cut, people of the village will die.

For the human being, a normal, peaceful, regulated life is a major factor in his accumulation of spiritual power. Living according to the calendrical cycles, the ever-renewed passing of the seasons, and participating in these through *everyday religion,* leads one naturally to that marvelous old age which is the greatest happiness on earth before one joins the ranks of the ancestors. The final passage is marked by sumptuous, prolonged funerary rites, true festivals of succession celebrated by the families for their "beautiful dead."[15]

By virtue of its very complexity, the human body is eminently able to charge itself with energy and thus to transmute itself. "Of all beings, the human is the most spiritual" say the Taoist texts, for with a round head (like Heaven), square feet (like Earth), five viscera (like the planets), and so many other points of correspondence, every person has innumerable points of correlation with the surrounding universe which can be put into correspondence with a great many spatiotemporal cycles. He or she is able to preserve this body thanks to everyday religion, as well as to work towards its perfection by conscious, directed action. Thus, each person can not only live a healthy life, but also radiate energy, that is, become transcendent.

This virtue which confers divine power is obtained by cultivating oneself through *hsiu-yang*, a practice which enables us to acquire, on the basis of our natural dispositions, exceptional qualities. *Hsiu-yang* means to arrange, to smooth down any roughness or irregularities by repeating an action many times in harmony with the cosmic order, until perfection is achieved. The perfect and complete body is thereby nurtured, its energies strengthened; it thus becomes totally integrated into the natural and cosmic environment. From there, the way is led—by repeated, cyclical movements—to spontaneity, which is the essence of the Tao.

To understand this process, one has to realize that one's *body-person,* the ephemeral conglomerate of the diverse *ch'i* that make up the world, is not perfect at birth. The child's spontaneity is only an illusion. True spontaneity (*tzu-jan,* literally "as it is") is acquired through training and self-perfection. A classic example is the practice of calligraphy. A child does not know how to give Chinese characters that perfection of form that expresses so completely their essence and is so prized by calligraphers themselves. It takes daily practice and endless repetition of the same gesture, the same discipline and ritual procedure, to achieve the mastery that finally allows one to create perfect forms without any apparent effort. It is nature retrieved, spontaneous creation, the secret stolen from the Tao. Perfect calligraphy incorporates the cosmic forces so well that it is invested with spiritual power: a master of the art who has beautifully rendered the character "stork" sees the sign transform itself into a living bird that spreads its wings and flies away.

Moreover, the great vital and creative forces of exceptional living creatures (animals, humans, or demons) once captured, recovered, and directed towards the good—that is, towards *life*—will continue to expand indefinitely. Worship—perfect ritual action constantly renewed—contributes to the spiritual power of the gods which in turn results in the spread of their glory and influence. In the beginning, the worship of these demon spirits is primarily propitiatory and purely local. But a minor demon can, through the liturgy of the people, become a great god, a patron saint, a protector of a region or of an entire nation, an archangel, an emperor of Heaven.

Ma-tsu, for example, was at first the object of a small mediumistic cult in a temple at her birthplace where her mummified body was kept.[16] She was recognized in the twelfth century (she is believed to have lived in the tenth) as the patron saint of sailors for the whole coastal region of eastern China. As the result of a series of petitions, she was accorded an official title—a form of canonization—by the imperial administration, who named her "Saint of Diligent Assistance." In 1155 the Sung dynasty emperor Kao-tsung named her "Lady Source of Felicity," and, in 1160, "Lady of Illuminated Response and Benevolent Spirituality"—the length of the title being directly proportional to rank in the public registers of worship.[17] Later, in 1190, she was promoted to "Celestial Consort." Her title now included more than twenty characters, and her sanctuaries received imperial donations and were permitted the highest of decorative marks: yellow tiles, imperial insignia, and the like. A sacred scripture (*ching*), revealed in Heaven and transmitted here below, marked her acceptance in the great Taoist liturgy as patron saint of sailors. Taoism saw her as an emanation of one of the stars of the Big Dipper, thus identifying her as one of the cosmic *ch'i*. This scripture in honor of Ma-tsu was included in the *Tao-tsang* [*Taoist Canon*] of 1445.[18] In 1683, after having helped the Chinese reconquer Taiwan and subjugate the independent state that had been set up there, she was finally promoted to Queen of Heaven (T'ien-hou). Her cult now extended throughout China from Peking to Canton. It remains today especially vital in those places where it has not been forbidden and repressed, namely in Hong Kong and Taiwan. The fishing folk and peasants of Southern Fukien have succeeded in recent times—thanks to the liberalization of the official ideology—in rebuilding on Mei-chou Island part of the founding shrine for Ma-tsu's worship. This time the building has been constructed in stone (rather than wood, as before), so that it won't be burnt again.

The road to sainthood is long. The concentration of one's vital forces, maintained through self-perfection, makes one a formidable demon before one becomes a gentle and beneficial power. The career of each being, as carefully codified by the Taoist masters, leads from the status of minor local spirit, even from the spirit of a stone or a plant, to the summits of the heavens where spiritual strength becomes astral. All the same, those higher beings are capable of worldly feelings. Despite her elevated position, Ma-tsu still remains subject to her own whims, and Lord Kuan, who is just as illustrious since he is a Celestial Emperor, remains capable of turning his anger on those who fail to respect him. The demoniacal character of the minor gods is clearer still and is expressed in their iconography itself.

As long as they are gods, these beings remain subject to the rule of time. No investiture, not even a stellar one, lasts forever, for everything that has a beginning also has an end, and to concentration correspond dispersal and diffusion, which are the privileged actions of the Tao.

4

The Masters of the Gods

Puppets and Mediums

Taoist masters sometimes perform as puppeteers. The plays they perform with string dolls (*k'uei-lei*) are considered by some to be the oldest form of theater in China.[1] The ties between religion and drama are manifold. We have seen that stagings of sacred history form part of religious celebrations. In fact, only a hundred years ago professional theaters were rare in China; the usual time and place to see performances was at festivals, on outdoor stages set up in front of the temple. Even today in places where the religion is practiced openly, there is no true festival without theater.

The theater has a liturgical function, performances being divided into two parts, the first of which is purely ritual. Called the "review of the gods" (*pan-shen*) or "auspicious play" (*chi-hsiang hsi*), it is composed of a number of short, successive playlets: the Celestial Court; the Banquet of the Gods (with the monkey god who steals peaches belonging to the Queen Mother of the West;[2] the Emperor of Heaven's daughter and the pious Tung Yung,[3] the divine couple who are the parents of the god of music; and, finally, the Heavenly Officer[4] who comes to present his compliments to the community.

It is only after these preliminary scenes that the performance of the historical plays selected for the occasion can begin. While these plays are not ritual, there is always a link with religion. Thus, the actor playing Lord Kuan in the epic of the Three Kingdoms[5] is subject to certain dietary and sexual restrictions. As befits a representative of the divine administration, his character speaks entirely in official Mandarin[6] even if the play itself is in dialect or in a regional language.

The religious role of marionette theater as performed by the masters is even more pronounced than that of ordinary theater which features human actors. Puppets are rarely called in just for the show; their power is such that they are considered invaluable aids in the battle against evil influences. A troupe is called on to exorcise these influences in the event of disaster such as fire, flood, drought, or epidemics. They also come to purify newly built houses and temples or to consecrate important offerings, either to the gods or to the orphan souls. This is because the puppets do not just represent the gods: they *are* the gods.

As a rule, a marionette ensemble consists of thirty-six bodies and seventy-two heads. Together, these add up to 108, which corresponds to the total number of constellations. The puppets, therefore, represent all the essences of the universe. Before the play begins, the marionettes are consecrated in the same way as the statues of the gods and the tablets of the ancestors. They are thus infused with the spiritual force of the gods they represent. So fearsome is their strength that when they chase away demons with their chants and dances, and assail invisible devils with their miniature weapons, no one dares to look. The orchestra plays, the master puppeteer recites sacred formulas, the puppets move about, but the place in front of the stage remains empty and the common people stay home behind closed doors afraid that, in a panic, the demons might take refuge in their homes, or even in their bodies.

The stage—boards and canvas—is a sacred area. At the back is an altar for the cult of the puppets, represented by the most powerful of them, the clowns. In the four corners of the stage, talismanic symbols (*fu*),[7] written in sacred characters on bands of yellow paper, call on the protecting gods to come and surround the stage. A fifth symbol, corresponding to the center of the sacred area, is carried by the master puppeteer. Here, at the heart of the microcosm of the stage, he stands as the main axis. He is the intermediary between the divine and human spheres, the invisible master who makes the puppets (mostly the clowns) perform the gestures of the exorcism, gestures which on other occasions are performed by himself or by a medium whom he directs.[8]

All this is interrelated: the structure that governs the relation between puppet master and puppet—between the one hidden in the shadows who pulls the strings and the other who occupies center stage and, while the show lasts, holds the attention of the audience—is the same structure found in the relation between masters and mediums, men and gods. The gods are puppets. Like the figures of White Impermanence and Black Impermanence in processions, the statues in temple niches often have movable limbs. They are completely outfitted, with under-garments, shoes, gowns and hats, fans and scepters. They can be moved around and seated at a table to be served real feasts on their birthdays. In this game, men play with the gods, and the temple becomes a great dollhouse.

Active religious communities each have their "children," the name given to the mediums, those who are possessed by or are interpreters for the gods.[9] When we looked at the festival of the autumn moon, we saw how common trances were. They are first part of children's games and then part of the adolescents' initiation. At the age of sixteen, boys undergo several months of training at the village temple, where a master teaches them the history of the world and the gods, cosmology, and techniques of concentration and trance.[10] The boys learn to experience the influence of the divine power, experience they will need when they carry the tutelary saint's sedan chair in processions. The master also teaches them boxing techniques and other martial arts, which are all considered to be religious work and are therefore called "meritorious action," *kung-fu*.[11] Thus trained, these young men form teams of boxers and sedan chair bearers. During festivals they show off their accomplishments, parading in strategic formations that repeat the cosmic diagrams: the Eight Trigrams, the Five Cardinal Points, the Dragon-and-Tiger. Their collective trance makes them invulnerable, ready for anything. These were the troops that bravely defended Chinese culture against Western colonialism during the "Boxer Rebellion."[12]

While the boys are trained as divine soldiers, at home the girls learn the different forms of female worship and are initiated by their elders into the arts of massage and healing, the secrets of the bedchamber and the delivery room. At the New Year, along with the other women of the household, they invoke and are possessed by the Lady of the Privy, the little bride who committed suicide to escape her mother-in-law's harassment.[13]

Anyone can be possessed and become a medium. It is generally during the young people's training period that the community recruits, according to its needs, those who have a particular gift for trances. Such a person then becomes the mouthpiece of the god of the community, his or her representative and incarnation.

Dressed like a child, barefoot and stripped to the waist, his stomach covered by a lozenge-patterned cloth—the undergarment worn by babies and women—the medium is carried in a procession on the sedan chair of his gods where he is placed behind the statue (which is to say, carried like a baby on its mother's back). Standing thus, he shows off the invulnerability that comes with being possessed by applying to his body the symbols of the gods of the Five Cardinal Points, in this case thick steel needles ending in sculpted heads portraying the Guardian Generals of the ritual area.[14] Two through the cheeks, two through the arms or the calves, and the remaining one corresponding to the Center, through the tongue. In one hand, this divine baby holds the vanguard flag of the heavenly armies led by the generals, which are present in his body; in the other, his exorcist's sword, with which he chases away demons by striking himself on the forehead and the back.

He is a bloodied child, wounded in his divine body by the stigmata of the Five Cardinal Points, Center of the universe, Lord of the heavenly armies, sacrificed and immortal, his blood purifies the world of any evil influence. At any given festival, there are many of these epiphanic saviors who free the community from negative and hostile currents and who chase away the demons brought there by past sins.

The seances, which take place after the processions or independently of the festivals, are more peaceful. Wearing the scanty outfit of ritual nakedness or dressed in the costume of the god he represents, the medium speaks in the shrill voice of the Chinese theater actors, using the language spoken by civil servants. His stream of words is sometimes broken by improvised chants. Those who have come to consult him do not grasp the content of this dignified speech, so his "impressario" stands beside him and interprets, respectfully translating the divine words, backing them up with a commentary, and adjusting them to the question, for the oracles rarely speak directly to the point. Rather, a medium's speech is extremely general, moralizing, and broad. In some cases, though, when asked about an illness, the medium may give a prescription, or even write down talismanic symbols, sacred characters representing the secret names of gods.

The "impressario," who is usually called "he who stands at the end of the table," directs the seance. On the surface, he plays the role of an assistant: he dresses the medium, helps him to fall into a trance,[15] and brings it to a close by abruptly picking him up off the ground—for as soon as the "child's" feet leave the ground, his power leaves him. However, the assistant is actually the master of the medium. He is almost always the one who has taught the latter his trance techniques. From the master's point of view, the medium is merely a disciple, an interpreter of the art, an instrument of his power, filling the place that a doll might occupy in other circumstances.

Indeed, the master can have his "children" carry out in a trance the simple rites of the liturgy in the vernacular. In this case, the text is sung by a chorus of young people, the sedan chair bearers and boxers mentioned earlier. They stand in two lines facing each other, each one with a percussion instrument—drum, gong, or bells—and sing in unison the verses of the ritual, an epic describing the voyage to the land of the gods.

When the ritual reaches the end of this journey, the seance takes place. The singing breaks off and the faithful ask the medium what he sees in the other world. After a while, the ritual continues, this time in order to bring the medium's spirit back to earth. In this way, rituals can be transformed into theater, without changing their fundamental structure. Even if the common person sees only the medium, focuses only on the puppet without paying attention to the puppeteer, or gazes at the deity's statue without asking how its divinity was revealed, the source of what is expressed here nevertheless always lies in the master.

The Barefoot Master and His Ritual

The masters of the mediums, these discreet celebrants of the vernacular rites, are shamans. They invest their strength in their assistants and make them their instruments: in Fukien, mediums are called *dang-ki* (in Mandarin, *chi-t'ung*), which literally means "the divining-stick-child." The masters and their mediums belong to the same group, that of the "boxers," the initiatory age groups of the local communities. According to need and opportunity, the community, speaking through its elders, allows an especially talented young man (in some cases, a young woman) to seek divine investiture. This search is generally accompanied by illness and existential crises which are taken as the signs of a master's vocation.

The apprentice takes up residence in the local temple, where he eats and sleeps. Through constant (but not exaggerated) devotion and good behavior, he tries to win the confidence of the local gods, who eventually reveal themselves to him, usually in his sleep. The local gods, among whom the Earth God of the village is very important, teach the adept the mythical and sacred history and geography of the gods and demons, the forces present in the village and its surroundings, and the identity of the spirits and wandering souls. The gods revealed in these initiatory dreams later become the adept's protectors. He may call on them to aid him in overcoming evil influences. When his vocation is confirmed, the adept seeks a master who, in exchange for services, will transmit the necessary ritual skills.

The master's ritual costume is essentially the same as the medium's for the simple reason that the medium is none other than the alter ego of the officiant. Indeed, rather than "costume," one ought to call it a ritual "undress": he has a bare chest and bare feet; around his head he wears a turban of red cloth; his stomach is covered by the little red lozenge apron which is the characteristic women's and children's undergarment; and his waist is wrapped in a white "cavalier's skirt," opening in the front. In his left hand, he holds the command banners of the spiritual army; in his right, a buffalo horn to call the gods.[17]

This barefoot master is called a "magician," *fa-shih,* or, because of his headdress, a "red head." The rites that celebrate his installation as master provide the occasion for him to demonstrate the skills he has acquired from his divine protectors. He shows his invulnerability by walking on a bed of live coals and climbing a ladder of sharp knives. This is not just a trial: the thirty-six rungs represent the levels of heaven and the ascent is a voyage to their summit. There, face to face with the lord of the pantheon, the Jade Emperor (Yu-huang), the disciple introduces himself to the divine court and receives their investiture. This takes the form of an individual covenant with each of the gods, a pact sealed by a document in which the divine authority promises his protection and aid by virtue of the law which obliges the gods to work for the benefit of mankind.

While a vast crowd watches his progression on the sharp steel blades of the ladder of knives, the disciple, on reaching the summit, drops two oracular blocks. These blocks are asymmetrical, one side convex (*yang*), and the other flat (*yin*). If they fall to the ground each with a different side up, one *yin* and the other *yang,* the disciple is accepted and he becomes a new master. If not, he must begin again. Success thus seems to depend on the gods. But things are not what they appear to be: it is perfectly acceptable to start over as many times as necessary to obtain a favorable answer, to force the gods to agree. In the end, the gods depend on men, on the alliance that they must make with the master.

Indeed, at the time of his investiture, the disciple establishes bonds not only with the deities of heaven, but with all the different categories of spiritual beings. Following his initiatory dream, he tries to enlist all the spiritual powers of the region. For this purpose an announcement is posted at the investiture site, proclaiming:

Master So-and-So introduces a disciple who wants to become a master, and whose duty it will be, once he has been initiated and purified by fire, to aid and succor all men. He still presently needs a few more soldiers in his contingent to strengthen his ministry. On this very day, we therefore have established a ritual area and have announced to the local Earth God and to the other spirits who make possible communication between the world of the dead and the world of the living that all dead souls not yet dissolved into the air, evil ghosts from the outside and foreign demons, all sprits having neither dwelling nor support and who are in the prime of life, with good vision and without infirmities, should come and enlist in our troops. Be quick! Take the exam!

The monthly wages are four bushels of rice, two taels, and two cents in silver, (in exchange for which) you will spend all your time aiding and relieving the people, you will obey the call of the drum and the buffalo horn, you will greet the living politely, you will lead to your superiors the dead souls who carry symbols [fu] which you have verified. But you will fight without mercy the pernicious demons, evil spells, ghouls, and perverse spirits who attack our ritual area.

Everywhere, and without questioning, you will follow the disciple in his work to save the people, to fight evil and heal the sick, and when the day comes you will be rewarded and promoted according to your merit.[18]

In this way, the barefoot masters, who themselves belong to the lowest rank in the Taoist hierarchy, win over these demons, orphan souls, and other dangerous powers, who are thus able to take a first step up the ladder of merit which leads to heaven. Henceforth, these demons are *yin-ping*, soldiers of *yin*, of the nether world. They are under the command of the generals of the Five Cardinal Points whose garrisons are located at the four corners of the village territory and, for the Center, in the local temple.

For each ritual the master summons these generals by blowing on his buffalo horn. The Garrison Generals and the other gods with whom the master has established a covenant surround him and with their troops make a barrier around the area. This area is always in the open air and bears no sign except for the five talismans (representing the Generals' names) placed on bamboo stakes at the Five Cardinal Points. The calling up of the spirit armies, their review at the beginning of the ritual, and the dismissal at the end must be performed by the master in person.

On the other hand, for the main part of the ceremony, which takes place between the invocation and the dismissal (the concentration and the dispersal) and which varies according to the occasion, a medium or a puppet may replace the master as the officiant.

Inside the spatial and temporal circle created by the armies, the ritual action becomes a dramatic performance. The action may take different forms, including that of *the journey*. For example, when the ritual is performed to thank the local deities for their aid and protection, the officiant is called upon to transfer a large amount of sacrificial money to the divine authorities. His voyage beings here on earth. After crossing a vast desert plain, he enters a mountain through a cave which leads to the underworld and which he must cross at his own peril. Time and again he finds his way blocked by the guards of the hells. Fortunately, he knows their names and presents his talisman (*fu*) as his passport. Having crossed the underworld, he goes up to the heavens. He identifies himself by listing his name and quality and by showing his talisman to the deities at the gates. Finally, he enters the heavenly chancellery, where he finds the inspectors and clerks. There he deposits the contributions, duly counted, from the members of the community.[19]

Similar journeys may lead the officiant to different parts of the other world, for example, to the Flower Garden where each woman here on earth has her plant. The plants have red and white buds. A red blossom means that she is pregnant with a girl, whereas a white flower signifies a boy. The garden is watched over by a Mother to whom one must bring a few small offerings. There are also a couple of gardeners who should not be forgotten, for their task is to fertilize the plants so that they will flower. When new flowers have to be planted, the officiant takes care of this with the help of the deities in his command. Each month has its particular flower:

> In the first moon the spring grass is green,
> The dragon clouds bring rain,
> The trees come into bud,
> Anise is the first to flower;
> It waits 'til spring has come to bloom.
> The flowers of the first month are planted,
> Let's pass the basket!
> Here come the flowers of the second moon.[20]

Having planted the flowers of the annual cycle, the officiant picks one which he places, symbolically, in the hair of a woman who wishes to become pregnant by means of a paper flower.

Similar rites exist for the annual cycle of periodic crises that everyone goes through. In order to guard against their effects, one can make a preventive pilgrimage by crossing twelve times (for each of the months) a wooden bridge set up in the center of the ritual area under the protection of the deities who surround it.

The infernal world is where quarrels between the living and the dead are settled, and a great many misfortunes in this world originate in the complaints lodged by the dead before the underworld authorities, especially against members of their families. To settle the disputes, it is often necessary to make a journey to the hells to carry gifts to the deceased and to the clerks. On these occasions, the medium can be useful in establishing a dialogue between the dead and the living. The officers of the other world frequently like to express themselves in written form, in which case the officiant has access to mediums who specialize in automatic writing: A miniature sedan chair held by two people, one of whom is in a trance, becomes the deity's seat. The movements of the chair, dictated by the deity, trace lines on a platter of sand or rice, which are interpreted as written signs.[21]

These forms of communication can include other deities. The officiant is able to communicate with a great number of gods, including the patron saints of the popular pantheon. Indeed, he knows the secret names of all the gods and how to write these names using the secret talismanic signs. He also knows their legends and calls them by reciting verses that allude to their history:

I respectfully invite the Holy Mother Lin,
Queen of Heaven, who saves the people.
At dawn, as the cock is crowing,
She dresses, holding a mirror.
And combs her hair into a bun
Held up by twelve hairpins.
. . .
The Queen of Heaven journeys over the seas,
She defies the winds and storms.
With all her might she comes to help.
Then she returns to Mei-chou, to her temple,
Where every day men and women pay her their respects.
The Holy Mother appeared there, at Mei-chou,
Her birthday is the twenty-third of the third moon,
But all here present sincerely invite her,
Holy Mother of Heaven, descend!
Obey my command, in the name of the law![22]

Similar formulas exist for all the other gods, and in spite of the respectful words, the summons is real. A law requiring the gods to obey the master is the result of an agreement between the master and the gods: those who obey will be promoted and honored, the others will be persecuted. The gods are thus forced to manifest themselves in the medium or the puppet, or to reveal themselves through inspired writing. In the ritual of the barefoot "red head" master, the divine presence is contained within a precise context: during the time the forces are concentrated inside the ritual area, the medium in trance is their vehicle. He can be used, as we have seen, for divinatory purposes, but also to accomplish other feats.

For example, when the authorities of hell show themselves to be less conciliatory than usual, or if they withhold the soul of the deceased despite the pleas and offerings of the family, it is sometimes necessary to intervene. The journey to the underworld is then transformed into a military expedition. The officiant, together with the gods he has been able to summon, lay siege to hell and manage to rescue the unfortunate soul and return it to its family. The appropriate rites (which are beyond the barefoot master's capability) then put the soul on the right path towards paradise and reincarnation within the family.[23]

Similar punitive expeditions can be launched with the help of mediums or puppets against the demons that have invaded a faithful's dwelling and body. These are dramatic rites, with sword dances and military music, intended to chase the demons out. And when the demons do not want to let go, when it appears they have attacked their victim for good reason, as an act of justice sanctioned by the divine bureaucracy, it is still possible to offer them a substitute. The master then fashions a "substitute body," a puppet made of straw or paper, which receives the breath, the name, and the birthday of the patient. This puppet is sent to the kingdom of death and abandoned to the wrath of the demons, who leave their original victim free and unharmed.

The texts of the barefoot master's rites are long ballads in the vernacular. In the case of the journey, these ballads take the form of epics that describe the voyage and its dangers, while cyclical rites, such as the Passage over the Bridge or the Flower Planting, borrow the literary form of folk songs describing the agricultural year or the hours of the day. When dialogue is introduced, the text can assume a theatrical aspect. In the Flower Garden, for example, the text may include an exchange between the emissary and the Mother who guards this garden.

In many cases, the ritual is also enlivened by gestures and dances. But the ritual's most dramatic action occurs when the medium takes the place of the master. At the appropriate moment, his gestural and vocal language transport the gathering directly into the world of the gods. The language is spontaneous and improvised but, thanks to the master's direction and to the ritual code, it adopts a precise and easily recognizable form. When the medium takes the place of the officiant for journeys into heaven and hell, he dances just like him but in a livelier way; he truly mimes the voyage as he follows the narrative sung by the choir of acolytes.

In the case of an expulsion, the theatrical aspect of the rites predominates still further. The plague demons, for instance, are first propitiated with various offerings and then placed on a boat—often life-size—which is burned or set adrift on a river or at sea. The medium or mediums—for it is customary to use several on these occasions—carry out the expulsion with a great many cries and struggles, replete with realistic gestures, against an enemy whom they alone perceive but whose presence they manage to make felt.

During the procession intended to purify the region of evil influences, the medium leads the way, striking out at the demons that cross his path. The blows he strikes against his adversaries are also turned against himself. At regular intervals, he strikes his own body—child and madman of the gods—to show his invulnerability (or so the people say) and also to release the aggressivity of the group whose Center he is. He takes on, and atones for, the sins of the community. He is the divine child who, as a "substitute body" for the faithful, makes a public act of expiation in order that all live in peace. Demons flee at the sight of this blood offered for the good of all men and women. The faithful understand, for they come and lay sheets of sacrificial paper money on his wounds. Soaked in blood, these small sheets will be stuck onto the lintels of houses so as to ward off all evil.

The texts of the barefoot master's rites are, as we have seen, in the vernacular, and for the most part are composed in rhymed verses of seven feet. This form is also used by the blind bards in the popular ballads they sing, which recount the legends of the saints, romances, and epics of national and local history.[24] In a form scarcely altered but interspersed with dialogue, these same ballads also form theater libretti.[25] From a literary point of view, the worship of the gods, the ritual in the vernacular, the popular tales in the form of ballads, and the theater all form an interrelated and integrated whole, which constitutes one of the richest aspects of Chinese culture. At its source, we find *the cult* or, in the words of a contemporary scholar, "the shamanistic substratum,"[26] just as in the medium and his master we recognize the shaman (*wu*) and the invocator (*chu*). of classical China. The shaman called down the rain by dancing, but also knew how to journey in the heavens. The invocator recited formulas to call up the gods and ancestors, who were closely associated with each other in the cults of the ancient kingdoms. As with their predecessors, the "red head" master and the medium of today are allies, interpreters and promoters of the gods. But they do not transcend the gods. They belong exclusively to the local communities and do not organize as a separate group. There is no guild or even any informal society of *fa-shih*. At all times, they remain bound to their temple and to its local community. This is not so for those who are called *tao-shih,* and who are, properly speaking, the true Taoist masters.

The Dignitaries of the Tao

The masters of the mediums, puppet masters, and boxing instructors belong to public worship. They themselves recognize the *tao-shih,* "Dignitaries of the Tao," as their religious superiors. The latter consider shamanism vulgar, though they do not challenge the worship of gods and patron saints. Between the barefoot masters and the Dignitaries of the Tao there exists a rather complex relationship, comparable to that which exists between members of the same family whose leanings, education, and social status might be very different.[27]

Yet, another element obscures the situation for us: if the designation *tao-shih* is widespread, it is not always very easy to understand to what it corresponds. There remain many aspects of Taoism of which we know too little, and today it is not always easy to do research on them. For some time now, foreigners have been able to visit the monastery of the White Clouds, Pai-yün kuan, in Peking, which was once one of the historical, institutional centers of the Taoist school known as Ch'üanchen.[28] After 1949 the monks were expelled and the buildings turned into a temporary prison, for prostitutes in particular. Several years later the government founded a national association of Taoism which it located in the Pai-yün kuan. There young cadres received basic training in the mysteries of Taoism, albeit in order that they might then combat the "superstitions." After the Cultural Revolution, this experiment was renewed.

Elsewhere, on Ch'ing-ch'eng mountain near Ch'eng-tu (Szechwan province), a few monks have returned, out of the hundreds who lived there prior to 1949. After almost forty years and several internal upheavals (none of which was favorable to Taoism), there remains almost nothing of the ancient traditions: virtually no books, no great ritual, musical, or spiritual tradition, no trace at all of any religious life apart from the building, now designated as a historical monument and filled at all hours with crowds of tourists. The same is true for most other Taoist monasteries where any building remains. We, therefore, know virtually nothing about Taoist monasticism, not only after the holocaust but also before it. We do know that the modern Ch'üan-chen school, which originated in North China but extended its influence over the whole country during the sixteenth and seventeenth centuries, was essentially a monastic organization. On the whole, these institutions were very close to those of Buddhism. The great monasteries, like the Pai-yün kuan in Peking and the Luo-fou shan near Canton,[29] were training centers where Taoists received instruction, following the example of the Buddhist training centers (*Shih-fang ts'ung-lin*).[30]

Other schools maintained sanctuaries that were mainly places of pilgrimage and ordination, such as Mao-shan, not far from Nanking, or Lung-hu shan, headquarters of the Heavenly Masters, in Kiangsi province. For these older schools, the monastic rule of celibate life in a community made up exclusively of people of the same sex was found only in the main centers and never applied to Taoist masters living in the world. Actually, the latter have always formed the vast majority of the "Dignitaries of the Tao."

On the basis of historical and contemporary observations, we can state that Taoism never was a monastic religion, for celibacy is, in fact, inconsistent with its fundamental conception of the body. From the early times of the independent local communities of the Heavenly Masters' movement, the *tao-shih,* men and women, were married people. Traditionally, and even today, marriage is one condition for becoming a Great Master. Taoist monks are the rare exception.

Rather than his way of life, then, it is his liturgical function, his role as ritual specialist, that defines the position of the *tao-shih.* To be a Dignitary of the Tao is first of all to fulfill an office. At first sight nothing distinguishes the *tao-shih* from the ordinary person. Furthermore, while he dedicates himself entirely to his office, his family—which has the privilege of providing, from every generation, several Dignitaries of the Tao of the local community—may be peasants, merchants, or even literati.

Although the contrast between city and country is often less sharp in China than in the West, it is in towns and urban areas that one most frequently finds the families of *tao-shih*. The fact that the office is hereditary contrasts sharply with the situation of the "red head" masters, who are recruited by vocation and are also more common in the rural villages. The Taoist masters bear the title of Dignitary since they are the administrators of the divine or spiritual world, just as the imperial bureaucracy governs this world. Their status used to be recognized officially, and is still today acknowledged socially. The *tao-shih* belong to the lettered class; they are minor notables. For them, there are no initiatory dreams, no recruiting of local spirits, nor seances and mediums. Their hereditary investiture derives its legitimacy from the investiture bestowed originally by the Heavenly Master, the universal head of the liturgical tradition, without distinction of school or congregation.

The Heavenly Master (the "Taoist pope," as our missionaries used to call him) is in fact only the representative of the first family of the hereditary masters. He is the protector par excellence of the liturgical tradition. That tradition, as defined by that lineage, goes all the way back to the first investiture conferred by Lao Tzu[31] on the first Heavenly Master, named Chang Ling (or Chang Tao-ling), in 142 A.D. The Chang family line still exists and the current Heavenly Master represents its sixty-fourth generation. The Heavenly Masters bestow hereditary office on the *tao-shih,* who thus become the priests of the regional and local lay organizations. This bestowal takes the form of an investiture document, about which I will speak later. Thus constituted, the body of the *tao-shih* is a confederation of masters, not a church. The descendants of the Chang family are not Holy Fathers; they have no doctrinal or dogmatic authority and are only the symbolic heads of an ecclesiastical administration.

The same holds true for the *tao-shih*; he has no community, or rather, is not the spiritual leader of a congregation. His position is in no way comparable to that of our Catholic or Protestant clergy. Moreover, as we have seen, the community is simply the group assembled around the incense burner and the temple, without any leaders other than the "heads of the incense burner," appointed yearly by a simple divinatory process; a throw of the *yin-yang* blocks. In each local group, however, a council of Elders is formed spontaneously from the patriarchs of the village clans and the neighborhood families, the notables and the scholars, elected to form a permanent authority for the running of things. For them, the temple is a club where, because of their age or situation, they can gather daily.

The Dignitary of the Tao belongs to this informal group but has no special status within the community: "Around the incense burner everyone is the same." Today hereditary *tao-shih* are always men, whereas many who become masters by vocation are women. But this situation does not derive from Taoist principle. The liturgical tradition of the Heavenly Masters grants women a status identical in every respect to that of men, and a mastership is accessible to both. In the Middle Ages the practice of the ritual required an equal number of men and women dignitaries, and wives held the same religious rank as their husbands. Even today the hereditary transmission legitimizing the officiants may be passed on through the maternal as well as the paternal line. The disappearance of female secular *tao-shih* is simply the result of a modern society that requires a masculine presence in transactions with lay organizations such as guilds. The *tao-shih* belongs to the same social level as the local leaders. In our society, he would be considered a member of one of the liberal professions, not very different from a doctor or a lawyer.

Like the latter, the Dignitaries of the Tao are grouped in professional associations, in guilds that exercise an unofficial but effective authority on the local level. Viewed this way, the hereditary tradition seems less exceptional. Indeed, many specialized professions—pharmacist, geomancer, doctor—are passed on from father to son. There is even a Chinese proverb that says one should trust only doctors of the third generation. Nevertheless, the situation of the *tao-shih* is not exactly comparable. For them it is not solely a matter of an aptitude passed on within a family, and the quality of mastership concerns not just the social body, but also the physical body. One must have "the bones," the skeleton of an Immortal, to qualify for the dignity of being the representative of heaven and the master of the gods. This genetic quality is not exactly a question of physiology or of physiognomy (although a *tao-shih* must be of sound mind and body); "the skeleton" is a hidden quality, an inner quality that expresses itself, perhaps unexpectedly but nonetheless significantly, in the special privilege of being the keeper of the sacred writings.

Later we shall see what constitutes the basic, cosmic nature of the Taoist texts (they reveal the fundamental structure of the universe, the True Form of things), but for now let me simply note that the legitimacy of a mastership rests in part on ownership of the manuscripts for liturgical use: books for reciting, rituals, collections of formularies, secret formulas, talismans, and diagrams, passed on from generation to generation within families. As a visible manifestation of the master's legitimacy, each family's collection of manuscripts represents a real treasure, jealously guarded. It would be inconceivable for these books to circulate in printed form, accessible to anyone who might wish to buy them.[32]

As a rule, the manuscripts are recopied only when the family renews its hereditary tradition by having one of its members ordained as a Great Master. Indeed, even though the office of Dignitary of the Tao is hereditary, the rank of Great Master, that of the true initiate among the *tao-shih,* is not obtained automatically. It is neither a privilege of age nor a prerogative of social position. Anyone among the descendants of a family passing on "the bones" may solicit ordination, but his chances for success are slim, since a great number of conditions must be met. In addition to various physical qualities, a noble presence, a good voice, moral virtues, and intellectual abilities also count. There must also be room for a Great Master in the local community, that is, his liturgical services should be needed. The Elders must elect him, and his family must be wealthy enough to finance the ordination, which involves a pilgrimage to the Heavenly Masters on the Mountain of the Dragon and the Tiger to renew the investiture, and the organization of a festival at home to celebrate the ordination. In addition, one becomes a Great Master only after a long apprenticeship, usually lasting twenty years. Finally, custom dictates that Taoist families produce only one Great Master per generation. The latter are therefore rather exceptional people, which accounts for the following proverb: "Every three years there is a first laureate [of the imperial exams]; but even in ten years it is hard to find a Great Master."

Few descendants of the *tao-shih* families thus attain this position. The great majority are never ordained but are entitled to perform minor rites (similar to those of the barefoot masters, though without the aid of a medium). However, they can never preside over major rituals; at these they serve as acolytes.

The respective roles of the Great Master and his acolytes in the liturgy, as well as the stages of initiation into the ritual, will be examined further on. First we must try to clarify a complicated issue: that of the sacred writings of the liturgical tradition handed down by the Taoist families. These writings clearly do not correspond to the known Taoist works—the *Tao-te ching* or the *Chuang-tzu,* for example—for in this case, secret, handwritten transmission would make no sense. The texts held by the families generally include no doctrinal works. Nor do they contain any esoteric treatises, apologetic literature, nor magic or alchemical recipes—subjects usually associated with a secret tradition. The manuscripts of the *tao-shih* are exclusively liturgical (they never pertain to individual worship) and are tied to the social function of the master. As we shall see, this function can be summed up in these words: "To effect transformation on behalf of Heaven."[33]

Families possess these texts, yet to be the legal owner one must also be initiated and ordained as a Great Master, and that implies receiving the so-called register of scriptures (*ching-lu*). As a rule, the register is a list of names of the transcendent forces contained in the sacred scriptures. The Chinese character (logogram) as such is already a symbol representing the name of a thing, of a phenomenon.[34] In the case of Taoist scriptures, considered as spontaneous creations of the universe, these characters are the essences, the cosmic energies with their primordial force intact. But one must be an initiate in order to know and make use of these energies.

I shall speak again of the nature of the Taoist scriptures. For the moment let me simply state that only he who knows how to grasp the authoritative influence of the texts is fit to use them, much as in the case of a given painting, where only the person with the capacity to understand the true meaning of the painting can be considered its true owner. Can one explain a work of art? Likewise, initiation into the "Register" is not the result of discursive reasoning, even less so today when the register, whose transmission entrusts the care of the Scriptures to the *tao-shih* and bestows the rank of Great Master, is a fictitious document. All the more reason for us to examine it in depth!

The Register

In ancient China the nobles received from their king, along with the deed certifying their title to a fief, a list of subordinates who were in their service, but for whom they were responsible in return. It is doubtless here that one must seek the origins of the Taoist masters' registers.

Within the liturgical tradition, the origin of these investiture documents goes back to the first Heavenly Master, Chang Tao-ling. In A.D.

142, while he was living as a hermit in one of the sacred mountains in northern Szechwan province, Lao Tzu revealed himself and conferred on Chang the office of Heavenly Master of the Three Heavens. Here is how an ancient text relates this event:

It was in the first year of the Han-an era, the period of the cycle being *jen-wu,* the first day of the fifth moon, when the Old Lord,[35] in a grotto in Ch'iu-ting mountain of the Shu Commandery [northern Szechwan], came to the *tao-shih* Chang Tao-ling to take him to the great diocese of the K'un-lun of the Most High Newly Appeared [the latter being none other than the Old Lord himself in a new manifestation]. The Most High said: "Men of the world do not respect the true and the orthodox, but honor only pernicious demons. That is why I have taken the name of Old Lord Newly Appeared." Then he installed Chang as Master of the Three Heavens, of the Orthodox One energy of Peace of the Great Mysterious Capital; he revealed to him the Way of the Covenant with the Powers of the Orthodox One. The order of the Old Lord Newly Appeared was to abolish things from the era of the [demoniacal] Six heavens, and to install the orthodoxy of the Three Heavens, to banish the superficial and the flowery, and return to the simple and true. . . . [The Heavenly Master] made a contract with the Three Officials of Heaven, Earth, and Water respectively, as well as with the generals of the star of the Great Year, so that they then entered the orthodox system of the Three Heavens and no longer oppressed the faithful. [The terms of the covenant stipulated that] "the people would no longer worship other gods in a disorderly, lascivious way[36] [that is, gods outside the covenant], that the souls of the dead who are worshiped would neither drink nor eat, and that the masters would receive no salary."[37]

The gods of Antiquity, those of the official as well as the shamanistic cults, who were worshiped with bloody sacrifices, were banished as "dead energies." The arrival of Lao Tzu thus marked a new era, that of the One energy which rectified all, gave peace to all who entered the alliance, and put an end to the extortions and injustices of the old religion. This new energy came with Lao Tzu from the K'un-lun mountain of the primordial chaos to create a new world with the Heavenly Master, his representative among men. The One energy gave rise to the Three Heavens, the three spheres of the universe, and the three divisions of the body:

The Tao transmitted subtle energies (*ch'i*) of three colors. They are the Obscure, Primordial, and Initial Energies. The Obscure is blue-black and Heaven; the Initial is yellow and Earth; the Primordial is white and Tao. In the center of these three energies, a distinction was made between high and low, which then gave rise to the Father and the Mother of the ten thousand things. . . . In the universe, each being is born of these three energies, and the beings who live a long time are those who are capable of keeping the Tao and conserving the energies.[38]

The three levels of the body were oriented in space according to the eight points of the compass and the placement of the Eight Trigrams. Hence the differentiation into eight energies for each "Heaven," twenty-four energies in all. This is a perfect number, for it corresponds to the twenty-four energies of the annual solar cycle (the twenty-four calendrical stations).[39] These energy centers along the sun's path were represented on a sort of compass with concentric rings to represent the different categories: the four winds, the four seasons, the eight trigrams, the twelve months, the twenty-four calendrical stations. This compass was thus a diagram of the energies, a cosmic model illustrating the differentiation of all things outward from the Center.[40]

Each of the subdivisions, each of the categories, which could be multiplied infinitely, had its *essence,* expressed in a spontaneous sign as a *fu,* tessera, symbol, and "true image"; a somatic structure or skeleton. The compass of the energy cycles was composed of an arrangement of these initiatory symbols into a diagram, which constituted an emblem and a token of universal power. To each symbol (*fu*) corresponded a sound, the vocalization of one of the body's energies, the true and secret name of a cosmic force. The knowledge of these names and the ability to write the corresponding *fu* allowed one to master the energies of the universe.

The system of the Three Heavens is the basis of the new cosmology, which Lao Tzu revealed to Chang Tao-ling when he invested the first Heavenly Master with the One energy. It clearly seems from the historical sources, as well as from the ritual of transmission which shall be examined below, that this One energy was none other than the presence of Lao Tzu, the first being to come out of original Chaos, in the body of the Heavenly Master himself.

From this One, the First Master created the powers of the new cosmology, the gods of the Orthodox One (*cheng-yi*), and thereby concluded, in the name of this principle, a covenant with the forces of the old order. The new world was that of the Great Peace (*t'ai-p'ing*).[41] The new kingdom would rise from the ashes of the old, peace would be born from combat, order from disorder. The world would be destroyed by floods, epidemics, armies—the scourges of civilization, so familiar to the rural population. Those who had already entered into the new order would survive as the chosen ones, the Seed People of the kingdom of the Great Peace.[42] The Heavenly Masters (Chang Tao-ling and his successors) would prepare the peasant communities by having them "pass" (*tu*) here and now into the system of the Three Heavens.

The religious organization of the Heavenly Masters was patterned on the cosmological order of the body and of time, derived from the Diagram of the Orthodox One of the Twenty-Four Energies. This diagram (*t'u*) is both an outline and a constitution. The movement of the Heavenly Master established twenty-four dioceses, the twenty-fifth, that of the Center, being Lao Tzu's great diocese, on Mount K'un-lun.

The word *chih*, which we translate as "diocese," means to adjust, put in order, tend, heal. The written character, which depicts embankments and water, suggests the work required to straighten waterways, work like that which Great Yü, the god-hero at the dawn of Chinese civilization, undertook to reorder the world.[43] Each diocese had its holy place, its mountain, where members could gather and take refuge. Heading the twenty-four communities were twenty-four officers, men and women, called Libationers (*chi-chiu*)—a title traditionally designating the dignitary chosen from among the Elders and charged with the responsibility of the sacrifices (the libations of wine to the Earth God). The Libationers were selected from among the initiated believers, that is, those to whom the One energy, Lao Tzu's body, had been transmitted by means of the register of this energy. Only the Libationer received the diagram. At the head of the diocese, he or she stood as the equivalent of the Heavenly Master, the latter being only a first among equals.

The Diagram was made up of *fu*, those symbolic writings which correspond to the individual energies. The master conferred these *fu* on each of the believers according to the latter's personality or "fundamental destiny" (*pen-ming*), determined at birth by the stars and planets. When the master gave this talisman to the adept, he caused him to "pass" (*tu*) into the system and become a member of the Orthodox One community, making him one of the "Seed People" who would survive the end of this world in the Kingdom of Great Peace.

The *fu* symbol given to the adept incorporated the energy breath from the master's body, as well as the transcendent authority of the heavenly order. Through the ritual of transmission, the adept was identified with this essence, which became a protective force for him, as well as one of control and censure. As stated earlier, each essence had its own sound, a "name" which is revealed to the adept. This protective force also assumed a human form, which the adept had to learn to see. Through meditation and invocation, the adept could activate its presence and obtain its protective influence.

This protective essence is called the "agent" (*kuan*), a hypostasis of the One, of Lao Tzu's body. The Agent manifests himself not only in his own image, but also through a given number of subsidiary projections called Generals and Clerks (civil and military functionaries), who depend on his "administrative body." The adept invested with a *fu* also received a "register" (*lu*) listing all these powers, the subsidiary emanations of the agent's energy. Thus, each individual had at his disposal a small corps of lesser gods whom he could mentally invoke and call on by name to protect him. Moreover, through the sign and the corresponding register (*fu-lu*), he found himself integrated into the diagram, the constitution of the social body.

On receiving his register, the adept addressed a written memorial to the Chancellery of the Heavenly Masters:[44]

In such and such year (date, place), I, on receiving the Register corresponding to such and such rank, declare that my body, in its original state, has been invested with the energy of the Old Lord Newly Appeared, but that I am as yet unable to distinguish it[45] myself. Therefore, I have today prepared tokens of my faith and have come before the Master of the System[46] to ask him to transmit the register to me. . . . Henceforth, I know that my Agent is so-and-so.[47] Having had this recorded by the authorities, I pledge henceforth to respect the rules of the Covenant.

The registers were graduated. The lowest were intended for children who, beginning at age six, might receive the protection of a single General and had to promise to observe the fundamental interdictions. Around age twelve, a new confirmation brought the number of protective gods to ten; at the age of marriage, to seventy-five. Marriage between two adepts allowed them to join their energies, for a total of one hundred fifty gods, the highest number possible for beings of this world.[48] The rite that effected this union of the body's cosmic forces was of a sexual nature and made the adepts eligible to be invested with the Diagram and the Libationer's duties.

But, if the powers of the Diagram of the Orthodox One protected the adept, they also function to censure and control: the Generals protected, the Clerks controlled. By contracting an alliance with the Agent of the Orthodox One, through the intermediary of the *fu*, the adept found himself subject to certain rules of conduct, on pain of exclusion from the system and of falling into the sphere where the "dead energies" of the Six Heavens (as opposed to the new energies of the Three Heavens) exercised their diabolical tyranny. These rules primarily governed morality, but also concerned the individual's attitude in the world (giving primacy to the feminine attitude) and the protection of nature. The number of interdictions increased with each new register, for a total of 180 for the Libationers. I shall return to this point later.

The practice of the Diagram and its individual subdivisions—the adepts' talismanic symbols—required periodic renewals of the covenant. Certain days of the liturgical calendar were accordingly reserved for the renewal of the powers of the covenant and for the assembly of the diocese members. This calendar followed the patterns of the physical and social body; the three major annual festivals corresponded to the Three Principles of Heaven, Earth, and Water. They occurred on the fifteenth of the first moon (Heaven), of the seventh moon (Earth), and of the tenth moon (Water). There were eight minor festivals and twenty-four Energy-Nodes.[49] At the great festivals, all those invested with a register gathered at the holy place of the diocese. There the Libationers verified the lists of the community members and received their contribution in grain.[50] These revenues served to cover the expenses of the festive banquets and the running of the diocese in general.

Through their participation in the festivals, their regular worship, and their practice of the register, the faithful were constantly integrated with the powers of the universe at every level. The assemblies of the adepts were to some degree the constituent meetings of all elements incorporated in the Diagram. In addition, the recurring action of concentration and dispersal, following the rhythm of time, was in harmony with the cyclical movement of the Tao. This resulted in the accumulation of the transcendent force expressed by the notion of merit (*kung*). As community leaders, the Libationers were also Merit Inspectors (*tu-kung*).[51] It was therefore up to them to lead this liturgical organization, in which the same integrated system governed the physical body, the pantheon, the calendar, and the social body. These Dignitaries of the Tao maintained the population record of the communities and distributed the individual "symbols-and-registers" (*fu-lu*) according to each one's classification.

This classification of beings, not only human beings and gods, but, in principle, all the things of the world according to their "fundamental destiny" (*pen-ming*), their merit and their function, is the work of the masters. It is their work, their liturgy, called, in Chinese, *k'o*: to class, to divide, and also degree, promotion, exam, or competition for an official position in the imperial administration. The same word is also used for dramatic action in the theater, since theater is intended to cause the gods to manifest themselves in the festival, the community assembly. The liturgy thus aims at integration and order, and moreover to "pass" all beings to a higher level in one vast movement, so that the whole world may obtain the natural, spontaneous order of the heavens, and be at one with the cosmological system.

Within this system, all beings have a beneficial effect on one another, for the accumulation of merit contributes to the elevation of all. Invested with the Diagram, the master incorporates the One energy, from which he creates the categorical energies, or Agents, which he bestows—by way of the *fu* symbols—on each of the adepts according to his or her fundamental destiny. The merit acquired by the faithful adds to that of the social body whose source is in the master's body, since it is through him that the passage of beings is accomplished. All this constitutes a dynamic of emancipation and ennoblement, beneficial to everything and to everyone: the progress of each affects the entire group. This idea is expressed in the definition of the function of the Dignitary of the Tao: "To effect transformation [or: spread civilization] on behalf of Heaven" (that is: the natural order): *tai-t'ien hsing-hua*.

After this necessarily succinct description of the liturgical organization of the Heavenly Masters in the first centuries A.D., let us return to the *tao-shih* of today. The secular masters are still called Libationers and among their different titles is found, as before, that of Inspector of Merit. But, instead of registers based solely on the Heavenly Masters' *Diagram of the Energies of the Twenty-Four Dioceses,* the current Dignitary of the Tao is invested with a more general register of the sacred scriptures. The difference may seem unimportant; still, it deserves an explanation.

Since the beginning of the Heavenly Masters movement, the liturgical tradition has been enriched with sacred texts from different schools, in accordance with the literary and social developments of each period in Chinese history. These texts often introduce new names for these heavens and gods and use different vocabularies to describe the system. The definition of communities changes too. The twenty-four dioceses no longer have a direct relation to the localities of northern Szechwan, but became, a long time ago, cosmological categories. Today, the dioceses are located in the stars, for the local religious organizations of the earlier Heavenly Masters, with their democratic control, have long since disappeared, defeated by the imperial governments.[52] Now it is the laity who, through their unofficial associations, direct local political life, albeit within the liturgical framework of Taoism.

The sacred scriptures of later Taoism, such as the *Book of Men's Passage,*[53] the *Book of the Birth of the Gods,*[54] and the *Book of the Dipper Stars,*[55] are not doctrinal treaties. They present a renewed cosmology based on the ancient model, but with different names. Most important, they are considered to be spontaneous cosmic creations. Each book contains a central part in symbolic *fu* signs that is considered to reproduce a form of original cosmic writing. These cosmological writings—the *True Writs,* as they are called—are to some degree only new versions of the Heavenly Masters' *Diagram of the Energies of the Twenty-Four Dioceses.* The new texts are initiatory in the same way that the diagram and the registers of the early Heavenly Masters movement were. But these later sacred texts are intended to be recited; the vocalization of the names of the divine essences is equivalent to the actualization of their creation and should therefore be performed by a master, and then only in an appropriate ritual context. The scriptures (*ching*) combine talisman and sound, symbol and name, both diagram and register.[56] As for the register as a document of investiture, it no longer corresponds to a document in particular.

Even if the list of gods is no longer transmitted as such, the necessity of a ritual of investiture remains to ensure the legitimacy of their use. Taoist books ought never to be divulged except to the person who is entitled to receive them. Almost all the ancient texts end with these words: "To be transmitted only to those whom it may concern, at the risk of punishment to yourself and your ancestors back to the ninth generation. Take care! Take care!"

There used to be certain rules governing the transmittal of each scripture or group of scriptures belonging to the same school: a certain number of pledges of faithfulness to be given by the disciple to the transmitting master, so many days of purifying fasting to be observed, particular prohibitions to respect, the time between each consecutive transmittal being so many years. This is still the case. For a long period before the ceremony, the postulant to the rank of Great Master observes a ritual fast. Living in seclusion, he copies the ritual texts of his family or of other masters willing to lend him some. A considerable sum of money must be spent for the construction of the ritual area (where an Initiating Master[57] is to perform the ordination rituals), as well as for the ordination offerings. The disciple also must agree to respect a great number of commandments.

The ordination of a Great Master is a *chiao,* a ritual offering lasting one or several days. The main purpose of the ceremony is to introduce to the hierarchy of all the divine authorities the person of the new master so that his name is known to them. Documents drawn up specially for the occasion are addressed, by burning them in the ritual area, to the Celestial Chancellery. In return, the adept receives from the initiating master the commission of his office, his Immortal's Certificate, a condensed version of which follows:

IMMORTAL'S CERTIFICATE,

conferred by the Chancellery of the Three Heavens, granting admission to rank and office.

Respectfully, it is noted that the Tao is unique and venerable as the creator of the Three Heavens, that, of the ten thousand practices, keeping is the most precious.[58] Thus, neither the tin staff (*khakkara*) [of Buddhists monks] nor the white robes [of sect members] can be considered admirable; only that which is transmitted secretly between allies and is capable of forging a True Heart[59] may be considered fit to promote civilization and bring glory to the country, to bring peace to the family, and to preserve oneself.

On this day, there is in this prefecture disciple so-and-so, heir to the ritual [tradition], whose Fundamental Destiny is controlled by his birth in such and such year (full date), and controlled from above by such and such star of the Dipper constellation.[60]

Considering that the above-mentioned disciple has sought refuge with his whole heart in the Orthodox Tao, that he intends to serve the Mysteries, and that he wishes to receive the transmission of the liturgical rites, without, however, having found an Eminent Master,[61] and fearing that his name might not be known in the Palaces of the Heavens, and that he might not have any authority in the Offices of Hell, he was fortunately able to find heads of the community (their names are inserted here) who took from their own possessions to prepare the appropriate ceremonies. They have observed that the above-named disciple has a respectful behavior, that he is fully and firmly resolved, and that, consequently, he deserves that ordination [literally: "passage"] be conferred on him.[62]

The disciple has respectfully presented incense and pledges in order to invite so-and-so, as Initiating Master, to come into the house [of the disciple] to install a ritual area and to lead the rites of transmission there. Henceforward, when the above-named disciple—who has taken the oath "to effect transformation on behalf of Heaven" and to save men and benefit all beings—performs any liturgical services, at his home or elsewhere, we hope that he will obtain an immediate response, that by the solemn rites the gods will rejoice and the demons will submit, and that by the acts of purification all will know peace.[63]

The document then details the different rites that fall under the future master's domain: fasts (*chai*), offerings (*chiao*), the rites of union and birth, the worship of the stars,[64] and the barefoot master's rites in the vernacular. Indeed, the Dignitary of the Tao is equally entitled to pronounce the latter's invocations and perform his dances, without, however, resorting to mediums or trance techniques. But the reverse—a "red head" performing a classic, orthodox ritual—is unthinkable.

The rank the disciple receives today at his ordination is still that of the Heavenly Masters: "Universal Inspector of Merit and Libationer of the Register of the Canon [the Sacred Scriptures]." This holy office entails other specified functions, as well, which are different for each individual, for example: "Immortal Officer, keeper of the doctrine of the Three Heavens, in charge of executing the decisions of the Ministry of Exorcisms." Along with these lengthy titles, the ordinee also receives a new, religious, name.[65]

In addition, the Certificate mentions his investiture in a stellar diocese and names his altar and his pure chamber.[66] These are chosen, like his diocese, in relation to his Original Destiny. A registered, authenticated signature, to be appended on documents transmitted to the Chancellery of the Three Heavens, is also recorded on this document. Finally, we find an inventory of clothing, ritual instruments, and other implements, as well as a list of gods who accompany him wherever he goes, and with whom he has a personal relationship. Among the latter, we find the major saints of the popular pantheon: Lord Kuan, Ma-tsu, the God of the North, et cetera. These gods do not belong to the Taoist pantheon proper, that is, the abstract powers of the inner universe. They therefore are not truly related to the register of sacred scriptures. These popular gods entered the covenant in order that they might progress in the merit system of the *k'o* (liturgy). The *tao-shih* is their master and, thanks to his liturgy, the gods may "pass" (*tu*). Any of their actions favorable to mankind are duly recorded so that they may gradually transcend their demoniacal identity.

The ordination service of the future Great Master is conducted by the *tao-shih* of the local Taoist guild. This service differs from other services only in the content of the memorials, petitions, and convocations, which all proclaim the ordinee's merit so as to publicize his name as a new master.

Following the service, the installation ceremony takes place. It begins with the investiture, that is, the donning of the priestly clothing. The ordinee, who has been standing in the lower part of the ritual area dressed simply in the Taoists' black gown and wearing cloth shoes, his hair unbound, now receives the robes of Great Master. First his shoes are replaced by thick-soled boots—a sort of buskin—embroidered with cloud patterns. The formula accompanying this gesture goes as follows:

> Shoes that soar through the clouds as flying geese,
> With you I shall climb the nine steps of the altar of Mysteries;
> My exalted wish is to roam in the Three Worlds,
> To ride the winds all over the sky.
> Today I vow that with these shoes
> I shall proceed to the audience before the Golden Countenance.

Afterwards his hair is gathered and knotted in a bun on top of his head. The knot is covered with a crown—variously called *golden crown, golden lotus,* or *crown of stars.* The words that accompany this gesture are:

> Brilliant crown of the seven stars of the Dipper,
> Your radiance descends from Heaven.
> I, who receive you, hold the Certificate
> And am destined to be an Immortal.
> Today I vow that, wearing you,
> I will live as long as the Great Oak.[67]

An apron embroidered with the emblem of the Cinnabar Field[68] is then wrapped around the candidate's waist, covering his stomach and the front of his legs. Finally, he receives the *robe of feathers,* also called *vestment of the descent,* which is a sort of large, sleeveless chasuble, made of a square of embroidered cloth with a vent in the front; only the Great Masters wear this robe and then only for the most solemn rituals.

> Vestment of the Immortals on High,
> Robe of spontaneity, treasure from Heaven,
> Marvelously light and beautiful,
> Surrounded by the effulgence of the Three Luminaries.
> Today I vow that, wearing you,
> I shall roam freely in the land where there is no death.[69]

The entire surface of the robe is embroidered with a great variety of images: constellations, palaces, gods mounted on all sorts of animals, mountains, trees, waves, and fish. It depicts the three spheres of the world, the Three Heavens, and the principal deities who serve as intermediaries and guardians of the ritual area. In fact, the robe reveals, at least in part, the inner world of the master's body and the gods of his register. *The diagram of the Heavenly Masters* can no longer be found as a written document, but it is still present in the representations on the master's robe—as an expression of the universe which he shapes within himself.[70]

The candidate then receives the main ritual instruments: the sword and the bowl of lustral water, which he holds for a moment, the sword in his right hand and the bowl between the fingers of his left. These are then taken away and he receives the audience tablet, a long, curved ivory rectangle, which he holds respectfully with both hands in front of his chest so that the upper edge comes up as high as his mouth. In this position, standing at the center of the altar, he will receive the final consecration.

This is administered to him by his Initiating Master, normally an older *tao-shih,* who is renowed in the area and is a guild member and friend of the family. The latter begins with a ritual similar to that of "the opening of the eyes" for statues and ancestor tablets, transferring his own vital energy to the ordinee.[71] Afterwards, he reads aloud the Immortal's Certificate, which he then transfers to the ordinee. The disciple then kneels before him with bowed head. The Initiating Master takes a flame-shaped pin which he sticks onto the top of the ordinand's crown. This converral of the flame, which completes the consecration, is a gesture full of meaning. The flame, Flower of Gold or Flaming Pearl,[72] illustrates the One energy, the original vital breath (*ch'i*) emanating from the disciple's body. Now that he is ordained, he is able to recognize and externalize this energy, to make his body shine and to create his own universe, a place of order and peace, a sanctuary in which all beings passing through will be transformed.

5

Ritual

The liturgical tradition of Taoism is first of all a great structuring system (*fa*) which pursues the autonomy of the social body. The integration of individuals into this body is achieved through ritual, the *k'o,* a word that combines the meanings of class, division, grade, examination, and dramatic action. The etymology of the character *k'o* is "measure of grain," a synonym for bushel, *tou,* which is also the name of the Dipper (*Ursa Minor*) constellation. In Chinese astrology, this constellation is the "Controller of Destiny."

The dipper of the constellation is present everywhere in Taoist ritual: its image is engraved on swords to scare off demons; as a receptacle filled with rice,[1] the dipper is a pure and purifying container where ritual instruments and sacred writings are placed and preserved to protect them against evil influences. The bushel, *tou,* is also the ritual measure for offerings, or pledges of faithfulness, brought by the faithful; the bushel filled with rice grains can also be used as a base for the votive oil lamps that symbolize the stars of fate and vital energy; the central Pole Star of the Big Dipper (i.e., "Bushel") constellation[2] is represented in the flaming pearl that shines from the Great Master's crown; *bushel* is the symbolic name given to the belly and the womb, center of the body.[3]

The bushel stands symbolically for an exact measure, a closed space, and a perfect standard; transposed in the sky as a constellation, the Bushel (Big Dipper) is a heavenly clock marking the cycle of the seasons by its rotation.

The Dipper constellation is the seat of the celestial bureaucracy, the location of the Great Mysterious Capital, and its ministries and chancellery. When performing his many duties, the *tao-shih* represents the divine authorities of the Dipper stars at all the major turning points of life—birth, puberty, marriage, death—as well as at all the events of public life, for he knows how to tie and untie, to pass and integrate all beings into the space of the Tao.

This space is wherever he is, which means that, in daily life, it is mostly at his home. Many *tao-shih* have an office there to receive those in need of their services. This office, called *Tao-t'an*, the "altar of the Tao," is not a public sanctuary, but a room in the center of the master's residence where his family's household altar is found along with statues or paintings of Lao Tzu and the first heavenly Master, the patron saints and keepers of the liturgical tradition.

The first thing the master does is listen, in a kindly, reserved way, to the misfortunes and illnesses of those who come to see him. When the patient, the "lay friend" (*su-pan*), has finished speaking, the master dips a brush in red ink and quickly draws an incomprehensible sign on a little piece of yellow paper. This *fu*, talismanic symbol, is the divine name of a particular energy drawn from the master's body. It is either carried by the patient as long as the complaint lasts; or it is burned, the ashes then dissolved in water and drunk; or else it is rolled into a little ball, dipped in honey, and swallowed whole. The *fu* is a specially selected energy distilled from the master's vital powers to alleviate the lack of the same energy in the patient. This is called "distributing the energies," *pu-ch'i*.[4] The master takes from his own life force to nourish the life of others. He offers this service free of charge, not only because it is so common, but because no fee would ever be able to compensate for such an intimate gift.

Other services, notably the small exorcisms and individual purifications, require a small voluntary contribution. The most frequent is the healing of "childhood fears." Whether the child has suffered a real trauma,[5] causing a sudden loss of his life forces, or he suffers from some general indisposition whose causes may be attributed to some evil possession, the first thing would be to take him to the master. The latter listens to the parent explain what happened and then exorcises the demons and purifies the child.

Treatment is simple: demons are loudly cursed in the name of the ancestor masters, and the child is showered with a mouthful of lustral water. This water is prepared specially by mixing ashes from a purifying talisman with water over which invocatory formulas have been recited. The master fills his mouth with this water, makes the signs of *One* and *heart* with his hand over the child's head,[6] then, blowing hard, spurts the water from his mouth onto the child's face. In addition to these rites, it is common for the *tao-shih* to prescribe medicines.[7] The parent, who is really only the intermediary between healer and patient, compensates the master for his effort and time by a small gift of money wrapped in red paper.

Children are subject to evil influences because their energies are still weak and unstable. By contrast, the adult may have no need for protection or purification if he has taken care not to waste his reserves of energy. Unfortunately, it is common for the adult's share of life to be dissipated by passion and greed. As Destiny's agent, it is up to the *tao-shih* to repair the damage and restore the diminished energy.

The most common procedure involves setting up oil lamps to represent the stars of the Dipper: seven for the main stars, two for the secondary ones. Three lamps are added on top, representing the constellation of the Flowery Canopy which forms heaven's roof and symbolizes the original Three Energies of the Three Heavens. There are thus twelve lamps in all, with one lamp corresponding more particularly to the patient's "fundamental destiny" (by virtue of the ties existing between his date of birth and a particular star of the Big Dipper). The ritual is designed to revive the lamp's flame and thereby reinforce the deficient vital principle.

The worship of the Dipper stars and, in a general way, all the rituals for individual happiness fall within the domain of all *tao-shih*. These are the "small rites" that are part of daily practice and most often are combined with other methods—considered secondary by the masters—like medicine (drugs and acupuncture), astrology, and geomancy.[8] The patient's disorder is cured first by ritual, then by the other techniques.

By contrast, the great ritual transcends both simple individuals and the secondary techniques of medicine. It concerns groups of people: on the one hand, lineages and extended families, on the other, local communities. The great ritual is divided into two distinct canons, according to the group involved, and concerns either the "passage" of family ancestors or that of the local gods and the leaders of the communities.[9]

In the first case, the Taoist liturgy is an essential part of family funerary rites,[10] and in the second, concerns the local communities and their temples. The services for ancestors are called "somber" (*yu,* an epithet relating to the world of the dead), those for the gods, "pure" (*ch'ing*, descriptive of Heaven). The great ritual never takes place in a master's household sanctuary, but requires the construction of a special ritual space, "the Tao's Enclosure" (*tao-ch'ang*), most often inside the deceased's house or in the temple.

Each of the great services, "somber" or "pure," include many different rituals and are therefore very long. The funerary, or "somber," services may last from half a day and a night up to three consecutive days and nights. Furthermore, these services are repeated at regular intervals: once every seven days for forty-nine days after the death (thus seven services in all),[11] then again on the hundredth day after the death, and finally, one year later. As for the "pure" services, they take at least one whole day, but more often two, three, five, or even seven. Here, too, the ritual can be prolonged up to forty-nine days.

Although the two kinds of services are separate, requiring, in theory, two distinct collections of instruments, vestments, paintings, and manuscripts—to be kept in different trunks—the sequence and form of the two ritual canons are similar.

The funerary services, like the "pure" services, consist of: (1) rituals for the Installation of the ritual area; (2) rituals to obtain "merits" (*kung-te*), called rites of fasting (*chai*); (3) rituals of communion and covenant, called offering rites (*chiao*); and (4) rituals of the dispersal of the ritual area.

The most important part of the funerary services is the fast, through which one seeks to accumulate merits by recitations from the sacred scriptures (*ching*) and penitential litanies (*tsan*). By contrast, the essential part of the "pure" service is the offering, that is, the covenant banquet. This is why funerary rituals today are generally called "fasts" (*chai*) and communal services, "offerings" (*chiao*).

An exhaustive description of the two liturgical canons is beyond the scope of this work. As I have just indicated, the great services are a succession of many distinct rituals, and each ritual is in turn made up of a great number of rites. By way of example: A two-day service (*k'o*) for a local community consists of some fifteen rituals. Each ritual (*i*) corresponds to a distinct manuscript. In addition to the performance of these rituals, some twenty handwritten volumes of the canonical books and litanies are recited.[12] A ritual may last from one to several hours. It invariably includes a succession of rites (*fa*): purification, invocation, prayers, consecration and offering formulas, hymns, dances, perambulations, et cetera. The whole ritual is very complicated. Each Great Master and his acolytes know by heart—according to my experience—some fifty separate rituals from the two canons, funerary and "pure."

What could explain this great profusion of rituals? The rites are often redundant: each new ritual begins with a series of rites such as the singing of an introit, purification, offerings of incense, or invocations to the gods. These rites are practically the same everywhere. They are repetitive as well; those who understand the different stages in the development of Taoism can detect in these repetitive rites (e.g., successive purifications) successive additions made by different schools and branches. As in many other great liturgical traditions, Taoist ritual has undergone a great deal of accretion.

Taoist liturgy has constantly been renewed and elaborated throughout history, but this evolution rarely entailed the suppression of ancient forms. This process has resulted in a phenomenon of accretion, with new layers of rites superimposed on the old and new gods added to earlier ones. Everything has been preserved and integrated into the general structure, so that within the articulation of the ritual syntax, one can detect a real stratigraphy of discourse.

As I have said, the ritual remains basically the same for both canons and for all services, be they long or short. Each *k'o* is a whole, made up of the four great ritual articulations, sometimes varying in form; these articulations are again present in each ritual.

The Installation of the ritual area is the first articulation and is accompanied by actions considered to represent the creation of the world. Part visible, part invisible, a perfect model of the world is created, where all the time cycles and spatial categories of the space-time continuum are integrated. The ritual area itself is a mapping of "Heaven," a mandala.

The fast, *chai*, of the ritual is supposed to represent the "passage," the journey in this closed universe, where one accumulates transcendent forces by completing cycle after cycle.

The offering, *chiao*, celebrates the covenant with all the divine powers of the world: the banquet consists of offerings of wine and cooked or dried meats. For the Heavenly Worthies, the gods of a purely abstract pantheon,[13] these offerings are replaced by substitutes—meats modeled in dough, and sugar water in place of wine.

The dispersal of the ritual area entails the ritual oblation of the sacred scriptures, or parts thereof. The tailsmans in holy writing which oriented and delimited the space are destroyed by fire, immersion, or burial. This auto-da-fé also includes the documents and inscriptions that marked the location of each god along the perimeter of the ritual area (see below), as well as written prayers giving the names of the community members and specifying the purpose of the service. This "sacrifice of the writings" indicates the fulfillment of merit[14] and the promotion of all participants to a higher rank. For the gods, this implies another rung on the ladder of perfection; for the souls of the dead, it means a promotion to the rank of ancestor.

In the funerary services, the dispersal of the ritual area includes the specific ritual of offering a register intended for the deceased. The sacrifice effects the transmission of the register to the beneficiary of the ritual, who is thus able to enter the Tao and obtain the rank of Immortal. The jailers of the underworld must now allow him to leave. A written memorial, called a document of pardon, is attached to the register (which is accompanied by a talismanic chart). The document of pardon shows that the merit necessary for obtaining this rank has been accomplished and that all the errors of the deceased have been abolished. The ritual "dispatching" of this document to the authorities of the other world is of a highly dramatic nature.

This ritual of "dispatching" is not the end of the service. A long series of small rites—similar in part to those of the repertory in the vernacular of the bare-foot masters—intensifies and elaborates on the preceding liturgical action. A siege of hell (ta-ch'eng) represents the deceased soul's deliverance from the dark prisons of the underworld. The rites of the bath and the dressing indicate the reappearance of the soul in the world of light. Actions and gestures borrowed from alchemy mimic the molding of an immortal body (lien-tu). The deceased receives a pass for the world of the blessed. The family discharges the debt which the deceased had contracted for the purchase of a human body at his birth.[15]

The moment has then arrived to say farewell: the master makes a long speech addressed to the deceased, warning him against the dangers awaiting him on his voyage and reminding him of all that has been done for him. It is the moment for everyone to remember the virtues of filial piety and conjugal love. The master makes a series of "speeches to the common people" (su-chiang)[16] recalling the ethical principles governing human relations, as well as the examples handed down from the great men of the past. Then he lets the disciples take over and they act out the voyage of the Buddhist monk Mu-lien, who went to hell to save his mother,[17] the adventures of the Taoist master, Lei Yu-sheng (Master "Thunder Noise"), to save his father, and finally, Lady Meng

Chiang-nü's pilgrimage to the Great Wall in search of her husband.[18] These are simple theatrical plays, among the most ancient in China. The epic of Mu-lien still maintains a certain seriousness, but the *Story of Master Lei Yu-sheng* is very comical (indeed, he fails miserably in his mission), and the *Mystery of Lady Meng Chiang-nü* is the occasion for especially bawdy word plays. The somber rites are dissolved in laughter.

Finally, the moment of separation arrives. A short ritual helps the deceased to cross the bridge separating the world of the living and the dead from the universe of happiness and rebirth. In that paradise a sumptuous dwelling awaits the deceased, bought for him by his children. On his departure he is given the house and the titles to the property. A paper house, a masterpiece of Chinese craftsmanship, bursts into flames and burns in a few seconds. It is the final act of the service: the family has a new ancestor.

The enhancing of the classic ritual by small rites in the vernacular also occurs at the *pure* services held for the communities. But in the latter case, they are much less fundamental, and the theatrical aspect is almost absent. On the whole, the pure ritual is very solemn and hieratic. The celebration of these services requires all the participants to observe very strict moral and physical interdictions.

Aside from the Great Master, his acolytes (usually four), and members of the orchestra, one finds only a few Elders (five or so) attending the service as community delegates. They have often paid a great deal for this privilege[19] which consecrates them as leaders in the eyes of the people. The ordinary people of the community are not admitted. In their stead, each family places the statues of the gods and saints of their home altar in the sacred area. The presence of the leaders is also not really required, for the pure ritual is a matter between the master and the gods. Such holy procedures are most awesome for simple believers.

The installation of the altar for the pure services begins with the sending of written requests to all gods of the pantheon, asking them to assemble inside the "Enclosure of the Tao."[20]

The rites of creation represented by the installation of the ritual area are performed with great solemnity. The great purification (*chin-t'an*), preceding the consecration of the *Five True Writs (an chen-wen)*, enacts the occupation and the closing off of the ritual space. Harmful influence, represented by an acolyte wearing a demon mask who tries to conquer the altar and to make off with the community's incense burner, are expelled. After a lively dance and a simulated battle, the demon (represented by his mask) is imprisoned in a magic well constructed in the northeast corner of the area. From then on he will be the guardian of the altar and begin a career as a god.[21]

The rites of the fast or retreat enact a journey inside the ritual area. The journey is followed by "hearing" (*chao*) with the Three Heavens, a court ceremony including the presentation of a request before the Heavenly Worthies, with dances and offerings.[22]

The offering, which is seen as a great banquet (*chiao*) celebrating the covenant with the celestial gods, follows the fast. Its importance varies according to the circumstances. In the case of services intended to protect communities against epidemics, a special supplementary *chiao*, "banquet," is held to establish the covenant with the gods of the plague.[23] Similarly, when the service is held for the consecration of a newly built or restored temple, a separate "covenant banquet" is offered to the Earth gods. These secondary and subsidiary *chiao* are nevertheless complete services, inasmuch as they always include the four main articulations: installation, fast, offering, dispersal.

In the case of the *chiao* for the gods of the plague, the final offering and dispersal are performed in one of two ways: a boat, on which statues representing the plague gods have been placed, is sent out on the waters of the sea, a lake, or a river, or it is destroyed by fire. Made expressly for this occasion, the statues represent the "true form," the *body* of the particular power to be sacrificed here.[24]

Finally, to accompany the covenant banquets in the pure services, a great feast for the orphan souls is set up outside the ritual area and the temple. This exhibition resembles the offering made annually at the festival of the seventh moon. No one, no spirit, no god, no demon, is thus excluded from the celebration; all beings are united in the great covenant, and the pledge to establish the kingdom of the Great Peace is renewed.[25]

The high services of the Taoist liturgy are always accompanied by exceptional celebrations. Families do not honor all the dead with the seven consecutive *chai*: these are reserved only to those worthy of becoming ancestors, especially grandparents with many descendants. It is customary that the seven consecutive services be paid for by different categories of relatives: sons, daughters, and sons-in-law, daughters-in-law, and their families; each group is supposed to organize and finance one or several services. One of the groups may decide for reasons of its own to invite, instead of Taoists, Buddhist monks to read requiem masses. These are equally considered to generate merit and indeed often resemble Taoist services[26]. In the past, in patrician families in Peking, it was considered good form to have requiem ceremonies performed simultaneously by representatives of four denominations: Taoists, Buddhists, Muslims, and Tantric Buddhists (Lamas).[27] It was also customary that the last ceremony in this series of merit services be performed by Taoists.[28]

But what could be the purpose of these many long, burdensome rites? Would a single service not suffice for the "passage" of the dead into paradise? A ritual's function is often different from what is expressed by its action or given as its explanation. In the case of funeral services, what is expressed by the ritual itself (especially in the small vernacular rites, like the siege of hell, the settlement of debts, etc.) does encourage real participation by the mourners through collective expressions of joy or sorrow. But on close scrutiny, the aim of the ritual is not in the *k'o*, which raises the ancestor to the rank of the Immortals. Rather, the performance of the rites makes it possible to distinguish—within an extended family, often including many different factions—the worthy heirs who best fulfilled their obligations towards their deceased kinsmen. The funeral services are to some extent the families' general assemblies and festivals of succession.

Funeral services are the responsibility of the Buddhist monks as well as the *tao-shih*. By contrast, the *pure* liturgy of the community assemblies belongs exclusively to Taoism. Only the Officials of the Tao are able to assemble the gods and organize them into hierarchies (for each has his place in the ritual area), as well as to empower and promote them. The great assemblies (generally called *ta-chiao,* or, in Northern China, *huang-hui*) may bring together the local organizations of cities or entire regions. Some regions, made up of tens or hundreds of villages, meet every three, five, or twelve years to celebrate the covenant.[29] Other communities do so at irregular intervals. At least once every generation, each temple association must organize a *chiao* to celebrate the temple's restoration. This is done with the help of communities which are interconnected through the "sharing of the incense" or through some other form of affiliation.

The *chiao* is exceptionally expensive. The *tao-shih* do not receive a salary, but a voluntary donation which normally amounts to far more than any ordinary remuneration.[30] But the largest part of the expenditures does not go to the masters. Aside from the altar and the rituals, the *chiao* is an enormous celebration attracting huge crowds. Theatrical plays (with several performances at a time), processions, military parades of the "boxers," giant offerings to the orphan souls, and construction of secondary altars in the homes of members of the community (important leaders may even build real towers, several stories high, where they display their family treasures)[31] stir up the rivalry between families, and sometimes lead to financial ruin.

The basic expenses for the *chiao* are covered through a more or less obligatory donation from all households, calculated according to the number of individuals. But a leader must prove his generosity. The few places reserved to community delegates are especially prized and give rise to considerable bidding in the way of promising high donations in case one is chosen. The community may also choose a judge who, in the name of the assembled gods, has the right to decide all the disputes laid before him during the *chiao*. Obviously, those who present themselves for this honor enjoy an untarnished reputation, but the candidates must also dispose of wealth and backing.

In addition to this competition of expenses for the *chiao,* the leaders have to undergo the test of participation. Under the eye of hundreds of gods and representatives of the heavenly bureaucracy in charge of destiny, the leaders follow the ritual. That is to say, they make offerings of incense when the acolytes present them with lighted joss sticks; they offer libations when told to do so; they kneel and stand with the Great Master. But they understand almost nothing of what is going on. The ritual is in classical Chinese, a language which is comprehensible only when seen in writing. The significance of many of the movements is also difficult to understand for the uninitiated. The leaders only recognize their own names and titles heading the list of community members on the memorial and petitions read aloud by the acolytes. It is hard to hold oneself straight and steady without moving for days and nights on end, with only a few hours' break at night. But the sacrifice of the scriptures and the announcement of merits consecrate their leadership. The *chiao* is a real sacrifice to Heaven and its execution establishes the legitimacy of the local leaders, just as the imperial sacrifice used to consecrate the Son of Heaven's mandate.[32]

If the *chiao* is a test for the leaders, it is even more so for the Great Master. During the whole service, he must obey very strict interdicts.[33] The rituals follow each other at a rapid pace, each one different from the rest. Everything is predetermined, from the smallest gesture or step to every facial expression. Not one mistake is allowed for fear of having the greatest of divine gifts, the master's astonishing memory, withdrawn.[34] If he becomes confused, if the sequence is broken, the whole thing must come to a halt, along with his right to lead a *chiao*.[35] The great community services are also exceptional opportunities for the masters. Normally, a Great Master will carry out no more than a dozen *chiao* during his lifetime, and even the greatest of these masters conduct only three or four a year at the most.[36] And yet to attain this goal, endless years of training are necessary!

Becoming a *Tao-shih*

In the beginning each *tao-shih* receives the same training, and the apprenticeship begins very young. In former times, this used to be as early as age six. Nowadays youngsters normally go to school (before the compulsory school system, they went to a master of classical Chinese) and practice calligraphy at home. When the opportunity arises, the older ones take along the younger ones to attend high services. The future *tao-shih* at first simply puts in an appearance. He is welcomed affectionately, caressed and praised for his bearing and intelligence, but there is no question of having him undergo a trial period just yet.

Almost right away, as though in a game, he is taught the first words of the *tao-shih*'s secret language[37] and is given the apprentice's instrument, a small bronze gong suspended in a metal frame and struck with a horn-tipped stick. Despite its modest appearance, it is an important instrument and is used to accompany all the recitations, beating time with a high-pitched sound *("chiang!")* twice as fast as the rhythm of the wood block, the principal percussion instrument.[38] The *"chiang!"* player sits in the orchestra, between the drum and the gongs, while the wood block is played by the chief cantor (*tu-chiang*), the head of the acolytes. The block accompanies all the recitations as well and a great number of chants and hymns. It leads the whole orchestra.

The monotonous task of beating the little gong twice as fast as the wood block requires the unflagging attention of the young disciple. Recitations of the sacred books, and even more so, the rituals themselves emphasize changes of rhythm and tempo that have to be followed. In reciting the sacred books, a single priest chants the text, accompanying himself on the wood block. The reading is perfectly rhythmical, with two words per measure. During the chanted or recited parts, only the little gong accompanies the recitation. The smallest mistake may disturb the one reciting and upset his concentration. This is especially true of the great rituals, when the recitation of the acolytes is accompanied by the inner work of the Great Master. A mistake on the gong may break the harmony necessary for the conformity of "inner" and "outer" rituals.

While the officiating and reciting priests relieve each other, and other instrumentalists play only at certain moments, the young disciple must stay in his place for the whole service. This seemingly simple task is really quite hard and thankless. During the recitation of the great sacred books, which may last for hours, only he and the reciter sustain the cadence of the ritual. It is not rare, especially during the high services of mourning which last for days and nights, to see the boy with the little gong fall asleep on the job, exhausted.

But his work is very useful to his apprenticeship. He is introduced to the Taoist ritual through its music or, more precisely, its rhythm, and right from the start he learns to recognize the basic transitions that articulate each ritual. Accustomed to the melodies, he learns through osmosis the most frequently used chants. His neighbor, the drummer, explains the different parts and phases of the ritual and teaches him the language of the Taoists.

We still know too little about the practice of Taoism to be able to confirm the claims of the *tao-shih* of Taiwan and South Fukien that their patois is understood by their colleagues throughout all of China. It does seem that some words have affinities with the dialect of eastern Kiangsi province, site of the mountain of the Dragon and the Tiger (Lung-hu shan), headquarters of the Heavenly Masters.

At puberty the young disciple is promoted from the orchestra to the rank of acolyte.

At the central table of the ritual area, four assistants surround the Great Master, the "venerable of the middle." The place on the far right is that of the youngest, the incense attendant, who lights the sticks and distributes them, fills the incense burners and maintains them. In addition, he has passages to recite and sing, and even solo recitations are assigned to him in the great Taoist ritual, which resemble an oratorio. The reading of the sacred scriptures is also part of the duties of the incense attendant. As we have seen, this is done by a single person, whereas the rituals are performed by five *tao-shih* (a Great Master and four acolytes) acting out a complicated and elaborate scenario to the music of an orchestra—also made up of five members.[39] These great texts vary according to the occasion.[40] Their reading also varies in length, taking between thirty minutes and several hours.

The technique is simple, but typically Taoist: the reciter reads aloud, enunciating clearly and rhythmically each word. To keep time, he accompanies himself on the wood block, tapping out sharp, percussive beats with his left hand in a steady, regular rhythm while pronouncing two syllables per beat in andante tempo. The reading is clear but monotonous except in certain places where the punctuation, indicated by a tap on the bowl-shaped gong with the right hand,[41] allows for modulations on a syllable, or when poetry replaces prose and melodies are introduced. These hymns are numerous, difficult, very beautiful, and give the young master a chance to show his gifts as a singer.

Taoist recitation has two very striking characteristics. First of all, it forces the reader to pronounce each word clearly, to punctuate the text, and therefore to understand it. This last point is important, for many Taoist texts are written in a difficult language which even a good Chinese scholar cannot always understand at first glance. A rhythmical reading, especially if it is repetitive, allows one to penetrate the text in successive stages. It compels the reciter to concentrate and enables him, with each reading, first to grasp the surface meaning and later the deeper meaning of the text. Thus proceeds the Taoist instruction. At no time do the senior *tao-shih* try to teach doctrine to the young disciple. He does not receive any theological training, neither now nor later. The teachings of the Tao are passed on through the rhythmical, concentrated reading of the texts. It is up to each individual to understand them according to his efforts and intellectual abilities.

The other remarkable aspect of Taoist recitation is physical. The reciter must stand perfectly straight. His breathing is deep and regular, while his hands are busy beating percussion instruments that accompany the reading—with his left hand, the wood block, with his right, the gong. The mental concentration and this physical exercise make the recitation a complete activity. One's whole person is caught up as sounds, words, and their meaning take hold, measure by measure, gradually accelerating as the reading continues and transforms the tempo from andante to vivace. The last sentences are read rapidly, the voice rises, and the gong beats follow in quick succession. Once the reading is over, the disciple accompanies the final hymns with dances, prostrations, and, depending on the texts, quick steps and leaps to imitate the joy the gods felt when they first heard the revelation of the holy scriptures.[42] In the true Taoist manner, intellectual activity is here inseparable from body techniques.

These techniques get more complicated with each stage. Opposite the incense attendant, at the other end of the central table, stands the acolyte who ranks just above him. He is called the group leader (*yin-

pan). As his title indicates, he heads the processions and dances that are part of the major ceremonies: beginning and ending each ritual, at the entrance and departure from the ritual area, there are dances and processions that follow an intricate pattern, with whirlings, farandoles, and other dance patterns.[43] The group leader must know the whole sequence and lead the way for the others. He is also the herald of the Great Master at crucial moments of the ritual. He precedes him and opens the way for him to climb up onto the outer altar to assemble there the armies of his register and perform the sacrifice of the scriptures. This ascent is again a dance, but of a particular kind. With a limping step, dragging first one then the other foot behind him, the master follows the outline of a constellation or of a cosmic diagram. Through the dance, he is taking possession of the constellation's or the magic square's forces.[44] The course is first marked out with a purifying dance by the group leader.

As he masters the choreography, the disciple is promoted to second cantor (*fu-chiang*), to the right of the Great Master. He is in charge, not only of the sacred scriptures, but of all the other writings as well: the memorials, petitions, orders, appeals, letters, mission assignments, orders, summons, and passes that are all part of the administrative activity of the *tao-shih* as officers of the celestial bureaucracy. Indeed, in Taoist ritual every prayer is offered up in a written form. To call all the gods to the ritual area, an individual letter is addressed to each of them. Petitions inform the Heavenly Worthies of the celebration; lesser deities receive memorials, and the servant spirits get summonses to appear.

Within the Tao's Enclosure, each of the gods has his place. This place is indicated by yet another document, a certificate of participation with rights to the offerings and merits.[45] The place of each god constitutes a unit in the arrangement of the ritual area: services may include 60, 120, 240, or 340 units. The greatest rituals can include up to 3,600. The places are located along the circumference of the space, with the Heavenly Worthies along the north (the noble side), the gods along the east and west walls, the lower spirits and the popular deities on the south (behind the officiants and thus in an inferior position to them).

The Taoist ritual area is moveable. It can be set up around an incense burner anywhere, for as the patriarch Pai Yü-ch'an (beginning of the thirteenth century) said: "You have only to set up the incense burner for the divine empyrean to be present."[46] The priestly vestments, the ritual insignia and instruments, the texts to be recited all fit into two wooden trunks which a single man can carry. For this reason we speak of a "travel altar."[47] In actual practice, however, the great pure services in the life of the community are held in the courtyard of the local temple. In order to install the Taoist altar, some changes are necessary. The statues of the gods are taken out of the niches in the north wall, the noble side, opposite the entrance, and placed on the south, opposite their former position, on the most humble side. The community often protests this apparent demotion of the gods.[48] The statues of the temple gods are set up on ledges inside the entrances, closed during the service, and next to them are placed all the statues from the household sanctuaries, which are said to be there "to review the ritual." In fact, as we have seen, they represent the families and other groups (such as guilds) for whom the service is held.

Aside from these adjustments, the ritual area is built essentially with one or several incense burners, five bushels filled with rice, and paper objects: (1) rolled up letters in rectangular envelopes, placed all along the walls to mark the seats of the gods and form the Enclosure; (2) *True Writs* marking the five cardinal points; (3) paper statues representing messengers, guardians, patriarchs, and saints; (4) talismans, memorials, summonses, and passes which are put on specific seats. All these objects are burned either at different moments of the service or else at the final dispersion. The altar is, moreover, adorned with paintings of the Heavenly Worthies and the gods, which are hung on the walls, corresponding to the seats of the gods on the enclosure, so as to visibly illustrate the assembly of divine powers in the ritual area.[49] This is rarely done in a complete fashion, for the painted scrolls belong to the families of the Dignitaries of the Tao who exhibit them sparingly. The most essential aspects of the ritual space—such as its division into an inner and outer altar, its ten gates, and its orientation according to the Eight Trigrams—remain invisible.

After the gods have been called to their places around the ritual area, the real Installation rites begin. At the end of the day, all the fires in the ritual area and in the community are put out and a new fire is lit in an archaic fashion.[50] The new flame is brought in procession into the altar, and used to light the lamps one by one as the officiants recite from the *Tao-te ching:* "The Tao gave birth to the One, the One gave birth to the Two, the Two to the Three, the Three to the Ten Thousand Beings."

After the lighting of the lamps comes the harmonizing of the sounds of the universe: the gong on the central table and a bell suspended in the orchestra are struck a certain number of times. The bowl-shaped gong makes the sounds of the Earth; the bell, those of Heaven. First the gong is struck twenty-four times, then the bell twenty-seven times. They are then chimed in unison thirty-six times (the total number of heavenly energies). Finally, the gong is struck six times (a *yin* number), and the bell nine times (a *yang* number): Heaven and Earth are in place.

The next stage establishes the center. In the middle of the space, right behind the central table, a painted scroll is hung, the only one that is not merely decorative and that has a real function in the ritual. The acolytes unroll it carefully, then partially roll it up again. The only image in the painting is the character for "gate" (*ch'üeh*) which refers to the palace gate, the Golden Gate of the Jade Emperor (Yü-huang shang-ti), head of the pantheon and highest of the gods, who is seated on the threshold of the Tao.[51] He is the One, the axis, the mediator, and the center toward which everything converges. The whole ritual and all the petitions are directed towards this presence, which after all is really just an opening.

After the rites of purification and enclosure of the ritual area comes the final phase of the installation: the placing of the *Five True Writs* (*wu chen-wen*). These are documents drawn up entirely in talismanic symbols which are supposed to have been revealed spontaneously at the creation of the universe. The text of the ritual recalls their appearance:

The *True Writs,*
heavenly treasures in vermillion writing on jade tablets,
were born before the original beginning,
in the middle of the void cavern.
The universe had not yet taken root,
sun and moon did not yet shed their radiance.
Obscure! Dark!
No originator!
No lineage!
Now marvellous writs appeared, they gathered and mingled,
now present, then absent.
Yin and yang nurtured them into distinctness,
the great *yang* assisted them in obtaining brightness.
Thereupon these marvellous writs began to revolve,
these auspicious images started their revolution.
Riding the clockwork, responding to the cycle,
they became permanent.
When Heaven and Earth obtained these writs,
they also became permanent.
When the sun, the moon and the stars obtained them,
they became radiant.
Marvellous writings! So luxuriant!
Their light penetrating into the realm of the highest purity,

illuminating the heavens of the dark beginning.
Their colors were not yet fixed according to their orientation [in space] and the shape of the characters was bent and crooked; thus they were impossible to understand.
The Tao of the Original Beginning forged them in the lodge of Pervading Yang, smelted them in the Hall of Streaming Fire, and thus brought out their correct script. Dazzling brightness shone forth from them, and when they began to shine, the myriads of divine ancestors came to pay homage, flying through the air, dancing in the void, circling through the palace on high, burning incense, scattering flowers, chanting the marvellous stanzas contained in these writs. . . .
Then the Way of the Original Beginning took up its mandate, the supreme immortals wielded their writing brushes, their jade concubines prepared the space, gold was melted into tablets and the writs were engraved thereon. . . .
These writs are the high texts of the Nine Heavens, not things that can be understood by human spirits. Heaven treasures them and thus can float; Earth hides them in its bosom and thus can be stable. . . . The high sages worship them for obtaining perfection, the five sacred mountains follow them to become divine, the Son of Heaven holds unto them in order to be able to govern, the heirs to the land (the local leaders) sacrifice them so as to obtain the Great Peace.[52]

The phases of creation described in this text correspond to the rites of Installation of the ritual area: at the four points of the space and on the main table the bushels filled with grains of rice are placed.[53] As we have seen, these are perfect vessels, for the bushel is the measure of life, and rice is the food of life. Rice grains represent "the essence," absolute purity. A bushel measure full of rice grains thus is a perfect symbolic container for the *Five True Writs*. According to the liturgical manuals of the Taoist Canon, the *Writs* were to be copied on wooden boards in the colors corresponding to the five cardinal points: blue-green for the east, red for the south, white for the west, black for the north, and yellow for the center. In the liturgical tradition that I was taught, these *True Writs* are simply blank sheets of paper, the symbols being so sacred that a human being, even a Great Master, could not write them. Next to the sheets, a brush, a stick of ink, and an ink stone (for rubbing ink) are placed in the bushels with the prayer: "May the patriarchs come install the *True Writs*."[54] This prayer expresses the faith that the founders of the liturgical tradition themselves will come and write out the sacred signs, a kind of writing that will nonetheless remain invisible to mortal eyes.

The Sacrifice of Writings

Invisible too is what separates the ritual area into inner and outer altar. And yet this division is important to each stage of the ritual and governs the actions and gestures of the officiants. Turned toward the ideal "north,"[55] the noble side, the *tao-shih* are "within," in attendance at the heavenly court. Their attitude is reverential, the officiants bow and prostrate themselves. Facing the Golden Gate which indicates the center, at each ritual the second cantor respectfully presents a written memorial on which are inscribed the place, the date, the program of the rites, the blessings and merits requested, as well as the name of the Great Master and the elders who represent the community.

But when the masters turn around and face the gallery of gods and the area reserved to the lower spirits, they find themselves in the outer altar and they assume an attitude full of authority. They give orders to the generals of the celestial armies and entrust to them the transmission of the memorials just presented to the heavenly chancellery. The generals, as a group, receive a written mission order (*kuan*) and a pass (*fu-ming*) for the Golden Gate. To send off these emissaries, the Great Master, preceded by his herald, the group leader, "climbs up to the outer altar," symbolized by his performance of the Dance of the Stars discussed above. The Great Master then ritually purifies the memorial and cries out:

> Smoke of five colors, the memorial rises to the sky!
> Energies of five colors, the memorial goes all the way to the Jade Emperor.
> Lower supernatural agents and old energies,
> you must not impede this mission;
> my emissaries, carriers of symbols, hurry along in your task!

The second cantor then reads the mission order. The two junior acolytes bring in a horse (made of paper) and a messenger (also made of paper); they offer hay to the horse and serve three cups of wine to the messenger in the saddle. The Great Master sings a drinking song, bursts out laughing, and his acolytes mime drunkenness. Then they carry off the documents and paper statuettes to burn them outside the ritual area: a blaze, a few firecrackers going off, a stack of sacrificial monies thrown into the flames, while the Great Master, holding his command baton cries out a final warning to the emissaries: "Hurry!

Obey my orders! Any idleness or negligence will be punished! But if you have any merit, your name will be carried to the celestial registers!" Then, taking up a paper pass decorated with a talismanic symbol that will enable the agents of Heaven to recognize the messengers, he burns it and scatters the ashes in the air. This concludes the sacrifice of writings, one of the specific traits of liturgical Taoism.

From its beginnings, Taoism has rejected and proscribed the sacrifice of victims[56]—the immolation of living beings of any species—but has opted instead to open a way to the sacred through the oblation of written documents. At each of the rituals included in the great services, there is a central, coherent, presentation of the sacrifice of the memorials. Sacred books may also be burned after being recited.[57] Also sacrificed, at the end of each service, are the documents indicating the seats of the gods, as well as the cosmic *Five True Writs* (the white sheets) which consecrate the ritual area.

This gesture is defined in terms of "transformation" (*hua*),[58] meaning that the oblation is a transmutation that allows the essence of the sacrificed object to be distilled and refined; it is made divine, sacred, and powerful. To sacrifice is to make *real,* which means that the power obtained will remain active for a certain period of time. The ritual area— where, for a moment, all the powers of the universe have been concentrated and materialized in the sacred *True Writs*—is, at the final moment of the dispersal, consumed in a great blaze. Between the installation and the dispersal, the beginning and the end of a service, a day or two have elapsed. This represents an incredible shortening of time with respect to the temporal cycle of the cosmos and allows the world to benefit from the spiritual force released by this action.[59]

Let me emphasize once more the role of writings. We have seen the transcendent aspect of Chinese calligraphy: the perfect sign can even be changed into the being it designates. The symbolic *fu* characters of the *True Writs* represent the archetypes of all things.[60] First copied by the gods, their subsequent "transformation" by fire causes the signs to return to their original state. In addition to the oblation of the cosmic model of the *five True Writs,* such messages as the memorials, petitions, and commands, are addressed to the heavens. This practice might be hard to take seriously if it were not so respectably ancient in China.

In this area, as in so many others, the Taoist ritual reflects a fundamental fact, namely that Chinese writing was used first for communication between men and the gods before it was used among men themselves. The most ancient specimens of Chinese writing are the oracular inscriptions on bone. In ancient China, in the second millennium B.C., divination was practiced by observing cracks in the scapular bones of sheep and later in tortoises' shells. These were first subjected to preliminary preparation, then to heating and cooling by fire and water.[61] The resulting cracks were thought to be the writing of the gods in response to a question inscribed first on the bone by the diviner.[62]

Even when the use of writing was secularized and extended to all forms of literature, its ritual function was not forgotten. Emperor Wu, whose long reign (141–87 B.C.) marked the height of the Han dynasty, made a sacrifice called *feng*, "investiture," in 110 B.C. at the top of the greatest of the sacred mountains of China, the T'ai-shan.[63] By announcing his merit to Heaven, the emperor hoped to obtain immortality. A petition addressed to the Heavenly Emperor was written and buried at the top of the mountain. The fact that burial can replace combustion as a means of oblation in Taoist practice demonstrates that the famous sacrifice by Emperor Wu was indeed of the same type as that of the Taoists today.[64]

The Altar

There remains, however, an important difference in the way the "sacrifice of writings" was performed: to perform the *feng* sacrifice, Emperor Wu went to the summit of the highest mountain of eastern China, the sacred peak of T'ai-shan. There, where the sky and earth meet, and thus where the ruler was as close as possible to the gods from whom he sought investiture, Emperor Wu set up an altar to sacrifice the writings. The Taoist ritual, on the contrary, is performed within the ritual area where all the gods are gathered. This ritual area may be set up anywhere; there is not need to make a pilgrimage. The Master does not leave his homeland.

The taoist altar is itself a mountain. An enclosed space, secret and covered (thus "inner"), it is called *tao-ch'ang*, "place or enclosure of the Tao." Nonetheless, to enter this place of retreat in order to perform the rites is called, in the language of the *tao-shih*: "to go into the mountain." The taoist liturgy of the middle ages had so-called "silent" or "pure chambers" (*ching-shih*), in which a retreat or fast was performed. These were enclosed spaces (except for a single opening, a small doorway), without any decoration or any painted or sculpted images. Aside from the mats to sit on, the only furnishing was the incense burner placed in the center of the room. As we have seen, the incense burner represented a *mountain* in miniature. The fuel consisted of different aromatic herbs mixed with wax, which released smoke and flames when burned. The incense burner was used primarily for the purifying fumigation, similar to that performed during the big annual cleaning in peasant homes in ancient China.[65] The name "pure chamber" no doubt derives from the incense burner and the *smoke baths*. The flames themselves must have produced luminous effects, turning the incense burner into an incandescent lamp to light the room and a shining signal to guide the gods toward the meeting place. The radiant mountain was also the focus for the ecstatic journey of meditation. It represented the world of the Immortals, the K'un-lun. The smoke curled out through openings in the lid (like the Chinese notion of caverns giving birth to the clouds) to be transformed into dragons, winged messengers who carried prayers to the gates of heaven. Here, the mountain is located *inside* the pure chamber, under our eyes. To move towards it implies a movement towards the *inside*.

Today the incense burner, an instrument of purification and communication, continues to occupy a central place in the ritual area. The representation of the mountain has become more complex but not essentially different. The ritual area is called not only "space" or "enclosure of the Tao" (*tao-ch'ang*), but much more commonly "altar" (*t'an*). This designation for a closed and covered space, however, poses serious problems of interpretation.

According to all the ancient written sources, an altar is a square mount of several steps, three or nine (like a ziggurat), meant to be in the open air, preferably on top of a mountain. The gods have their seats on these steps according to the sphere to which they belong. The offerings are placed before them. The altar is reached through doors located at the corners and on the sides, eight or ten in all. The altar itself represents a mountain, and during the service the officiating priests are supposed to go up *onto* the altar to perform the sacrifice there.

But if the ritual area is an "altar," it does not have, at least nowadays, any central structure with steps. In any case, the space of the Tao is an enclosed, covered place, and corresponds more closely to a *pure chamber*. The pure chamber and the altar are the *two* ritual places of Taoist liturgy. The ritual is performed in one or on the other. Meditation, prayers, and the fast are held in the chamber, and sacrifices and offerings, on the altar. Upon ordination the master is invested with an altar and a pure chamber which are recorded on his *Certificate of Immortality*. The master uses the name of his altar (for example, "Altar of the Congregation of the Gods of the First Principle"[66] for all his liturgical transactions, and this is also the name used for his office at home, even though this office is an enclosed place. As we have seen in the case of the great services (the funeral rites as well as the pure ritual), the ritual area is always called an altar, and never a pure chamber. According to ordination documents, the pure chamber does exist, but the masters never mention it. Every place where ritual is performed is an altar, and the question of where its complementary space, the pure chamber, is located remains unanswered.[67] How does one explain this? Looking more closely at the ritual area, one sees that, though there is no elevated structure, the decoration, especially on the noble north wall where the Heavenly Worthies are, suggests an incline with steps. By stacking offering tables on top of each other and covering them with embroidered cloths and paintings, the illusion of the side (the southern slope!) of a mountain is created, on whose summit one sees the images of the gods.[68] Standing in the center before the Golden Gate, the officiating priest can thus be said to be standing at the foot of a sacred mountain, the dwelling of the gods. But the decoration is not restricted to the wall facing the priests; it surrounds them on all sides.

The noblest of the gods are on the north side, while the others are seated in the east and west, and the patron saints of local communities and the lower spirits occupy the south wall. Together these different positions form a whole, a circle, a sacred enclosure. Along this enclosure are located the eight or ten gates which "open into" the altar.[69] The multilevel mountain—*the altar*—is located *around* the officiating priest rather than the priest being *on* the altar: he is *in* the mountain, the Space of the Tao.

All the essences are assembled here in this space. There remain, nevertheless, a number of seemingly contradictory elements. For instance, the Great Master gathers all the gods along the circumference of the enclosure, but to send them messages, he goes "outside." To send memorials and petitions addressed to the chancellery of the Great Dipper, the *tao-shih* go out into the open air and up onto a square platform. This place would certainly deserve to be called "altar," but that is definitely not the case; it is simply referred to as the "platform for the presentation of memorials." Even if, as the officiants go up onto the platform, the ritual action imitates the ascent of a mountain, this is not clearly expressed or made explicit. In fact, the open-air platform is only

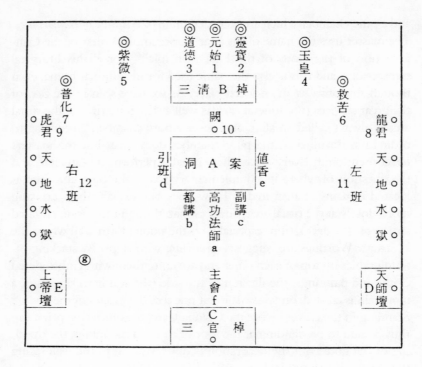

A: Central table
B: Offering table in front of the Three Pure Ones
C: Altar for the Three Officials
D: Altar for the Heavenly Masters (the patriarchs)
E: Altar for Hsüan-t'ien shang-ti, et cetera (the gods of the North)
a: The Great Master
b: The chief cantor
c: The assistant cantor
d: The group leader
e: The incense attendant
f: The heads of the community
g: The orchestra
∘: Painted scroll (image)
⊚: Painted scroll, with curtains and other ornamentation
1: The Yüan-shih t'ien-tsun (Heavenly Worthy of the Primordial Beginning)
2: The Ling-pao t'ien-tsun (Heavenly Worthy of the Marvellous)
3: The Tao-te t'ien-tsun (Heavenly Worthy of the Tao and its Power)
4: Yü-huang shang-ti (the Jade Emperor)
5–9: Other gods
10: The Golden Gate
11–12: Left and right walls with the seats of the lesser gods

a temporary *extension* of the ritual area where the sending of the scriptures is performed. Its use is neither systematic nor obligatory. The master might just as easily remain within the building to send messages and simply turn toward the outside, for "inside" and "outside" are only ritual directions of the ritual space. The enclosure of the Tao can be moved at any time and goes with the Great Master. Where he is, there is the altar.

The Great Master, "Universal Inspector of Merits Responsible for Spreading Civilization according to Nature's Principles" (*tai-t'ien hsing-hua*)," is popularly called the "venerable of the middle" (*chung-tsun*). His place is in the center of the ritual area. To his left stands his chief cantor whose role complements the Great Master's.

The chief cantor, the fourth and most important of the acolytes, is in charge of all the ritual recitations except those of the sacred books and the documents. He recites the formulas of invocation and consecration—which call on the Heavenly Worthies, the gods, and the spirits—as well as the texts of purification, elevation, and confession. He beats the wood block in front of him on the central table to indicate the rhythm. This is essential, for, as we have seen, the whole ritual is set to music. Imitating the external pattern of a hearing at the imperial court, with hymns, dances, presentation of petitions and banquets, the ritual is expressed in the most diverse vocal forms: recitations, psalms, chants, instrumental interludes, and elaborate gestures. The text of the ritual is there on the altar table in manuscript form and it is the assistant cantor's responsibility to turn the pages as the ceremony progresses; but the written word is a prompt, at the very most. The complexity of the ritual is such that it must be completely integrated by all the participants. It is through the music, and more precisely the rhythm, that this integration is achieved. The acolytes and the Great Master in particular identify the successive parts and exact moments of the action much more readily by ear than by notes in the manuscript.

Next to and a little behind the chief cantor, stands the Great Master, quiet and still. Holding his "audience tablet" (*ch'ao-pan*) in both hands, his eyes half closed, he quietly murmurs sacred formulas which, among all those present, only he and the chief cantor know. At times he puts down his tablet and draws his hands into his sleeves, where his fingers make invisible movements.[70] At other times he takes the incense burner,[71] makes signs above the hearth, and breathes in and out as he faces in different directions;[72] he lights and burns talismanic symbols; and with a brush dipped in red ink, he initials the documents that the assistant cantor presents to him.

All this is performed in silence with a minimum of visible gestures. For while the canor recites, the Great Master performs an inner ritual in harmony with the spoken text. What the cantor says, the Great Master accomplishes by meditation. As indicated in an ancient manual of secret formulas, the cantor is but the living aspect of the Great Master, because during his meditation the latter is "as if made of dead wood."[73] As he concentrates on the inner rites and murmurs the secret formulas, his mouth barely moves and his hands make invisible gestures. In the words of the manual: "The cantor must know the secret formulas so that his heart will be in complete harmony with the Great Master's; thus it can be said that the cantor is also a leader of the ritual. The ancients used to say: 'The living cantor is the replica of the Great Master.' "[74]

Here, at the heart of the Taoist ritual, we find once again the dual structure, that of the puppeteer and his puppet and of the barefoot master and his medium. A pair so closely bound together that what one of them thinks, the other says.

It is difficult to say which of the two is more important. The cantor represents the outer aspect of a universe whose inner dimension lies within the Great Master. The one cannot do without the other, even if the inner aspect remains more important in Taoism.

At the beginning of the ritual, during the consecration of the incense burner, the cantor chants slowly: "Sound the ritual drum twenty-four times!" During the brief time it takes the orchestra drum to beat out the twenty-four strokes, the Great Master, his eyes half-closed, stands still and murmurs:

> Nine spiritual palaces,
> The Great One guards the chamber;
> All the gods unite,
> The *hun* and the *p'o* souls are in harmony.
> Long life! Long life!
> The evil spells are broken!
> Urgent! Urgent!
> This is an order in the name of the energies of life!

Then he focuses his thoughts on the twenty-four energies of his body, eight for the lower body, eight for the chest, eight for the head; he calls on them as he grinds his (eight) teeth three times and inhales, directing his breath and energies from the Upper Palace (a point located between the eyebrows) to the Cinnabar Field (the lower abdomen).

Then the Great Master takes up the community's incense burner in his right hand, and the rite of the "lighting" begins as the Great Master follows step by step, through his meditation, the text chanted by the canter:

> Old Lord Most High of the Three Energies,
> Mysterious, Original, and Primordial
> Of the supreme Three Heavens,
> call from inside my body the Attendants to the Merits of the three (spheres)
>   and five (directions),
> the emissaries of the incense,
> the dragon-riding couriers,
> the golden little boy who guards the incense,
> the jade maiden who transmits the words,
> the officers who attend the symbols of the Five Emperors and who are on
>   assignment today,
> thirty-six people in all:
> "Come out!
> Come out, each one of you, dressed nobly in ceremonial costume, and stand
>   before the sacred officer, Earth God of this very place, to tell him that I
>   am here burning incense so that I may go up onto the altar and practice
>   the Tao for such and such a community.". . . And may the cosmic energies
>   of life descend and spread through my body, so that my sincere intentions
>   may be communicated rapidly before the throne of the Jade Emperor of
>   the Golden Gate in the vast heavens![75]

While the cantor recites this text, the Great Master meditates. At the mention of "Old Lord of the Three Energies," he directs his breathing and energies from the Cinnabar Field to the Upper Palace (opposite to the movement of a moment ago) and exhales as he evokes mentally the three colors: blue-black, yellow, and white. At "my body," he inhales again, turning towards the direction that corresponds to the star of the Big Dipper under which he was born. During the enumeration of the thirty-six gods of the body, he exhales while concentrating on the inner energies of each category.[76] While the cosmic energies of life are being mentioned, he inhales again and exhales when the Jade Emperor's name is pronounced.

To conclude this rite, the Great Master places the *hua,* a pin in the shape of a flaming pearl, in his crown. The meaning of this gesture is obvious: He has not only lit the incense burner held in his hand, but also the one he holds within his own body, in his Cinnabar Field, and from this one there now emanates a radiance up through his body and all around him.

The gesture of placing the flaming pearl on the crown recalls the moment of the Great Master's consecration during his ordination. Now he ceases to be an ordinary man. Having transformed his body,[77] he takes on his role of venerable of the middle. That is why, as soon as he has attached the pin to his crown, he lists his name and religious title, for the first time since the beginning of the ritual: "I, so-and-so, Immortal Officer, invested with the register of canonical scriptures, Universal Inspector of Merits of the Orthodox One. . ."

From his body of light, enlivened by the energies of life—the breaths of birth (sheng-ch'i)—the Great Master creates the gods of his inner pantheon and the deities of his register. He pronounces their names and evokes them in his thoughts, each with their proper attributes, costume, and distinctive signs. He reviews this parade like a general inspecting his troops. He lines them up in order of rank and creates a magnificent procession which precedes and surrounds him on his way to the gates of Heaven.

In the text read earlier by the cantor, an allusion is made to a message to be presented at the Golden Gate. Now that time has come. The sacrifice of the scriptures is performed according to the scenario described above. The emissary spirits from the "outer altar" are sent away with these words: "Your merits will be recorded in the books of the Most Pure!"[78]

Immediately afterward, the Great Master drops his imperious demeanor. He holds out his arms while the acolytes take his sword and bowl of lustral water, and hand him his audience tablet. The "venerable of the middle" slowly turns around. Briefly he performs a "dance on the stars," that is to say, he traces with is limping walk the outline of the Dipper constellation in the middle of the ritual area. Then suddenly he prostrates himself, his legs and arms folded under his body, his face resting on his hands, which hold the audience tablet. A three-footed cauldron is placed behind him and the attendant to the incense takes up the Grand Master's sword and holds it up vertically inside the cauldron.[79] The group leader takes the incense burner and turns it slowly, tracing figure eights (yin and yang), above the kneeling Great Master. The chief cantor starts singing a hymn and the assistant cantor answers him.

Curled up in the fetal position, the Great Master then makes a spiritual journey within his own body. First he visualizes a newborn child in the area of his abdomen, there at the site of the Cinnabar Field (tan-

t'ien), below his navel. Then he concentrates on his heart, where he rediscovers the newborn child, who is now called the True Person. He is dressed in red and two guards in military uniform stand beside him. They are "generals." He visualizes all three, standing on a terrace bathed in the light of dawn. Then, with an escort of other Generals, they ascend a twelve-story tower (which corresponds to the trachea) and present themselves before the Pass of the Tiger and the Leopard (the throat). They enter the mouth, then the nose and continue their path all the way to the Gates of the Sun and Moon (the eyes), which open into the point between the brows. Finally, they arrive at the top of the head and from there enter the cavity inside the crown. There stands the Golden Gate. On his knees, facing the flaming pearl—a white light emanating from the original energy—the True Person presents the memorial on which he has placed several *fu* or passes. Once the memorial has been accepted by the officers of the Heavenly Chancellery, the True Person turns back. But the journey to the heavenly regions has transformed him. Now he appears as a venerable old man, the Great Lord of Long Life, the stellar deity of Immortality, who slowly descends to reintegrate himself with the point of origin, the Cinnabar Field.

Thus concludes the ecstatic journey, called the "silent hearing," which takes place entirely inside the master's body (the crown is considered part of his body, as we shall see in the myth of Lao Tzu's birth), in another world, a new space which is added to the inner and outer spaces we have already seen.

Here we find the element that will finally enable us to understand the mystery of the ritual area. The closed space of the Tao is a world apart, but it is called *altar,* sacrifical mound, mountain. This mountain, however, has an inner face and an outer one. The surface of the mountain has been detached, so to speak, and now encircles the "place of the Tao." The mountain has become concave instead of convex.

In the middle of the ritual area then, we find ourselves inside a mountain; but since we perceive its surface, we must also be standing outside it: we are both "inside" and "outside."

We also see the sphere of the altar as something continuing outward from the master's own body. Moving "towards the outside," he projects from his body transcendent forces which radiate and surround him in concentric circles, in an infinite number of finite spaces. Moving "towards the inside," the master finds a place of retreat *within himself.* And that is where we at last discover that most intimate space, the world of silence: the pure chamber.

6

The Inner Landscape

"The human body is the image of a country," say the Taoists. There they see mountains and rivers, ponds, forests, paths, and barriers, a whole landscape laid out with dwellings, palaces, towers, walls, and gates sheltering a vast population. It is a civilized state, administered by lords and their ministers.

The vision of the human body belongs both to Taoism and to Chinese medicine. The fundamental work of medical theory, the *Simple Questions of the Yellow Emperor,* describes the body thus: "The heart functions as the prince and governs through the *shen* ["soul"]; the lungs are liaison officers who promulgate rules and regulations; the liver is a general and devises strategies."[1]

At first sight this appears to be only a metaphor: the functions of the body are like officials of a country. But in classical literature, the word *kuan,* "agent," means "organ" as well as "official."[2] It is clear that beyond the metaphorical level, a whole system of correspondences is intended here which the *Simple Questions* explain in detail. The image of the country is only one aspect of this system. We tend to refer to these representatives as macrocosm and microcosm: the body—microcosm—is meant to correspond in all respects to the outer world and reflect it faithfully. In consequence, some authors have even insisted that if Chinese doctors never performed dissections in a systematic way, it was because they had no need to, for the whole human body, its organization, laws, and transformations were to be found in the universe: they had only to observe the sky to understand the body's organs.

This simplistic equation is not supported by historical evidence, and in fact Chinese medicine is based just as much as ours on empirical observation, in the area of anatomy as well as pharmacology and hygiene. Many medical manuals transmit only this empirical knowledge, whereas the classic *Simple Questions of the Yellow Emperor* is an attempt at systematizing knowledge, especially that based on the cosmological doctrine of energies, and provides a theoretical foundation for medical practice.

But Taoism goes further. "The human body is the image of a country" implies a relation that transcends the simple metaphor. The emphasis on *country* reflects the interdependence of the human being and his environment, as well as Taoism's fundamental teaching that favors the interior over the exterior.

The Environment

Traditional thought in China recognizes a deep relationship between a physical setting and the nature of its inhabitants. Taking stock of the world's riches, the ancients always included human diversity in their catalogue by observing that:

Each region produces its class of beings. Thus the wind of the mountains produces many males; that of the lakes, females; obstructed winds produce mutes; heavy winds, deaf people; in the forest one finds many stooped people, for the breeze of the woods makes one hunchbacked; people living under rocky shelters often have inflated bellies, for the winds of rocks make one solid; in very hilly areas people often suffer from goiters. In hot climates people die young, while cold climates confer longevity; winds in the valleys bring on rheumatism, those of hilly areas drive one mad, fertile lands encourage goodness, . . . the land of the middle produces many sages. Thus, in every case (men) are in the image of the wind (of their environment), for everything corresponds to a category. That is why in the south one finds the herb that keeps one from dying and in the north the ice that never melts.[3]

According to its intrinsic power (or "virtue," *te*), each region of the world will produce a particular type of people, and knowledge of these characteristics is the key to good government. The prince, who stands at the Center, receives in tribute from each part of his country the fruits that represent the material, emblematic essence of those regions. The regional specialties of ancient China are part of the seasonal fare in the lord's diet which, according to the system of universal correspondence, is to sustain a Power worthy of the Universe, who will be the most whole and the most One, the least material and the least perishable, such that this Power may be seen as being the source of endless radiance. To respect this principle of influences, one has only to gather at the proper time and place the essence of all that lives in the universe.[4]

Marcel Granet, from whose work on Chinese ancient thought the above quotation was taken, describes the entire ritual system governing each instant of the temporal cycle intended to bring the sovereign into harmony with his environment: his clothing and his nourishment, as well as the exercise of his authority. The ultimate expression of the "cosmologization" of the person of the sovereign is the *ming-t'ang,* the Hall of Light or house of the calendar, as it was conceived in ancient China. This was a dwelling built on the model of the universe, with a round roof on a square base, and in which the king was to move from room to room according to spatiotemporal correspondences. At the New Year, in early spring, he would occupy the room in the east, in summer, the one in the south, and so forth. The third month of each season being dedicated to the Earth, he would at that time go to the central room. The colors of his clothing, his food, everything had to be in keeping with the cosmic cycle so as "not to interfere" and to insure universal harmony. Being thus fully united with his territory, "the lord forms a single body with his realm," or so the Classics said.[5] This ancient theme is echoed in the words that the great Taoist master Ssu-ma Ch'eng-chen addressed in A.D. 711 to an emperor of the T'ang dynasty. The emperor had summoned the master to question him on arithmetic, and the master replied: "Study brings progress daily, the practice of the Tao brings loss. From loss to loss, one arrives at Non-Action.[6] Why do you tire your mind with arithmetic?"

"To care for the body, to practice Non-Action is all very well, but who will govern the country?" asked the emperor.

"The country is like the body: follow the nature of things, don't let your mind harbor any partiality,[7] and the whole world will be governed." With these words, the master took his leave of the emperor and went home to his mountain, some two thousand kilometers from the capital.[8]

"Who governs his body, governs the country." This teaching which the master passed on to the Emperor is in keeping with the ancient concept of the state discussed above. To absorb the essences from all directions and thereby to integrate the cosmic order is the fundamental principle, both of governing through the ritual of the Son of Heaven, and of the Non-Action (or non-intervention) of the master. "To intervene" means in effect to violate nature by going against the spontaneous process with actions inspired and influenced by our partial view of things. Imbalance results from this intervention. The disruptions of nature, droughts, floods, epidemics, famines could all be attributed to the loss of universal harmony in the behavior of the king. In ancient China he was considered personally responsible for these calamities, and when they occurred, he was judged guilty and had to redeem himself through confessions, fasts, and sacrifices.

In Taoism, the idea of the responsibility of the king towards his country is extended to the responsibility of each person towards his environment. To be sure, the ordinary person is influenced and molded by his environment, but for one who has received the initiation of the body and who knows the laws of nature, the flow of influence is reversed. He is no longer simply the product of his environment, but dominates and transforms it. By saying "the country is like the body," master Ssu-ma seems to have turned around the Taoist saying stated at the beginning of this chapter, according to which "the body is the image of the country." In fact, he has expressed the very heart of Taoist thought in relation to both the system of correspondences of medical science and the concept of the state and the king of ancient China, that is to say: the fundamental role of the human body. It is pointless to try to act on the world outside oneself so long as one's inner order is not established; otherwise, whatever is achieved will not endure. For Chuang Tzu, "the action of the sage is directed within. He does not seek to impose on the world rules, values, rites, or laws that he himself has invented."[9] The only valid law is that of nature, which explains Taoism's love for the natural sciences. For a human being to rediscover his spontaneity, he must first come to know the laws and secrets of the universe, beginning with those of his inner universe.

The Image of the Body

Up to this point we have encountered two ways of envisioning the body, two main approaches to the person. The first is theological and is tied to the notion of divinity and to the many transcendent principles, where the multiple souls and spirits represent the essences and the energies (*ch'i*) of the body.[10] It depends on ontological and cosmological theories related in turn to the systems of correspondence that subtend medical theory and the ritual of the state. This set of representations is well-known to those who study China and has been examined in many publications.

The second approach is empirical and is the origin of the techniques of acupuncture, herbal medicine, and many other Chinese arts and sciences which continue to draw our attention. In the learned literature these empirical technologies have often been systematized through the philosophical and cosmological theories of correspondences. Among the practitioners and their professional corporations, however, these technologies exist without that conceptual and learned stock of knowledge. Therefore, this empirical approach can be said to constitute a separate dimension.

There is a third way of conceiving the body, which I shall call the symbolic vision. It is specifically Taoist. We have already encountered this vision in the description of the Great Master's inner vision of the landscape of the body. "The human body is the image of a country" is not just a proverb that expresses the twofold relationship between country and inhabitant and between king and territory; it corresponds above all to the Taoist vision of the inner world and to related physical exercises. This beautiful vision, which I will try here to describe, includes both the cosmological system of the theory of energies and correspondences, and the empirical knowledge of medicine; but what distinguishes it from the other ways of viewing the body is that it is related to a rich and meaningful mythology.[11]

The vision of the body as a symbolic land or country is alluded to in the oldest chapters of the *Chuang-tzu* (fourth century B.C.). However, it is not described fully until the first centuries A.D. In their broad outlines, these descriptions are all very similar and, despite additions and changes made over the centuries, they correspond to the inner vision as it is still practiced today. But if the techniques of introspection of today's Great Masters appear fairly simple, the same cannot be said of the descriptions passed down to us in the ancient texts of the *Taoist Canon*. These descriptions correspond to secret teachings intended for adepts, to complement oral teachings, and seem at first to be obscure, even incomprehensible. The many commentaries that exist for the most important texts often only add to the confusion, for they generally try to systematize the ancient mythological representations according to the abstract classificatory system of *yin* and *yang,* the Five Phases, the Eight

Trigrams and so on, an endeavor which results in many contradictions.[12]

Unfortunately, not a single text on the symbolic vision of the body has survived which has not been affected to some degree by the scholastic cosmological theories of the Han period.[13] Nevertheless, these theories did not succeed in masking the ancient mythology. The key elements of the inner world, such as the Cinnabar Field and the Yellow Court, have no counterpart in the outer world, the universe, the macrocosm. Generally speaking, the symbolic vision of the body, especially in the older texts, remains so full of logical contradictions, that it is useless to look for any "system."[14] At the same time, the fundamental themes recur with surprising regularity throughout all the descriptions of the inner landscape.

The least systematized description, the most disorganized, and yet the most authentic, is the one that I consider to be the most ancient. It is given in a text titled the *Book of the Center,* also known as the *Jade Calendar.*[15] Divided into two parts and fifty-five paragraphs, this work appears to date from the second century A.D.

The point of departure of the description of the inner world is indeed purely mythological: the great sacred mountain; the K'un-lun, pillar of the universe; the isles of the Immortals; the holy places, such as the altars to the Earth God; in short, the whole mythical geography as well as its corresponding pantheon. For instance, speaking about the Queen Mother of the West, the text states: "The human being also possesses her. She stays in the right eye. Her family name is Great Yin, her personal name, Jade Maiden of Obscure Brilliance."

One obtains the inner vision by looking within, by turning the pupils to the inside and keeping the eyes half-closed to let in light from the outside. The eyes not only relay light from the sun and the moon, but also are considered to add their own luminous energy,[16] so as to become themselves the sun and the moon of the inner universe. These sources of light are to be directed toward the center, in the head between the eyebrows. In the center, there is a third source of light, identified with the Pole Star (the third eye), which acts like a mirror and reflects the light of the eyes and directs it within.

What do we see there? The landscape of the head consists of a high mountain, or rather a series of peaks around a central lake. The lake lies midway between the back of the skull and the point between the eyebrows (the Pole Star and mirror). In the middle of the lake stands a palatial building, where there are eight rooms surrounding a ninth, central one. This is the Hall of Light (*ming-t'ang*), the house of the calendar of the kings of ancient China. In front of this palace and the lake around it, lies a valley (the nose). The entrance to the valley is guarded by two towers (the ears). Inside one, hangs a bell and inside the other, a stone chime.[17] Whenever someone passes, they are struck—something we perceive as the ringing of the ears.[18] At the far end of the valley runs a stream bringing water from the big lake into a smaller one at the other end, where it rises like a fountain (the mouth and saliva). A bridge (the tongue) crosses over the smaller lake to a lower bank where there stands a twelve-story tower (the trachea). It marks the border between the upper world and the middle regions.

These regions have their own sun and moon (the breasts). The middle world is covered by the clouds (the lungs) which hide the central constellation of the Dipper. Below it is a large dwelling, colored bright red (the heart). In front of this Scarlet Palace lies a courtyard of yellow earth (the spleen); this is the Yellow Court, the body's ritual area and the meeting place of its inhabitants. Opposite the court stands a simple structure called the Purple Chamber (the gallbladder), which is the place of retreat, the silent room adjacent to the ritual area. Farther on there is a tall building called the granary or warehouse (the stomach). Beyond the stomach, a forest indicates the location of the liver. In this area one also finds the altars of the God of the Earth and the God of the Harvests (the large and small intestines). Now we have reached the frontier of the middle region.

We now arrive in the watery lower world. Here again the sun and moon are found, this time in the kidneys. The cast their light on the great Ocean of Energies (*ch'i-hai*), which covers the whole of the lower body, and wherein a large turtle swims. In the middle of the ocean rises the K'un-lun, the sacred, inverted mountain with its narrow base widening towards the top, giving it the outline of a mushroom. The mountain has a hollow summit (the navel), which gives access to the deepest recesses of the ocean. There lies the Cinnabar Field, source of all life. The *Book of the Center* describes it in the following manner:

The Cinnabar Field is the root of the human being. This is the place where the vital power is kept. The five energies [of the Five Phases] have their origin here. It is the embryo's home. Here men keep their semen and women, their menstrual blood. Meant for the procreation of children, it houses the gate of harmonious union of *yin* and *yang*. Three inches under the navel, adjacent to the spine, (the Cinnabar Field) lies at the base of the kidneys. It is scarlet inside, green on the left, yellow on the right, white on top, and black on the bottom. It is four inches around. Its location three inches below the navel symbolizes the trinity of Heaven, Earth, and Humans. One is Heaven; two, the Earth; three, the Human Being; four, Time. That is why the (Cinnabar Field) has (a circumference) of four inches. It is modeled on the Five Phases, which is why it has five colors.[19] The Cinnabar Field is located in the region of clear water, in the village of the High Hill: it is also called the Palace-that-keeps-the-Essence.[20]

The Cinnabar Field gives access to the deepest regions of the body, at the bottom of the ocean, where a gaping hole siphons off the waters and also the vital energies of the Cinnabar Field. The most frequent names for this abyss are Gate of Destiny, Obscure Gate, Original Pass, or Terminal Exit (wei-lü). Chuang Tzu says: "The ocean is the greatest of the world's waters, the ten thousand rivers spill into it endlessly and yet it is never too full. Its waters escape through the Terminal Exit and yet it never empties."[21]

Some commentaries describe the Terminal Exit as a rock in the ocean that radiates an extreme heat. Water that comes into contact with the rock turns to vapor immediately. This juxtaposition of water and fire corresponds with that of the Cinnabar Field and the Terminal Exit. Chuang Tzu's static vision of the ocean is nonetheless not the most widespread today. Other theories, which are current today but which may have originated long ago, consider that the Cinnabar Field's energy diminishes and that our life withdraws through the "Gate of Destiny" like drops from a water clock. There are techniques that consist of blocking the Terminal Exit in order to recycle the Cinnabar Field energies. I shall speak of this later.

The vision of the lower region as described by the *Book of the Center* corresponds to that of a body reclining on its back, the usual position in ancient meditation. The highest point of the body, that is the hollow summit of the K'un-lun mountain, is thus the navel. The whole landscape of the body is organized around this central point: "The human destiny is the navel, called the Central Summit, the Great Abyss, the K'un-lun, the Solitary Pillar, also named the Five Fortresses."[22]

But the great majority of texts, beginning with the famous *Book of the Yellow Court,*[23] advocate the seated position and in this case the summit of the holy mountain coincides with the top of the skull. The elongation of the mountain—whose base is bathed in the Ocean of Energies—entails a different disposition of the elements of the inner world and of its division into spheres. The three levels—head, thorax, and abdomen—which correspond to the three worlds of Heaven, Earth, and Water, now appear as separate entities, and each of the essential elements, such as the Palace of Lights, the Yellow Court, and the Cinnabar Field, are thus found on each level. As a result, there are three Cinnabar Fields in the brain, heart, and stomach, and all three are considered essential points of the body, even though the "Lower Field" of the abdomen remains the "true Cinnabar Field," because of the generative function.[24]

This is an example of the confusion of body topology in later texts. This confusion increased over the centuries as reinterpretations and new systems were added and old elements had to be integrated.[25]

Already in the *Book of the Center,* the body appears as one and many at the same time. The head, thorax, and abdomen are described as distinct sections, and on each level one finds the sun, moon, and Pole Star (as well as the Dipper constellation with which it is associated). At the same time, each section retains its own essence and together the three form a complete landscape. Viewed as a whole, the body is a holy mountain;[26] it is the K'un-lun, pillar of the universe, and dwelling of the gods.

The painting reproduced here, by Liang K'ai (twelfth century), shows an anonymous Immortal whom I would identify as Lao Tzu himself.[27] The artist has painted him "as if he were a huge mossy mountain, enshrouded in rags of mist."[28] The brush technique used by the artist is that used in landscape painting, never for portraits.[29] It is a wonderful example of the human being seen as a mountain.

The Inhabitants

The mountain, like its homologues the temple (with its mountain-shaped roof) and the altar, are peopled with gods. Right above the top of the skull lives the Great One (T'ai-i):

Above the nine heavens, in the center of the Supreme Purity. Inside the Extreme Subtlety. I do not know his name. He is the Original Energies (*yüan-ch'i*) and that is all. As a god he has a human head and the body of a bird. He looks like a cock, a phoenix of five colors.[30] He is right above my head, nine feet from my body. . . . When I see him, I say to him: "Supreme Great One, Lord of the Tao, your grandson So-and-So loves the Tao with a pure will and prays for Long Life.[31]

An Immortal, by Liang K'ai (twelfth century). Palace Museum, Taipei.

Between the eyebrows dwells the Most High Original Lord of the Limitless:

This is the Lord of the Tao. Sometimes a being with nine heads, sometimes nine people, in both cases dressed in garments of five-colored jewels, wearing the crown of the Nine Virtues, he is the child of the Great Unity.[32] A child without having been born a child, he was created spontaneously of the Original Energy. He is right there, in my head, in the center of a purple cloud, under a dais of colored clouds. . . . His family name is Stupid-Red, his first name, Radiance, his poetic name, Ancestral Land. He is the first star of the K'ou-ch'en in the Great Tenuity (Tsu-wei, the Pole Star). He is called the Great August Emperor of Heaven. . . .[33] Human beings have him too; one can see him between the two eyebrows, related to the Mud Pill.[34]

The left eye (the sun) is the dwelling of the Father of the East, the *yang* energy of spring; the right one shelters the Mother of the West, the Original Energy of the Great *yin*. The Father is called "Non-Action," the Mother, "Nature." She reigns over Mount K'un-lun.[35] She is still called Reclining Jade or the Jade Maiden of Obscure Brilliance. Dressed in five-colored garments, she stands nine-tenths of an inch, or even three inches tall. The couple is found most often in the Yellow Court and in the Purple Chamber. From them was born a child, the True Person Cinnabar-of-the-North,[36] that is to say, fire of water, *yang* of *yin*. Essential being, this child is "my true self":

I am the child of the Father and the Mother Tao. Human beings have me too. I am not the only "self." I am found at the entrance to the stomach, in the esophagus. Seated facing the south on a bed of precious stones, under a canopy of yellow clouds. (I, child of the Tao) am dressed in garments of five-colored jewels. My mother stands on my right; she embraces me and nourishes me. My father stands on my left; he instructs me and protects me. My father is the Sunny Hill and is called Master Light. My mother is the Great Yin and is called Jade Maiden of Obscure Brilliance. My own body is Original Yang, I am called Cinnabar-of-the-North. . . . One must meditate constantly on the True Person Cinnabar-of-the-North, just as he is here, at the entrance to the stomach, facing south, eating yellow spermatic essence and red energy (*ch'i*), drinking from the liquid fountain [the saliva]. Original Yang Cinnabar-of-the-North, nine-tenths of an inch. But while meditating, one must view him according to the dimensions of his own body. His Father and Mother nourish him, and in this way he achieves immortality.[37]

The embryo of immortality, "the True Person Cinnabar-of-the-North," is born in the Cinnabar Field from the Original Yang, the vital energy that we transmit from generation to generation. The immortal seed, it is "my body" in its most primitive, essential state. Created by the union of "my parents' " breaths (*ch'i*), it is "my true irreducible self," but, as the *Book of the Center* says, "not my one and only self." Further on, the same book ads:

The Tao is me, it is the Supreme Lord of the central summit . . . the Pole Star which shines on my forehead, between my eyebrows, like the sun; (it is) the Great August Emperor of Heaven. It is my energy, I was born of that energy [breath].[38]

Obviously, the text refers here to the Most High Original Lord of the Limitless, Lord of the Tao, who dwells between the eyebrows and who was said to be "the child of the Great One." But the child is also the "Great One," by the same token as his ancestor: "The Lord of the Tao, Great August Emperor, central and polar star is the One."[39]

The title of the Great One (T'ai-i) is widespread and is also given to the bird-god above the head, the Lord of the Tao between the brows, the King of the East (the sun), the Old Man of the South Pole who dwells in the Scarlet Palace of the Heart, and the deity of the navel. The *Book of the Center* recognized three Great Ones: lower, middle, and upper, even though it gave this same title to many other gods. Confusion? Only on the surface. The body has three levels, so one can only expect to find the *One* on each level. The "self" is also present as three distinct aspects: "embryo" in the Cinnabar Field, "child" in the Yellow Court, and Lord of the Tao or "True Person" in the head. Everywhere in the body these hypostases of the Tao are called "One" and "Original Energy."

One concludes from this that not only are the *self* and the *One* multiple, but that they represent successive phases of transformation of the self, permutations of the One.

The variety of aspects of the One at every level of the self contrasts with the permanence of the Mother, Jade Maiden of Obscure Brilliance. We find her all over the landscape, always the same, easily taking on the roles of mother and wife, of Queen of the West and Empress of the North, presiding at the revolution of the Dipper constellation, the constellation of Destiny, without changing her name or aspect. As *yin* energy, she is the moon and the wife of the King of the East (the sun). As the North Pole and the Goddess of the Ocean (the element of water = North), she is the wife of the Old Man of the South Pole. At the center, she is the feminine part of the Tao, Mother Tao, wife of the Lord of the Tao (who is the summit of the center), the one with whom she shares the Yellow Court and the Purple Chamber. . . . The Lord of the Tao is again "me" and son the Jade Maiden of Obscure Brilliance. The mother is therefore both "my mother" and "my wife." Her sexual otherness is nevertheless relative, to the extent that *she too* is "Original Yang."

Partner and mother on every level, she reigns supreme in the abdomen, the sphere of the ocean. She is the queen of K'un-lun, in the body as well as in ancient mythology. She sails the ocean on the back of a large turtle, a fabulous creature on whose shell is represented the map of the world.[40] Accompanying her are the Six Attendants of Destiny, goddesses of the kidneys who are Merit Inspectors of the body. They are all Jade Maidens and "they note the mistakes and sins of the human being and report them to the August Emperor of Heaven the Most High Lord of the Tao" on appointed dates:

At midnight on the nights of the new moon, the solstice, the equinox and the four seasons, the drum is beaten in the Five Fortresses to assemble all the gods. The merits are then verified and there is a discussion of all actions, good and evil. For those whose records indicate [good actions], destiny is lengthened and all the gods are promoted. Those whose records are blank will die. Destiny's Attendant crosses them off the Book of Life.[41]

The spirits of the Fortresses are those of the four seas. They bear the names of heroes from Antiquity and are just as fearsome. They resemble other dangerous carping spirits of the body: The Three Cadavers and the Nine Worms. The latter are also supposed to make a report on the body they inhabit and they too can hasten its demise. The Three Cadavers are associated with the Cinnabar Field, a good example of the presence of the forces of corruption there at the very origin of life.[42]

In ancient mythology, the Mother, Queen of the West, was not only Lady of K'un-lun, the mountain of the Immortals, but also goddess of death and of epidemics.[43] In the *Book of the Center* her title is "Nature," as opposed to "Non-Action," the title given to her husband, King of the East. On the one hand, then, there is the One, which is transformed according to the phases and the levels of the body even as it remains in Non-Action; on the other, there is Mother "Nature," who embraces and nurtures, but who also governs the forces of death. She is the enveloping body, the agent who transforms the immortal child in her breast. This image brings to mind that of Lao Tzu's body.

A temple: the Palace of the Queen of Heaven (Ma-tsu) in Tainan.

T'u-ti, the God of the Earth, and his spouse: statues (and a simple incense burner) in a small village shrine.

String puppet performance at a village festival: the dance of the God of Music (T'ien-tu yüan-shuai).

Ritual theater on a temporary stage at a large festival. The dance by the masked actor represents the Officer of Heaven (T'ien-kuan) congratulating the community on the festive occasion.

Popular theater: a temporary stage opposite a village temple during a festival. Like the Taoist rituals that take place inside the sanctuary, the representations in honor of the gods continue day and night. Even in the wee hours of the morning, some spectators remain fascinated by the play.

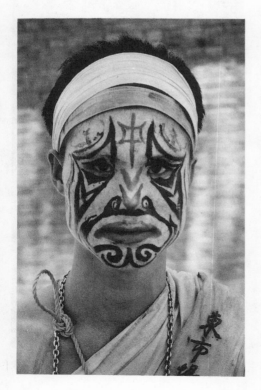

Boy actor impersonating a celestial warrior during a village procession. These actors often are in trance.

Martial arts group (*Sung Chiang chen*) at a village festival.

A *fa-shih*, ritual master of the "little rites," performing an exorcism. Note the buffalo horn in his hand and the snake whip around his neck.

A *tao-shih*: Great Master Ch'en Weng in his ceremonial robe, holding his court tablet. He is waiting for the beginning of an Audience ritual.

A heavenly emissary: paper statue of a celestial marshal, made especially for a large Offering (*chiao*) service and destined to be burned with the written memorial of the members of the community.

The outer altar, during an Announcement ritual.

Acolytes making a new fire during a Division of the Lamps ritual.

The inner altar, with the characteristic altar paintings with curtains and drapings. On the tables are the seats (*shen-wei*) of the deities.

Purifying the altar: the Group Leader (*yin-pan*) performs a sword dance.

Audience ritual before the Golden Gate.

Statues of the Three Pure Ones, the Taoist triad, in the Temple of the Altar of Heaven in Tainan.

7

Lao Tzu, the Body of the Tao

Let us turn again to the book of Chuang Tzu:

Confucius went to visit Lao-tan ["the Long-Eared Old Man," another name for Lao Tzu]. Having just bathed and let down his hair to dry, Lao-tan was sitting so perfectly still that he no longer seemed human. Confucius at first stood back and waited, but after a while introduced himself, saying: "Dare I believe my eyes? A moment ago, master, your body seemed dried out as dead wood, as if you had abandoned all things and left the world of men for solitude!"

Lao-tan replied: "I let my heart revel [in the realm] where [all] things had their beginning."

"How is that?" asked Confucius.

Lao Tzu said: "One may harrow one's mind, yet remain unable to understand; open one's mouth, yet be unable to express what [this experience] means. . . . We shall never know where life comes from or where death leads; yet I will try to tell you something about it. The utmost *yin* is stern and cold, the utmost *yang* is flaming hot. The stern and cold proceeds from Heaven, the flaming hot proceeds from the Earth. The two intermingle and interpenetrate, and from their union all things are born. . . . Their action alternates through the four seasons, through night and day. . . . Life has its place of germination, death has its place of return. This opposition of the beginning and the end creates an endless circle whose end no one knows. And yet, if not at this here, then where should one look for "the Ancestor?"[1]

In this speech of Lao Tzu to Confucius, the references to (the realm) where (all) things had their beginning" and to "the Ancestor" are ways of indicating the hidden and unknowable dimensions of the rhythmical

113

rite of the universe;[2] Chuang Tzu shows us that Lao Tzu was able to reach these fundamental dimensions in his own body. The same notion is also explained in an ancient inscription, which says: "Lao Tzu sometimes is one with the energy (*ch'i*) of primordial chaos, sometimes separates himself from it; he is coeternal with the Three Luminaries [sun, moon, and Pole star]."[3]

Another ancient text tells us that when the adepts meditated on the "body of Lao Tzu," they conceived this cosmic body in the following manner:

He exists at the origin of the Great Beginning, he walks about in the beginning of the Great Simplicity, he floats in the Obscure Emptiness, comes and goes through the outer door of Dark Tenuity, contemplates Chaos before its differentiation, the transparent (heaven) and the opaque (earth) before their separation. . . . Alone, without companion, he wonders in the times of yore, before there were Heaven and Earth. He comes out of his hidden state and returns there to dwell. Having vanished, he is the Primordial; being manifest, he becomes human. Elusive! Through the transformation of Heaven and Earth and of his spirit, he is made flesh in the bosom of Mother Li.[4]

In the mystical view of Chuang Tzu, as in the theology of ancient Taoism, the cosmic body of the Old Master is the image and the model of the entire universe. These very ideas can already be found in an ancient myth, a few fragments of which have been preserved:

Lao Tzu transformed his body. His left eye became the sun; his right eye, the moon; his head became mount K'un-lun; his beard, the planets and constellations; his bones, dragons; his flesh, four-footed creatures; his intestines, snakes; his stomach, the sea; his fingers, the Five Peaks; his hair, trees and grasses; his heart, the Flowery Dais; as to his two kidneys, they were united and became one, the Real and True Father and Mother.[5]

This same myth is also known in another version. Here the subject is not Lao Tzu, but a primeval being called P'an-ku:

Long ago, when P'an-ku died, his head became the Four Sacred Peaks; his eyes, the sun and the moon; his fluids, rivers and seas; his hair and beard, the grasses and trees. At the times of the Ch'in and Han [between the third century B.C. and the third A.D.], it was commonly said among the people that P'an-ku's head was the Sacred Peak of the East (the T'ai-shan), his belly that of the Center, his left arm that of the South, his right that of the North, his feet that of the West. Scholars of yore maintained that P'an-ku's tears formed the rivers, that his *ch'i* was the wind and his voice the thunder, whereas the pupils of his eyes became the lightning.[6]

I have quoted the version of the P'an-ku myth with that of Lao Tzu, not in order to demonstrate its universal nature, but to show that, according to these tales, the world was created as the result of the *death* of the First Being. In other words, the differentiation of energies out of the original chaos and the birth of our universe are somehow tied to death. This concept is also illustrated by another mythological text preserved by Chuang Tzu:

The ruler of the Southern Sea was called "Rash," the Ruler of the Northern Sea was called "Crash" [allegorical figures of *yin* and *yang*], and the Ruler of the Center was called "Chaos." Rash and Crash at times met on the lands of Chaos, and on these occasions Chaos treated them very well indeed.

So Rash and Crash got together to decide how to repay Chaos's goodness. They said to each other: "All humans have seven holes with which to see, hear, eat, and breathe; he alone has none of them! Let's try to pierce him some!"

They pierced one hole a day, and on the seventh day Chaos died.[7]

In other words, when *yin* and *yang* procreate, the result is the end of the Wholeness of Chaos and the birth of man. What was in a diffused state becomes something distinct. With the bursting of the matrix, the energies are divided and thus we perceive things as separate. Conversely, when the fragmented perception is abolished and is unified, one becomes *like dead wood* and returns to the beginning of things. About this beginning, Chuang Tzu says: "That which causes things to be things is (in itself) not a thing" (chap. 11).

This alteration between creation and chaos, between life and death, is only a rhythmic beat which rouses its own echoes, just phases in the work of the Tao. Chuang Tzu tells of a sage of ancient times, who in regard to this exclaimed:

"Oh my Master (the Tao)! My Master! You who harmonize the Ten Thousand Things without the idea of Rightness, who benefits the Ten Thousand Generations without moral principle! Older than the most remote antiquity and yet not 'aged'; embracing Heaven and Earth, fashioning endless shapes, and yet not 'skilled.' This is the joy of nature [or: 'heavenly joy'] and thus it is said that: 'for those who know the joy of nature, life is spontaneous action and death the transformation of things.' "[8]

The statement that "death is the transformation of things" explains not only death; it also helps to define the passage between different states of consciousness, such as the two states in which Confucius found Lao Tzu: first, in meditation, "dried out as dead wood" and then, awakened, as a reasoning individual. The well-known anecdote of Chuang Tzu dreaming he is a butterfly actually explains the same thing:

Once upon a time I dreamed I was a butterfly, fluttering about most happy and content as a butterfly would and unaware that it was me. Suddenly it woke up, surprised to find it was me. Who knows now if it is I who dreamt he was a butterfly, or a butterfly who dreams it is me? However, between me and the butterfly, there is necessarily a distinction, and it is this kind of separation which is called "the transformation of things."[9]

This concept of change (*hua* or *pien-hua;* also: mutation, transformation, and flux), is one of the very basic ideas of Taoism and one of the keys for understanding it. It finds its natural expression in the ways Lao Tzu's body is envisaged and also constitutes the principal theme of the myths and legends concerning Lao Tzu. This is illustrated by the fact that books concerning the story of the Old Master have titles such as *Book of Lao Tzu's Transformation, Book of the Endless Mutations of Lao-chün,* and so forth.[10] One of the oldest of these texts has the Old Master say: "I transform my body, passing through death to live again. . . . I die and am reborn, and each time I have a [new] body."[11]

These continuous mutations, this joyful changing according to time's cycle and the nature of things, constitutes in fact, according to the Taoist texts, a subtle mingling of alternating phases which are not easily understood.

When Lao Tzu died, his body was transformed into a landscape, the same landscape we find within ourselves as the domain of the infant, source of life as well as fruit of the union of the elements that make up this inner landscape. The child is again Lao Tzu himself, the immortal child in his mother's breast. According to an ancient hagiography, before he was born, Lao Tzu went through nine transformations, following a nine-phase cycle. The number nine corresponds to the accomplishment of cosmic creation.

Lao Tzu is the body of the Tao. There is an inner as well as an outer body, the difference being the result of different circumstances to which the body is responding. The names we can give to the inner body are: "Ultimate One, True One, Mysterious One, August One, Primordial One, Ancestral One, Most High One, Natural One, Right One." . . . While having different names, these nine concepts have a common origin and refer to the same mysterious driving force. Therefore they are all called "One."[12]

Another ancient text gives the following nine names:

Primordial *yang,*
Ancestral *yang,*
Light of the ancestor,

Light of the child,
Sign of the child,
Growth of the child,
Beginning of the child,
Birth of the child,
Sign of the ancestor.[13]

The ancient philosophers also discuss the nine phases of the embryo's transformation:

The One gives birth to the Two, the Two to the Three, the Three to the Ten Thousand Beings. The beings turn their back on *yin* and embrace *yang,* and it is this harmony of energies (*ch'i*) that realizes their union.

This famous passage of the *Tao-te ching* (chap. 42) was explained in the second century B.C. by the prince of Huai-nan in this way:

At the first (lunar) month, it is like an ointment;
 at the second, like a tendon;
by the third, the embryo is formed;
by the fourth, it develops flesh;
the fifth, muscles;
the sixth, bones;
by the seventh, the child is fully formed;
in the eighth, it moves;
the ninth, it turns upside-down;
and in the tenth, it is born.[14]

Pregnancy is the paradigm for the creation of the universe. In nine stages the passage from the invisible to the visible, between the undifferentiated and the differentiated "things," from non-being to being is accomplished.

The non-being of the *incipit* cannot be expressed in ordinary words, only through repeated sounds without any other meaning than that of confusion and turmoil. In the *Tao-te ching* (chap. 21), the words used to describe the process of creation from chaos to distinct beings are: *Huang! Hu!* ("Vague! Ungraspable!"): "*Huang! Hu!* In the center, there are things. *Miao! Ming!* [Profound! Mysterious!]. In the center, there are essences, most true essences."

In the legends of the birth of Lao Tzu, as given in the above-mentioned *Book of the Transformation of Lao Tzu,* the gestation of the Old Child is described with the help of similar terms: "*Huang! Hu!* By the transformation of Heaven and Earth he is incarnated in the womb of Mother Li."[15] Cosmogony, the creation of the universe, and the pregnancy of Lao Tzu's mother do here coincide. Among the many other descriptions of Lao Tzu's birth, here is one that is both concise and typical:

The Most High Old Lord (Lao Tzu) is the sovereign ancestor of the origin of the Chaos. He was born of the Without-beginning; he emerged from the Without-cause; he existed before the Ten Thousand Ways; he is the ancestor of the Original Energy (*ch'i*). Without light, without image, without sound, without noise, without ancestors, without descendants. *Yu! Yu!* [Dark! Dark!]; *Ming! Ming!* [Mystery! Mystery!] In the center, there are essences, most true essences. So vast is he that there is nothing outside of him; hence his name of Great Tao.

The Tao is the Ultimate Sovereign of that which is thus-by-itself [the spontaneous]. At the center of the dark Non-being was created the Empty Cavern. This Empty Cavern is the True One. It is neither Non-being nor Being. From this one energy (*ch'i*) proceed the Three Energies.[16]

The Three Energies, which appear here at the very end of the process of mutation, are the same as those which play such an important role in the ritual of the Great Master. As we have seen, he invokes these when he consecrates the incense burner, saying: "Old Lord Most High of the Three Energies, Mysterious, Original, and Primordial, of the supreme Three Heavens . . ."[17] While pronouncing these words, he must visualize the three *ch'i* as three colors: blue-black, yellow, and white. These three energies form three spheres, three stages, and also three hypostases of the Tao as purely abstract and spiritual aspects. Together they express the essence of the Taoist pantheon since they correspond to the Three Pure Ones (*san-ch'ing*), also called the Three Heavenly Worthies (the Chinese word *t'ien,* "*heavenly,*" here has the connotation of "natural". But again, this triad merely represents three major aspects of the Tao, given that the Tao, which can never be wholly expressed or defined, has innumerable aspects. In fact, each *idea* is a "Heavenly Worthy," a god. This inner—and hence "pure"—pantheon is therefore always defined as groups and categories of different numbers, each time as a different totality: first 3, then 7, 9, 12, 24, 120, 1,200, 3,600, and so forth. Taoist theology often waxes mathematical.

Here we see the great difference between these gods and the gods worshipped by the people of whom I spoke at the beginning of this book. The latter are essentially *orphan spirits,* first propitiated and then made powerful through the worship they receive. The "pure" pantheon of the Tao, on the contrary, is made up of abstract gods whose common characteristic is that they have no power whatsoever. The Heavenly Worthies are not the gods of this world; they come forth from the chaotic confusion of Anterior Heaven (*hsien-t'ien*), that is, from the times of origin and of the matrix. In Taoist liturgy, properly speaking, we encounter solely these abstract hypostases, which appear in groups and function as rhythmic, structuring elements of ritual time. The "popular" gods are excluded from this inner universe.

In the meditation of the Long-Eared Old Man (as described by Chuang Tzu), as well as in the above-mentioned visualization of the Heavenly Worthies as three different colors, we encounter the notion of ephemeral, cyclical concentrations of *ch'i*, a form of spontaneous conception of "being," of "me" and of "the old child."[18]

As described by the earlier quoted *Book of the Transformation Of Lao Tzu:*

I was born before things received their form, I contemplated the Chaos before its differentiation, the transparent and opaque before their separation. . . . As I exhale I become [diffuse] *ch'i* as I inhale, a human being.[19]

The phases of this transformation are so many knots or markers (the nine stages of the embryo, as well as other time cycles) along the endless thread of time. They mean to give a form to its eternal progress so as to offset this eternal *becoming* from its opposite, the return, that is: the dizzying plunge back into the chaos of the matrix, the womb of the mother.

Birth

A person's conception is considered his birth, a point confirmed by the Chinese custom of determining a child's age not from the date of parturition, but from the beginning of gestation. Pregnancy lasts ten moons, and these ten lunations are considered equivalent to one complete year cycle. Hence, a child at birth is said to be one year old. Inner life in the womb is taken to be proportionately equivalent to the subsequent outside existence. The gestational cycle is, moreover, considered to be a perfect model of time; its length determines a person's life span in the world. The normal gestation is of course ten lunations, but exceptional beings have a longer inner existence. Divine heroes are carried for twelve months, great sages for eighteen. Lao Tzu, the Old Child, had an inner life (in his mother's womb) that lasted nine times nine, that is eighty-one years. In other words, his life span was equal to that of the Nine Heavens!

As an inner being in the womb, Lao Tzu is the body of the Tao and, in his oneness, he alone represents the pantheon of the Tao in its totality. The "nine inner names" mentioned above, as well as the nine stages of pregnancy, are but one way of perceiving this theophany. They are comparable not only to the Three Pure Ones and other Heavenly Worthies but also to the twenty-four energy nodes of the calendar, the 1,200 functionaries, the gods of the Great Master's register, and so forth. The Taoist pantheon is derived entirely from the True One, from the immortal embryo in its inner land, because, in Taoism, the inner precedes and determines the outer. This axiom, repeated many times by Chuang Tzu, is illustrated in the myth of Lao Tzu's birth. In Taoist books there are many versions of the story of his early life, but they always end with the same myth of the Mother, Mother Plum Tree (Mother Li), Jade Maiden of the Obscure Mystery.[20]

The narrative of the Old Child's birth is both scandalous story and initiatory tale. It belongs to oral tradition, and masters today still tell it to their disciples. Here is one version that I have been able to record:

There was once an old woman who belonged to the clan of the Pure Ones. The Old Lord[21] did not have a name. One might say that originally he was an incarnation. He was born in (the womb of) a chaste woman.[22] She had no husband, but had become pregnant after absorbing a drop of "sweet dew."[23] Her belly grew bigger, that is to say, during the day she was pregnant; but she was not pregnant at night, for then the Old Lord would leave her body to go study the Tao, and so he was not there.

This Old Lord was not just anyone! Having taken the form of an embryo in his mother's belly, he wished to delay his birth to the day when there would be neither birth nor death in the world. Thus he waited for more than eighty years, unable to appear.

The God of the Underworld and the God of Heaven spoke to each other, saying: "This here is the incarnation of the Constellation of Destiny.[24] How can we not let him be born? Let us choose a day when we allow neither birth nor death so that he may be born on that day."

It was the fifteenth day of the second moon. On that day the Old Lord was born. He came into the world through his mother's armpit.[25] At that very moment, oh! his hair and beard were all white. Since he knew how to walk, he set off right away.

His mother said to him: "You! My old child! Why are you leaving without letting me have a look at you? Why are you going off as soon as you're born? I won't even know how to recognize you later!" So he turned around abruptly, his beard and hair flying. . . . Seeing him, his mother took a fright. She fainted and died on the spot.

He [the Old Lord] continued to walk straight ahead, without stopping until he reached a plum orchard. There he leaned against a tree and said to himself: "I know neither my name nor my family. I am leaning against this plum tree [Chinese: *li*]. Why not take *Li* as my family name? And what should be my personal name? My mother called me 'old child!' So, my name will be 'Lao Tzu' [Chinese for "old child"]."

"Old Lord" is a title of respect. In fact, his name is "Old Child."[26]

This myth, preserved in the purest of oral traditions, is equally attested in literary sources since antiquity, though rarely in any explicit way. For example, the theme of Lao Tzu leaving his mother's body to go "study the Tao" may be compared to Chuang Tzu's tale of the "Long-Eared Old Man" who leaves his body behind to go and "revel [in the realm] where [all] things had their beginning." It should be noted, in this context, the Chuang Tzu has a tendency to present mythical themes in anecdotal settings.[27] By contrast, historiography, even Confucian historiography with its tendency to rationalize myth, has preserved many more exact elements of sacred thought.

Take, for example, the biography of Lao Tzu in the *Historical Records* (*Shih-chi*) of Ssu-ma Ch'ien (145–86 B.C.). This first great historiographer of China attempted to rewrite the sacred story of the Old Master and reduce it to a historical source so as to make Lao Tzu appear as an ordinary philosopher. His "biography" reveals nonetheless that Lao Tzu's family name was Li, "plum tree," a detail that comes straight from mythology. Indeed, no clan of this name ever existed in ancient China[28] and the very appearance of the family name Li late in antiquity is apparently linked to the story of Lao Tzu and early Taoism, as the Old Master was the first to have borne this name.

It would be possible to see traces here to a cult of the plum tree, and indications of such a religious custom do exist.[29] But this, in my opinion, is not what matters most. If Lao Tzu is called Li, and if he is the first to carry that name, the implication is that he had no father. The *Shih-chi* does not dwell on the circumstances of his conception, but makes no secret of the fact that Lao Tzu had no ancestors. After reviewing various aspects of the legends related to the Old Master, Ssu-ma Ch'ien concludes by saying: "Li-the-Ear [i.e., "the Long-Eared Old Man"] is the spontaneous transformation by Non-Action, spontaneous rectitude by purity and silence."[30]

Lao Tzu has no father, and mythology has him adopting the identity of the plum tree, or taking his mother's family name Li, "Mother Li." Commentators discussing this mythical theme often quote Chuang Tzu as saying that "in the oldest times, people did not know their father, only their mother."[31] There is no need to take this statement out of its mythical context in order to prove that ancient China was a matriarchy and thus conforms to the theories of Engels. Chuang Tzu only wants to say that in the beginning there was no father creator, only a mother to accomplish within herself the Work of the Tao. Here is what the Taoists themselves have to say:

In the matrix, he [Lao Tzu] sang sacred texts for eighty-one years. Thereupon he was born out of the left armpit of mother Li. At birth he had white hair, which is why he was called the "old child." . . . As to his reincarnation in the womb of mother Li, one must know that it was he himself who transformed his body from nothingness into the shape of mother Li, so as to return into his own matrix; there was never any other mother Li. People today are not aware of this fact and say that the Old Lord came [from the outside] to place himself in mother Li's womb. In fact, it was not at all like that![32]

Even if we did not have this text to tell us explicitly that Lao Tzu was his own mother, the consubstantiality between the two would have been clear from the description of the creation of the cosmos presented in several ancient documents. According to these scriptures it was the above-mentioned Three Energies that originally gathered together to produce the Old Lord. He then transformed himself into the Jade Maiden of Obscure Mystery (that is: the Mother); the Three Energies joined spontaneously within her to form a pearl. She then reabsorbed this pearl and this was the conception of Lao Tzu.[33]

Lao Tzu is his own mother, but this point requires further commentary. We see that the body of the Tao goes through successive and alternating transformations. First, there are repeated mutations between concentration and dispersion. Next, a form, a physical body, is shaped at each stage. Between these distinct bodies—Old Lord, Mother, Old Child—there exists a continuity that also constitutes a transubstantiality. This is conveyed in this myth by the fact that, when Lao Tzu is born, the Mother dies.

In the oral tradition, the mother's death is brought on by the sight of her offspring. In the literary sources of Taoism, her death is described in more pleasant terms: heavenly spirits come to meet her as she climbs into a chariot of colorful clouds and flies off to the sound of divine music. But all written sources mention another meaningful detail: during the brief moment between birth and apotheosis, the Mother reveals to her child the secrets of the art of immortality, of that "Long Life" which the Old Child has just experienced in his mother's womb.[34]

Indeed, there, where there was "neither birth nor death," a complete cycle of the cosmos was accomplished. What else could the Mother's revelations be but the very secrets of her woman's body and an initiation into her creative power (*te*)?

A scandalous tale, the myth of the Old Child's birth is also an initiatory narrative. It contains some of the most important themes of Taoist thought: a) the anterior existence in the womb, with the accompanying permutations of the One and the Self; b) the transubstantiality of the Mother and child, also expressed by the transmission of the body's secrets; c) the feminine nature of the Taoist body in its exterior form in this world. Let us take a closer look at these themes one at a time.

The real Taoist pantheon, that of the *true* gods, belongs to "Anterior Heaven" (*hsien-t'ien,* the universe before creation). This true pantheon reveals itself to us as the One and its different permutations, and also as different manifestations of the original cosmic energy. This point is essential to Taoist thought: "*Huang! Hu!* (Vague! Ungraspable!) In the center, there are things. *Miao! Ming!* (Profound! Mysterious!). In the center, there are essences, most true essences." This passage from chapter 21 of the *Tao-te ching* on the birth of the cosmos, which I quoted at the beginning of this chapter, closes with this question: "— How do I know that here are to be found the seeds of all beings? —By *this!*" "This" is the immediate, the present, that which is the closest to us—that is, our essential body, the womb, the embryo, "whose name never leaves it,"[35] (in other words, "the permanent name"). The first chapter of the *Tao-te ching* tells us that "the permanent name" is in fact "the Unnameable." This Unnameable stands for the original cosmic energy (*yüan-ch'i*) which is said "to give birth to the gods."

The manifold aspects of the One are conceived by the Taoist theologians as so many "Heavenly Worthies" (hypostases of the Tao in the Anterior Heaven) and as "Ancestors,"[36] and alternately as numerological categories corresponding to the body's functions. Thus we discover that the true Taoist pantheon exists within us, created by our vital energies. It is this pantheon—ungraspable vision of the eternal forces of nature—that constitutes the initiatory framework of Taoism. It situates the disciple, as well as all of Taoism, beyond the ordinary gods, the *shen-ming* of the people. The gods of the people are only human souls, born without fulfilling their destiny, dead without returning to the undifferentiated, outside the cycle of transformations and by definition dangerous.

This is what separates the Taoist from the communities of the faithful of popular religion. The Taoist carries his gods within himself; he can give them an external appearance, a certain form, at will and then make them return to the origin, to the undifferentiated. He may, like the Old Master (body of the Tao), either appear or disappear, reside in the world or cross the pass to return to K'un-Lun mountain,[37] to primordial chaos.

According to the *tao-shih*, the followers of the vulgar cults are forever fascinated by symbols they take at face value and engage in disastrous transactions with "old things." They are blocked, held back, and sink ever deeper into debt to their "gods" in exchange for the latter's protection.[38] Their situation resembles that of Kafka's story, *Before the Law*, where the hero ruins himself in trying to bribe the Keeper of the Gate of Law. For Taoism, these baleful gods must be overcome.

As a rule, however, the Taoist keeps his initiatory knowledge to himself and avoids any open conflict with those who worship the popular gods. He acts discretely in order to counter the unlucky effects of these cults on the communities who call upon him. When he accepts the invitation from the elders of the temple to lead the festivals, which the elders consider to be in honor of "their gods," he does not attempt to rectify this misunderstanding. He secretly neutralizes the influence of these gods through the workings of the liturgy, whereby he can reintegrate them into the energies of his own body and thus purify and "convert" (*tu*) them.

As we have seen, these energies of his body, distilled from the Great One, are related to the true inner pantheon, not only of the Heavenly Worthies and the "officers and generals" of the master's register, but also to those other categories of bodily *ch'i:* the five viscera and six receptacles, the joints and arteries, and even the energetic nodes of acupuncture (see chap. 3). There are too many areas of overlap between the ancient medical theories and the inner pantheon of Taoism not to see that they are related. It may well be the mystical vision of the body in Taoism that has served as a model of reference for Chinese medicine.[39]

I shall return to this last point more fully when I speak of the phases of the body. Let us first consider the second theme: the body of the Tao is first a woman, then a child, whereas the father is entirely absent from this genesis. Some texts do say that the mother is the product of the transformation of the Old Lord (Lao-chün), but this does not necessarily imply the presence of a masculine element. The word *chün*, which is usually translated as "lord," can designate a woman as well as a man. The etymology of the written character is uncertain. The generally accepted meaning of the word in ancient texts is "venerable chief" and is applied indiscriminately to elders of both sexes—to the father or the mother, husband or wife, king or queen. In mythology, however, the word *chün* is preferably reserved for *female* deities. Nothing allows us, therefore, to consider Lao-chün as a "father." Taoist theology understands the Old Lord as the divine aspect and the hypostasis of the Tao. In other words, Lao-Chün is Lao Tzu before his birth and thus simply one of the ways of apprehending the divinity of Anterior Heaven. This is precisely how today's masters still understand the matter: Lao-chün is the body of the Tao before birth; Lao Tzu is the Old Child and the Old Master of this world. We discover here once more the multiple aspects of the One as it passes from the invisible to the visible. It is the Mother in whom and through whom this transformation is accomplished. The Tao has taken form in her. Through her the Tao has been revealed. The instructions she gives to her newborn have to do precisely with this action of the Tao.

Their are many texts, some of which we shall look at later, which tell us about the revelations that took place when the Jade Maiden of Dark Brilliance took leave of her Old Child. These scriptures can be compared, to a certain degree, to the *True Writs* revealed at the moment of the birth of the universe. Let us recall the ritual of the installation of the altar with the rites of the True Writs: "The universe had not yet taken root, sun and moon did not yet shed their radiance. Obscure! Dark! No originator! No lineage! Now marvellous writs appeared." Thus does the marvellous essence of creation manifest itself.

This is the Canon, which appeared in the brief instant between the bursting matrix, the death of primordial chaos, and the constitution of the universe of the Ten Thousand Things. Chaos projects its archetypes; the Mother reveals the body's secrets. On the one hand there are cosmological theories, on the other mythological themes. But they are transposed by the Taoists into the concrete: cosmological theory becomes liturgy, whereas mythology—and this is the third point—is translated into the social body of Taoism.

The current theories concerning a matriarchy in ancient China are far from proven, and perhaps the very question of "matriarchy" is poorly framed. But what has been clearly demonstrated is the fact that in every period women have been the initiators into the techniques of the body. For example, in the ancient manuals of sexual hygiene, it is women, in this case two goddesses—the Dark Maiden (Hsüan-nü) and the White

Maiden (Su-nü)—who instruct the Yellow Emperor, founder of civilization, in the arts of love, healing, and begetting many children.[40] The
same goddesses also teach the Emperor strategy, which is a closely related science.[41] But here we are still in the realm of legend. That women
were the ones to teach sexuality to men is shown in a poem from the
beginning of the second century A.D. It described a young woman who
sings, as she prepares her room and her body for a night of love:

> I shed my robes,
> Remove my paint and powder,
> And roll out the [erotic] picture scroll by the pillow's side.
> The White Maiden I shall take as my instructress,
> So that we can practice all the variegated postures,
> Those that an ordinary husband has but rarely seen,
> Such as taught by T'ien-lao to the Yellow Emperor.[42]

Even today, at least in traditional peasant families, knowledge of sexual matters falls into the woman's domain. Traditional custom still forbids familiarity between father and son, and fathers therefore do not
ordinarily instruct their sons in the facts of life. Moreover, from puberty, boys live apart from their mothers. By contrast, mothers and
daughters enjoy a very close relationship which allows the mothers to
teach the secrets of married life to their daughters. It is the young girl's
job to know; furthermore, she must be expert enough to satisfy her
husband while also caring for his health, for sexual excess is considered
very harmful.[43] She also should not neglect her own pleasure. Chinese
sex manuals are the only ancient books in the world on this subject that
do not present sexuality solely from the male point of view.[44] These
books, though inspired by Taoism, must not be considered to represent
Taoist sexuality itself. I shall return to this later.

The same distinction between Taoist teachings and social norms holds
true for the woman's situation. Despite her role of initiator and partner
in "the art of the bedroom" (*fang-chung chih shu*), the social position
of women in traditional China was far from being equal to that of men.
Again, Taoism is different. The myth of Lao Tzu's birth, the transubstantiality of mother and child, all this is tied to practices relating to the
search for long life and "nourishing the Vital Principle" (*yang-sheng*).
Those who nourish the embryo of immortality, the "true self," *are mothers*.

This in itself, as a mythological or mystical fact, does not necessarily
indicate any real superiority of women. After all, the preeminence accorded the Virgin Mary, Mother of Christ, has not yet given Christian

women a dominant role in the Church. An important characteristic of Taoism is that it is not limited to the spirit of things, but "seeks reality in the body as it lives." Because the adept in this world holds "the True" within himself and cultivates this immortal principle, he is a mother, a mother with child, and must live this period of gestation in a concrete way by adopting a feminine personality.

This simple fact is stressed throughout the traditions of Taoism. Chuang Tzu, in an important and justly celebrated passage, describes the case of the adept Lieh Tzu who, when he experienced the revelation of primordial Chaos, goes home to take his wife's place in the kitchen. He feeds the pigs with equal care as the other members of the household and keeps away from all other affairs. He lives alone in his body, undifferentiated in closed completeness and in this unity he maintains himself to the end (of his life).[45] As so often is the case, this "anecdote" by Chuang Tzu could reflect a real religious practice.

The famous sixth chapter of the *Tao-te ching* says: "The Goddess of the Valley never dies. Her name is 'the Dark Woman.'" One of the oldest commentaries on the *Tao-te ching* explains this by saying:

The Female is the Earth, that is, a body of a peaceful nature. This is what woman is like, as she does not have an erection. As for man, he must concentrate his semen and he must pattern his mind after that of the earth and of woman. He must stay away from the affairs of the world![46]

From the same tradition as this commentary, there is a series of commandments intended for the adepts who received the *Tao-te ching*. The first of these commandments is: "Practice Non-Action, practice gentleness, keep your femininity; never take the initiative!"[47]

The phrase "keep your femininity" (or "observe the feminine") is here borrowed from the *Tao-te ching* (chap. 28): "To know the masculine and yet maintain the feminine is to become the valley of the world." Here the opposition between conscious awareness on the one hand, and on the other, the activities of keeping and caring, of protecting and nurturing as natural physical functions. This second mode calls on unconscious intuition and the vital impulses that spontaneously govern the creative process at work inside us. "To know the masculine and yet maintain the feminine" is completed in the *Tao-te ching* by a following sentence: "To know clarity and yet maintain obscurity (*hsüan*) is to become the measure of all things." And the same passage goes on to say that for he who is such a valley, such a measure, "the constant force [of the Tao] will never leave him; he will return to the state of the infant."[48] For Chuang Tzu, the words just quoted, "to know the masculine and yet maintain the feminine, to know clarity and yet maintain obscurity," contain the whole of the Old Master Lao Tzu's teachings.[49]

This was indeed how the Taoists of later periods understood Lao Tzu's teachings. The physiological practices of nourishing the Vital Principle require that one first realize the female which is in each of us.[50] In the next chapter we shall see many concrete examples of this. But the female attitude must also be constant in *daily life*. This is laid down in instructions to the masters, as can be seen in *The One Hundred Eighty Commandments for Libationers,* the religious leaders of the liturgical organization of the Heavenly Master: one must be cheerful, never raise one's voice, never stare, carry arms, hunt, or amuse oneself with cars and horses, and, sure sign of antivirility, never urinate while standing.[51] This last restriction is still followed today by Taoist masters and entail not only the adoption of a female posture, but also, due to certain exercises for nourishing the Vital Principle, the shrinking of the sexual organs (*ma-yin ts'ang-hsiang*), though not to the point of atrophy or castration.[52]

There are many anecdotes in the biographies of the Taoist saints to illustrate the abandonment of the male mentality. For example, the great patriarch of modern Taoism, Lü Tung-pin, used to visit one of the famous courtesans of the capital without ever making love to her. One evening, when the beautiful lady was rather tipsy, she tried to draw him to her bed. Lü said to her: "The *yin* and *yang* energies of Anterior Heaven are already joined in my body. The sexual union has taken place inside me, the embryo is already formed. I am about to give birth. Do you really think that, in my present state, I still desire exterior sex?"[53]

And what about women themselves? In the book of Chuang Tzu there were many women among the initiates. Later the movement of the Heavenly Master was organized on the basis of absolute equality between men and women who, as Libationers, shared in equal numbers the leadership of the liturgical organization. The Heavenly Masters themselves shared their duties with their wives. In the dioceses there were as many female as male masters. This balance was fundamental, even in the practice of perfection, inasmuch as the highest degree of initiation—that which qualified the adept for the rank of master—could only be obtained by a man and a woman together, as a couple. Celibacy was unthinkable.

Seen in the context of Chinese society of those times (the first centuries A.D.), the parity of men and women in the Taoist organization and practice suggests in fact a certain ascendancy, in the organization as well as in religious practice, on the part of the women. Let us not forget that the social situation of women, at least among the lettered classes, was far below that of men. All the lords had harems. Education for women was virtually unknown. The marital situation of the wives was extremely precarious, especially in the absence of any male children. Official morality embodied an outright misogyny.[54] What then to make of a religion that ruled out polygamy, made women the intermediaries, if not the keys to initiation, and allowed them the status of master in the same way as men, which implies a high degree of education? The origins of such an organization can only be found in a liturgical context where femininity was predominant.

We are too poorly informed about the period prior to the Heavenly Master movement to give any historical backing to this hypothesis. But this movement itself produced enough women to prove that the situation as described in the texts corresponded to reality. We have an example in the mother of Chang Lu, the third Heavenly Master, herself the wife of the second Heavenly Master, Chang Heng. She was an important, influential religious leader in the second century A.D.[55] Another example is the Libationer Wei Hua-ts'un, a married woman, mother of two, who became the matriarch of the Mao-shan school and is considered to have been its founder.[56] Taoism produced remarkable women in other periods as well.

We can now assert without any hesitation that in this world the body of the Tao is a woman's body. The female body, the body of the pregnant mother, is the only truly complete body, the only one able to accomplish the transformation, the work of the Tao. This fundamental truth also finds it expression in the social body: the masters, initiators in the art of Long Life, must cultivate a feminine personality. In principle this does not present any problem; in the eyes of Chinese science, we are all universal, and within each of us, there are female energies as well as male ones. But how does one realize this femininity when it has been devalued by society and when the reproductive (or transformative) functions, in China as much as here, are bound by prohibitions and taboos? How can one tend towards this inexpressible state? How can one be, oneself, the body of the Tao?

8

Keeping the One

For the Taoist master, the true gods are found within himself. This is the pantheon of *Anterior Heaven*,[1] of the child before birth, of the true being called the One, or, in liturgy, the Heavenly Worthy of the Original Beginning. To realize this mystery of the body is to experience a pregnancy and a motherhood and is called *Keeping the One*. This term covers not only a mystical experience, but also a concrete exercise of the body. Leading us from one towards the other, the Master-Who-Embraces-Simplicity[2] explains:

> Here is what I have learned:
> He who knows the One has accomplished everything.
> He who knows the One knows all.
> For him who does not know the One, there is nothing he can know.
> The Tao reveals itself first of all in the One.
> It is therefore of incomparable value.
>
> The [Multiple] Ones reside each in its own place, in Heaven, Earth, and Humankind.
> This is why we speak of the "Three Ones."
> Heaven attains the One in light;
> Earth attains the One in reproduction;
> Gods attain the One in transcendence.[3]
>
> Metal sinks in water, whereas a feather floats;
> Mountains stand tall while rivers flow.
> We look at it without seeing it.
> We listen to it without hearing it;

If we know how to preserve it, the One is there;
If we neglect it, the One is lost.
If we turn towards it, we find good fortune;
If we turn away from it, we meet disaster.
Those who know how to keep it will experience endless joy.
In those who lost it, life will dry up, their energies exhausted.

The Old Master says;
"Ungraspable! Vague!
In the center there are images!
Vague! Ungraspable!
In the center there are things!"[4]
This applies to the One.

This is why in the books of the Immortals it says:
If you want to attain Long Life, you must know how to Keep the One!
Think of the One, and if you are hungry, the One will give you food;
Think of the One, and if you are thirsty, the One will give you drink;
The One has a name and garments of certain colors.
In men, he stands nine-tenths of an inch tall, in women, six-tenths.
He resides in the Lower Cinnabar Field, two and four-tenths below the
   navel.[5]

From here on, the text confirms that the One is no other than the Child, the True Person Cinnabar-of-the-North, our true self. The Master-Who-Embraces-Simplicity says about the One and its identity:

This is what all Taoists consider to be most sacred. The names of the One have been handed down from generation to generation under the seal of utmost secrecy.[6]

He tells us, moreover, that the Way of the True One was first transmitted to the Yellow Emperor. This revelation included the description of the inner country and its landscape, where the One resides. Here we are on familiar ground:

Be aware that the human being is the most spiritual of living beings. But he must know himself and keep his spirits [within himself] so as to ward off all evil influences. Those who know this have no need to implore the help of the gods in heaven; it suffices to keep the gods of their body. That is why it is said: "The human body is in the image of a country; the chest and the stomach are like places and mansions: the four limbs are outskirts, the joints are the officers." . . . Those who know how to govern their bodies know how to govern their country. . . . They analyze the divine forces so as to protect their government, they reduce their desires to strengthen their blood and their *ch'i*. And in this way only can the True One be preserved. . . .

The One is found in the Great Ravine of the Pole Star. In front, there is the Hall of Light; behind, the Scarlet Palace. How high, the Flowery Canopy! How vast, the Golden Court! . . .

To know the One is not difficult; what is difficult is to keep it until the end, without losing it. If you are capable of doing this, you will be eternal.[7]

The Preliminary Stage: The Work of the *Ch'i* (*Ch'i-kung*)

On reading the preceding paragraph, one may have the impression that to Keep the One implies the "keeping" of a great many things! Indeed, "One," (*i*) in Chinese, also means "total" and "complete." Keeping the One thus also means "keeping together" one's vital forces, that is: to act in such a way that these forces remain complete and nothing is lost. Inside the body, the One (the true self) is, as we have seen, always multiple and multiplied. There are a great many places in the body which are related to the mutations of the One, and the list we made in the previous chapters is far from being exhaustive. Even the Master-Who-Embraces-Simplicity himself recognizes that all this is complicated:

I have heard my master state that the manuals of Taoist meditation . . . propose thousands of different systems. . . . and that for the inner vision of the gods who inhabit the body, the formulas are really innumerable. Each of these is effective in its own way, even though there are some in which one has to "keep" several thousand gods who surround and protect you, which would seem to me pretty fastidious.[8]

These complicated practices to which the author refers no doubt belonged to the School of the Heavenly Master with its registers listing thousands of "Officers and Generals."[9] He himself appears to have preferred to meditate on the True One, the inner child who "has a name, and garments of certain colors," mentioned above. This method may well have been rather similar to that of the vision of the inner country we already encountered in Lao Tzu's *Book of the Center*. He also mentions an exercise which is even simpler: the concentration on the Obscure One (Hsüan-i). This is a matter of putting into practice the words of the *Tao-te ching:* "To know clarity and yet maintain obscurity." It is done by first visualizing the sun and then concentrating on the shadows which it projects. These shadows are again so many projections of the self.[10]

How does this all work? Not just through meditation, for the inner and the outer being must act together, action and thought must agree. We have seen that, in his ritual, the Great Master dances, makes gestures, recites inaudibly, and meditates all at the same time. Such an integration and participation of the entire body is also necessary in the preliminary stage of Keeping the One. Today these exercises are called: the Work of the Ch'i (*ch'i-kung*, also written, in present-day Chinese transcription: *qigong*).

Let us now see what these exercises entail. Among the thousands of methods spoken of by the Master-Who-Embraces-Simplicity—all of which he considered efficacious—some are still known. The most famous is given in the *Book of the Yellow Court* (*Huang-t'ing ching*).[11] As we have seen, the Yellow Court is one of the most important places in the body. It designates the sacred area, the central space of the Inner World. The meaning of this term can also be explained by comparing it with similar sounding two-syllable terms such as *hun-tun* (chaos), K'un-lun (the mountain of the Mother and of immortality), K'ung-tung (empty cavern, a mythical place), Tung-t'ing (cavernous court, sacred space). Thus, the phonological similarity extends to the semantic level. The main theme of the book is indeed that of the inner and former life.

The *Book of the Yellow Court* is written in rhymed verse. Each line measures seven words (syllables). It gives a detailed, but sometimes difficult to follow, description of the Taoist body and its related practices. It was intended to be recited by the adepts.

> Lao Tzu, at rest, made these verses of seven feet,
> To explain the body and its forms, as well as all its gods:
> Above, there is the Yellow Court; below, the Pass of the Origin;
> Behind, the Dark Towers; in front, the Gate of Destiny.
> Breathe through the Thatched Cottage, all the way to the Cinnabar Field,
> And let the clear water of the Jade Lake asperse the Marvellous Root.
> Once you are able to practice that, you will enjoy Long Life![12]

Thus begins the *Book of the Yellow Court*. This opening shows how, by first setting out four major points (above, below, behind, in front), the spirit takes possession of the body. From these four points the location of the Cinnabar Field—the place of generation—is now determined. The Cinnabar Field is connected to breathing and swallowing saliva (the clear water of the Jade Lake).

These exercises belong to the first stage of the practice of Keeping the One. They entail the putting in order of the inner world through the control of the rhythm of breathing and of the circulation of bodily fluids through activation of the energy cycle. These are the preliminary steps, often seen as a general marshalling of one's energies—the gods of the body—for a general assembly, a "hearing."

The meditation, which consists in calling up the gods of the body and visualizing them as a kind of procession that leads them through the inner world, is an exercise which is also linked to particular days. Indeed, some gods are supposed on certain days of the year to report to the heavenly administration on the good and evil actions of men. This may lead to a lengthening or, more often, to a shortening of a person's lifespan. In order to prevent this, one must keep the gods under control and prevent them from leaving us. We are already familiar with the carping gods of the popular religion; they too exist in the inner world of the body. They are called the Nine Worms or the Three Cadavers, and they reside near the Cinnabar Field, at the very source of life. The Six Jade Maidens of the sixty-day (sexagenary) cycle, who watch over our destiny as well as our merits and faults, are also supposed to report on bad actions.

In everyday religion, certain "festivals" are closely connected to the reckoning gods. At the New Year, as we have seen, the God of the Hearth does his job of talebearer, and as a result a propitiatory offering is prepared for him. On New Year's Day everyone ages by a year, and the report made by the God of the Hearth, in his role as inspector of Destinies, is directly related to this progression towards death.

The gods of the body also have their specific days, the most important being *keng-shen*, the fifty-seventh day of the sexagenary cycle, on which they cause us to get nearer to death and dissolution. Indeed, the end of our life means for them liberation and the possibility of returning to the element of origin. In a way, this is true for all the constituent parts of the body. They all count on the centrifugal dynamics of the cycle in order to hasten the final collapse. But while the *hun*, the heavenly souls, are endowed with discernment and a sense of justice, the *p'o* are real brutes that seek only to harm the body in which they are enclosed. Spirits of the Earth, their cycle of action corresponds to that of the moon:

The nights of the first, the fifteenth, and the last day of the moon are the times when the *p'o* go roaming, steeping in corruption and filth. Some join with the eaters of bloody sacrifices [the demon gods] and associate with *kuei* (ghosts) and *mei* [demons of old things]; others become the allies of the Three Cadavers; sometimes they band together in order to attack the child [the embryo of immortality], and thus destroy their own dwelling [the body]; at other times, they report a person's faults to the Three Officers (of the heavenly administration) and to the Count of the River [Ho-po, divine superintendent of punishments]. They even induce *kuei* to enter the body through the breath, thereby introducing fatally harmful substances. All the illnesses of the living can be attributed to the *p'o*. By their nature, the *p'o* rejoice in the death of human beings.[13]

Indeed, there is something rotten in the Kingdom of the body and periodic crises are inevitable. The sole way to survive is to Keep the One, to collect oneself and, so to speak, keep oneself together. To keep all one's energies complete is first and foremost a search for equilibrium. This equilibrium is a preliminary condition for any bodily practice, spiritual or medical. It is obtained primarily through retreats and fasts (*chai*).

On critical days one should observe a *chai*. The rule here is to purify oneself and to avoid any foods that would strengthen the forces of death. The Three Cadavers feed particularly on cereals and the interdiction against them is one of the fundamental features of the Taoist diet.[14] One should avoid, at these critical periods, stimulating and strong foods like garlic. It is also necessary to be careful with all secretions, as excrements and death are symbolically related.[15] The retreat is held in a clean, sparsely furnished, place, away from all turmoil.[16] The practice consists essentially of concentrating oneself in order to inspect the gods of the body, call them by their names, visualize them, speak with them, confess to them the sins one may have committed, and ask their forgiveness.[17]

The retreat is a long vigil, for in general the spirits take advantage of our sleep to escape and report on us, thus making us age. One must not sleep on critical days. "Stay awake, day and night, and you will be immortal," says the *Book of the Yellow Court*. These fasting days are marked by a search for unity, by penitence and abstinence, and by a general inspection of the gods of the body. We see that the practices of Keeping the One are very similar to those of the festivals of the people: propitiatory offerings, confessions and penitential acts, banquets (where no rice is eaten),[18] processions of the gods and, finally, plays lasting all night. Once more we see the close relationship between the physical and the social body.

In individual practice the search for unity and equilibrium is part of the preliminary stage, the preparation for the great union. A preface to the *Book of the Yellow Court* comments on this stage, while at the same time explaining the virtues of the recitation of the text:

This text reveals the gods of the whole body, their dwelling places and even the location of the divine embryo. If it is recited regularly, the gods and their dwellings become clearly visible and well-ordered. The True Embryo is peaceful, the transcendent fluids flow abundantly and penetrate everywhere, the passage ways stand open, blood and marrow are plentiful. . . . All this due to the fact that you know the names of the souls and essences of the inner organs.[19]

While reciting the text, one should at the same time mentally evoke the images of the gods. This should be done as naturally as possible, and in harmony with one's breathing. Spiritual exercise is closely tied to the breath; calling on the main gods must be done in connection with breathing exercises.

Grind your teeth twenty-four times, swallow your breath twelve times, and repeat the following formula: "Five viscera, six receptacles, your true gods all go up to the great assembly in the Scarlet Palace."[20]

Grinding the teeth resounds inside the body as does beating the drum to summon the gods to assemble and participate at the great parade. Swallowing the breath is done in the following way: bend back the tongue so that the tip touches the palate, fill the mouth with saliva, inhale through the nose, hold your breath and swallow the saliva, exhale through the mouth. This breathing exercise knows all kinds of variations. Here is an easy one:

The Old Lord says: "The Gate of the Obscure Female is the root of Heaven and Earth; like a slender thread that unwinds forever, we use it without ever exhausting it."[21]

This means that the mouth and the nose are the gates of Heaven and Earth through which we inhale and exhale the energies (*ch'i*) of *yin* and *yang*, of life and death.

Each morning, stand up and face the South. Place both hands on your knees, then pressing softly on the two joints, exhale the impure *ch'i* and inhale the pure ones. This is called "exhaling the old and inhaling the new." Hold your breath for a long time, then very softly let it out. As a rule, rub yourself during this exercise with your hands on the left and the right, from top to bottom, in front and behind. As you absorb the breath, think of the Original *Ch'i* of the Great Harmony which descends to the genitalia and spreads from there to the five viscera and the four limbs, which all receive its beneficial action, like the mountain that absorbs the clouds, like the earth that drinks up the rain. When the breath has been properly diffused through the body, you will feel your belly stir lightly. When this happens ten times, the body is filled with a feeling of well-being, the complexion is fresh, hearing and vision are clear, appetite is good, and health complaints go away.

This method should be practiced between midnight and noon, when the energies are alive. During the other half of the day—from noon to midnight—the *ch'i* are dead; one should not do these exercises.[22]

This easy exercise can become the starting point for more advanced ones. Breath-holding can be rhythmical: taking the time necessary for normal breathing as the basic unit, hold the breath during a certain number of units—three, five, seven, or nine. These numbers correspond to the symbolic values of the viscera: heart, kidneys, lungs, and liver.[23] Each time the breath is held in this way, one should guide it *mentally* to the particular organ. Indeed, this mental function is that of the central organ, the spleen, which receives that symbolic number, *one*. This kind of exercises is called *tao-yin,* "guiding the energies (*ch'i*)." They are usually performed while lying on the back with the legs slightly apart and may be accompanied by massages that enhance circulation.

The *ch'i* which are thus guided towards the different organs may also be vocalized. While inhaling, clench the teeth and make the sound *shhii;* while exhaling, the sounds are:

—For the spleen: *hou!*
—For the heart: *kha!*
—For the lungs: *si!*
—For the kidneys: *tse!*
—For the liver: *su!*

The exact sounds are of course impossible to reproduce in writing. They must be learned from a master.[24] This exercise of the Six Breaths (*liu-ch'i,* one inhaling and five exhaling) is meant to heal illnesses of the viscera through the vocalized expulsion of air. More than a meditative practice, it is a rhythmical expression of the body's functions.

Guiding the energies (*tao-yin*) is not alone stimulated through concentration and massage but through physical exercises as well. One of the earliest forms of moving *tao-yin* was the Dance of the Five Animals in which certain stereotyped gestures of the tiger, the bear, the deer, the monkey and the owl are imitated. Among the manuscripts of the second century B.C. discovered at the site of Ma-wang tui there is a richly illustrated text on different exercises of this and other types. Intended to develop suppleness and relaxation and to improve circulation, these exercises were the origin of today's Taoist gymnastics, of which

T'ai-chi ch'üan ("boxing of the Highest Ultimate") is an example. This wonderful method of harmony and well-being is a martial art for the defense of the inner world. The slow, supple dance of *T'ai-chi ch'üan,* performed with no apparent effort, is for everybody an excellent initiation into the very essentials of Taoism.[25] It requires no special equipment, very little space, and no prior training, yet it is so efficient that even thinking through the movements provides some benefit. In the same way as reciting the *Book of the Yellow Court,* this form of "boxing" is a rhythmical expression which guides the breathing and which, through daily practice, conditions one for the Keeping of the One.

These preparatory exercises are not simple repetitive movements that can be done whenever one feels like it. They require precise timing. The day is divided into two halves: that of the living *ch'i* and that of the dead *ch'i.* There is, moreover, a system of correspondence between the hours of the day and the four directions and the center, and thus the absorption of the *ch'i* of the five viscera should be performed at certain times (morning for the liver, noon for the heart, et cetera). The sixty-day cycle is part of the spatiotemporal order, as are the twenty-four calendar-nodes. There is even a method for regulating the daily breathing exercises according to the sixty-four hexagrams of the *I-ching.*[26]

The daily exercises can and should be made to coincide with the time cycle. To every period of the time cycle corresponds a part of the body, to each hour a god with whom one can communicate through a kind of perpetual prayer. At every moment, the body changes; it floats through time, and the regulation of our life can never exist without the cyclical time structure. The daily preparatory exercises already constitute an entrance into the cosmic rhythm, a way of participating in the spontaneous evolution of nature. As soon as the practitioner enters into this universal movement, he becomes one with the great mutation of all beings.

This harmony with time, moreover, is necessary in order to realize one's female nature. Phases, periods, and critical days do belong much more to the existential experience of a woman than to that of a man. The *Tao-te ching* stresses this connection between the practice of Keeping the One, cyclical time, and female nature:

Can you keep the turbulent *p'o,* prevent them from leaving; embrace the
    One without its leaving you?
Can you control your breathing and make it as soft as a child's?
Can you purify your vision of the mystery so that it loses all distortion?
Can you, by Non-Action, watch over the people and rule the [inner] land?

Can you, by opening and closing (at given times) your natural gates, realize your female nature?
Can you, by Non-Knowledge, let the white light penetrate all the regions of the [inner] space?[27]

The cycles of fertility and gestation lead us to understand that the human body is a time machine. Chinese medicine does take this very much into account, in diagnosis as well as for therapy.[28]

The ordering of the inner world demands that one submits to the rules of time and continuously prepares oneself for the Work of the Tao, and this entails, so to speak, a "cosmologization" of the individual.

The initial and preliminary stage of Keeping the One concerns in the first place breathing exercises which allow one to restore the equilibrium and the harmony of the body's energies. This, as we have seen, is the Work of the *ch'i* (*ch'i-kung*). Practiced with regularity, these preliminaries are a way of setting the body to music. After a while, the exercises and the discipline become spontaneous and the integration into the cosmic rhythm is achieved with less and less effort, while the individual's spiritual strength increases with the natural completion of the greater and lesser cycles. "No need for divine aid to become immortal," says the *Book of the Yellow Court*. "The continental accumulation of energies, year after year, is enough."

Chaos: The Work of the Tao

The positive values of the search for equilibrium and harmony through the exercises of *ch'i-kung* are easy to understand: what could be better than this natural order and purity, especially since they coincide with the ideals of the social body, with the very life of society and its goals of autonomy and harmony? Furthermore, the methods of Taoism overlap with the precepts of personal hygiene and medicine to such a degree that it is sometimes difficult to tell them apart. Many famous doctors in Chinese history were Taoists. And over the last decades, many *tao-shih,* faced with the persecution of their religion, have been reconverted to traditional Chinese doctors.

But this is far from being the entire story. Keeping the One is more than a putting into order; it is a search for the center. With the practices I have called preliminaries, the preparatory methods of *ch'i-kung*, we are still within the realm of systems, precepts, even recipes. At that stage, everything is tied to rules, remains ordered and logical. The systems of correspondence of *yin* and *yang,* of the five phases, the eight trigrams, and all the other correlatives are allowed full play. There even exists, as we have seen, a system of great complexity that allows one to regulate his daily practice on the sixty-four hexagrams of the *I-ching*. The conceptual framework of all this is so convincing that, in spite of the pursuit of the female attitude, with all its connotes, the "work of the *ch'i*" never really escapes a certain formalization. In these systems we easily have the illusion of having found something absolute, if only because the time cycles, which play such an important role at this stage, seem to be eternally revolving according to an unvarying principle. Thus the ordering, which ought to be merely a means, soon becomes the final goal. The student of *t'ai-chi ch'uan* or of *ch'i-kung* is likely to consider that he has already found "it," that is, the long-sought harmony with nature. And so, with full confidence in an apparently faultless system, where everything is in place, clear, and well-centered, he then turns again to the *Book of the Yellow Court* for the next stage. But here he may well find something very different from what he initially anticipated.

> In the Yellow Court sits someone dressed in scarlet.
> The door is locked, its two leaves tightly closed.
> The Dark Towers rise to vertiginous heights.
> In the Cinnabar Field, semen ["essence," also used for female genetic secretions] and breath subtly mingle.
> Above, the clear water of the Jade Fountain flows abundantly,
> Making the Divine Root sturdy and hard: it will not ever weaken.
> In the Center Lake a noble person, dressed in red.
> Below lies the Field, three inches away; that is where the god lives.
> Lock the passage between the Inner and the Outer with a double lock.
> Always keep the Hut spotlessly clean.
> When suddenly you receive through the tunnel of the Mysterious Meridian the semen's signal,
> You should quickly retain semen and hold yourself together.
>
> There is someone in the House who never comes down.
> If you can manage to see him, you will never be ill.
> On the frontier of the Upper Sphere lies a one-foot-long barrier.
> Concentrate on that point and you will suffer no more harm.
> Breathe in and out through the Hut to recover your forces.
> Keep whole and hard: your body will benefit.
> Carefully preserve the contents of the Square Inch,
> Transmutation of the semen keeps one young!
> Then guide it through the Dark Towers toward the lower regions,
> So that it will nourish the Jade Tree and make it strong;

The highest Tao is not complicated, so long as you follow the right path.
The Tower of Gods opens onto Heaven and [below] is close to the Center Plain.
From inside the Square Inch, we reach the place under the Pass.
And in the Jade Chamber we find the Gate.
All this the Young Lord has taught me.

The Palace of Light opens onto the Four Directions, in the middle of a circular sea,
There is the True Person Cinnabar-of-the-North, and he [represents] me.
The Vital Spirit descends through the Three Passes.
If you do not wish to die, take care of the K'un-lun. . . .

Among the essential secrets of Long Life, the most important are those of the Bedroom.
Dismiss all lustful desires and concentrate on keeping your essence.
In the Field of the Square Inch and in the House of one Square Foot you can regulate your life.
Sit on your egg for a long time, with a peaceful heart.
Calculate with care where the Three Strange Forces are, those playful gods!
With them you will practice Non-Action, that is: the Great Peace.
Think constantly of the Nuptial Chamber and communicate with the gods therein.
At the right moment meditate on the Great Granary to suffer neither thirst nor hunger.
Then call up the Jade Maidens of the Six Ting signs;
But close the door of your semen; you will live a long time![29]

These are but a few passages. A complete translation of all 178 verses would be too long. Not much of essential interest would be added to what we have seen. The same images, within the same kinds of phrases, containing the same exhortations and cautions, evocations and incantations, are constantly repeated in no apparent order. At first, we recognize the already familiar places and figures: the Hall of Light, the Scarlet Palace, the Cinnabar Field, the True Person Cinnabar-of-the-North. These elements appear here in jumbled confusion, without any precise relation to the place or function they should have in the Inner Land. We go from the Yellow Court to the Dark Portico (the kidneys?), to the Jade Lake, then to the Central Lake (?). And so we wander around in a strange land full of unfamiliar elements.

So as to try to understand at least something, we turn to the commentaries. There is no lack of glosses on the *Book of the Yellow Court,* but unfortunately they rarely agree on the meaning of the names and terms and often even contradict each other. For example, take "Yellow

Court." We have seen that it is the central place and matrix of the body, where Lao Tzu lives and "where he comes in and goes out." For the most ancient commentator of the *Book of the Yellow Court, Yellow Court* means *the eyes;* a more recent commentary says *"three places in the head."* The same commentary states, on another occasion that *Yellow Court* is *"the spleen."* Yet another commentary comes with the following explanation: "The Yellow Court is the Gate of Life (*ming-men*)." Also found are "The Void," and "the Cinnabar Field." In short, one gets the impression that any part or function of the body can be associated with *Yellow Court!*

This impression is strengthened when we try out the commentaries on other terms, like Cinnabar Field: sometimes it is said to be the spot between the eyebrows, sometimes the mouth, or the heart, or a place under the navel, or the kidneys, and so on. Having spent time with the adepts of the practices to nourish the vital principle, I can say that according to them, the Cinnabar Field does not correspond to any exact place in the body, but "must be found by each for himself during meditation." According to them, nothing more precise can be said about it.[30]

The *Book of the Yellow Court*—and let me repeat that it contains one of the oldest and most celebrated methods for Keeping the One—does indeed start out by giving precise names to different places of the body and assigning functions to them. But we soon loose track of all this as we meet all kinds of creatures, sometimes officers and sometimes children, in the most unusual places. Those who are dressed in red and scarlet are all "I"; they represent "me." The *other* is the one practicing, doing the exercises, lying on his back, his legs spread apart, holding his breath, swallowing his saliva, guiding his energies around his body. That one is *you. You* "keep" *me* and *I* am the vital principle in the field of the square inch, in the house of the square foot, the Lord of the Tao, the child, the being of light, as well as the egg, which takes a long time to brood. This "brooding" is an activity during which—according to the text—one should call into action "those playful gods," the Three Strange Forces.

Who are these Three Strange Forces, *san ch'i-ling?* This question leads us to one of the most arcane facets of Taoism. The oldest commentary of the *Book of the Yellow Court* has only this to say: "The great Tao plays! Wonderful peace! Wonderful peace! Concentrate to the most utmost all your willpower in order to contemplate the True One of the Tao. The Three Forces stand next to him, playing the lute and the zither!"[31] But other ancient sources tell us that these strange musicians who accompany the inner life of the child in triple harmony are in fact gods of time, but not of ordinary time. They relate to the "hidden periods" (*tun-chia*), which occur at certain moments in which the cycle seems to forget itself.[32]

As we saw in chapter 2, one important method of computing time was to count days (and also years, but the *tun-chia* system stresses days) according to the combination of two series of signs, one of ten "Heavenly Branches", the other of "Earthly Stems." By pairing the two series, one obtains sixty different combinations, which are used to denominate a cycle of sixty days. This sexagenary cycle can be again subdivided into six periods of ten days, which each begin with the first sign of the series of ten, the *chia* sign. The first days of these six periods are thus called the "six *chia* (days)."

In every ten day period, we find two signs of the series of twelve that remain unused. These two signs are considered "orphan" (*ku*) signs, as they have no partner in the ten combinations of signs of the period concerned. When the twelve signs of the Earth are set out in a circle or compass, the eleventh and twelfth signs always face the fifth and the sixth. If now, for instance, the eleventh and the twelfth signs are "orphans," the signs opposite them on the compass—that is, the fifth and the sixth ones—are called "void" (*hsü*).[33] Thus, between the *first* sign of the decade (the *chia* sign) and the "void" signs, there are always three stations (numbers two, three, and four). These are the Three Strange signs (*san-ch'i*). Through various calculations relating the systems of correspondence involving the Five Phases and other criteria, the third of the Strange Signs is considered to possess *the Spiritual Force* (*ling*). This last sign corresponds to the fourth of the series of ten and is named *ting*. Here, *ting* is considered the antithesis of *chia*, the first sign and "leader" of the ten-day period. *Ting* is the absent ("void") value, a split, break, or fault. There are six ten-day periods, thus six *ting* signs. These are the six *yin* forces. Here is what an ancient Taoist text has to tell about them:

The Six *chia* are generals of *yang;* the six *ting* are deities of *yin.* That which is not used by the Six *yang* (that is, the non-used signs in a given decade), causes the Six *yin* to become "void." This void [*wu:* non-existent, non-being] is the very condition for the transformation; it can become being, it can become nonbeing, it can manifest itself through life or return into death; it embraces the hidden as well as the visible.[34]

Thanks to this break in the system, to this fault on the compass (and let us remember the sentence in the *Tao-te ching* which says: "the great perfection is like a defect"),[35] it is possible to find non-being at the heart of being or, as it says in the *Book of the Yellow Court*, "to go out by the Gate of Heaven to enter there where there is no space."[36]

Now, in the inner landscape, we have already met these Six *yin* deities, Jade Maidens of the *ting* period, in their role as assistants to the Mother.[37] In the preparatory *ch'i-kung* exercises, they appear as Destiny's agents, responsible for reporting mistakes. But here they are suddenly Mothers themselves who bring divine nourishment to the child. Under the mysterious name of Strange Forces of the Hidden Periods (*tun-chia san-ch'i*), they are also musicians and playmates of the Tao. Let me note in passing that the instruments they play are those of love and sexual union.[38]

In the *Book of the Yellow Court*, once the inner order has been achieved, it is again abolished. The constituent elements lose their symbolic value. By reversing the roles (e.g., from maidens to mothers), by the confusion and union of the elements, the text evokes images of disruption of the system, caused by agents who are deities of *yin*, of shadow, of Non-Being. They lead us into a vertiginous fall, towards the unknown region of Chaos, where the union can be consummated. It is Eros who drives us irresistibly towards this fall. Throughout, the *Book of the Yellow Court* mentions sexuality and describes arousal,[39] amorous intercourse,[40] and impending orgasm.

Keeping the One, at this second stage, is a practice which in principle ought to correspond to a mystical pregnancy—the gestation of the True Self, the immortal embryo. But now it appears that this pregnancy is also the act of love itself, as though coitus and gestation were one and joined in a single process. This is all the more remarkable inasmuch as the instructions given to the practitioner insist that the act should never be consummated. The *Book of the Yellow Court* constantly warns: "Restrain yourself! Conserve your seminal essences! And above all, take care not to succumb to the temptation to make love to the Jade Maidens of Hidden Time."[41]

Eros worshipped, Eros repressed—this paradoxical contradiction explicitly governs Taoist sexuality. Not only is sex everywhere alluded to in scarcely veiled metaphors, but it is also spoken about in direct and explicit terms. Taoism is aware of the central position of sexuality in life and nature and accords it this same prominence at every level of its thought and practice.

Because of this attitude, Taoism has lately inspired a number of popular works on the subject. Many of these works are rather poorly informed, and they all tend to conceal the contradiction mentioned above. They stress the open side, the explicit and the technical, of Taoist sexuality and do not give sufficient attention to the major interdictions. Misunderstandings regarding Taoist sexuality are therefore widespread. Given the importance of the subject, it is necessary to go into it more deeply here.

This is not an easy subject. How can the catharsis of Chaos be experienced under the coercion of repression? Is it possible to find freedom in constraint? Once the moment of Chaos has arrived, can it still be mastered? And above all, how can one maintain, in the face of these instructions, that Taoist sexuality is natural and spontaneous?

In order to unravel this paradox, let us have a look at the misunderstandings first. The very fact that they exist shows that there are problems, and not only for us Westerners. A Chinese text from the fourth century A.D. has an initiating goddess say on the subject of Taoist sexuality: "There is nothing more difficult for humans to understand than this."[42] However, these very problems and misunderstandings may help us to see where exactly the stumbling block lies.

Sexual Life in Ancient China by R. H. van Gulik is undeniably a serious work. The author, with the help of many texts, reconstructs a historical survey of the mores of the Chinese, emphasizing the Taoist aspect. For van Gulik China is, in matters of sexuality, the land of natural simplicity, thanks to the fact that it has remained completely ignorant of the Jewish and Christian belief in original sin. In China, the union of man and woman imitates the harmony of Heaven and Earth, and that idea certainly seems beautiful, good for the health, and right. And since this simple (albeit somewhat abstract!) openness of the texts which deal with sex contrasts so flagrantly with the great prudishness and the sexual repression so prevalent in China today, van Gulik puts the blame on the political and cultural changes that have occurred in the last few centuries. According to him, it was the last empire, that of the Manchus—and thus a non-Chinese dynasty—that spoiled everything by promoting Neo-Confucianism at the expense of Taoism.

This is a very simplistic way of looking at things. In China, as elsewhere, there was of course a certain relationship between politics and sex. But Confucianism and Neo-Confucianism have inspired Chinese governments of every period. As for the Manchus themselves, seminomadic Mongolian tribes of southern Siberia, how can one make them responsible for the reactionary mentality of Confucian schoolmasters?

In fact, there are many indications that show that, contrary to what van Gulik wants us to believe, sexuality was never very *natural* and nonproblematic in China. The very existence of a vast erotic literature, from as early as the second century B.C., as well as a great number of sexual handbooks (from which van Gulik gathered much of his wisdom), bear in themselves more than enough testimony to this fact. The current vogue of illustrated translations of these manuals (which are wrongly considered to be Taoist) and the very success of van Gulik's book show instead that the Chinese situation, for a long time now, has not been as different from ours as we would like to think.

It is nonsense to think that sexuality in traditional China was practiced freely. On the contrary, the central place which cosmology attributes to the concepts of *yin* and *yang* strongly indicates, as Marcel Granet liked to point out, that sex in China was always "far more sacred than for us"![43] Every union, even without the intervention of ecclesiastical or political authorities, was understood to be sanctioned by Heaven. Marriage itself was a very important event, loaded with meaning and religious interdictions. Let me mention only in passing that marriage in traditional China implied an alliance between clans which in itself was no simple matter. On the individual level, so as to warrant the cosmic agreement between the spouses, a first requirement was harmony between the spouses' horoscopes. An exact calendar was established for each stage of the betrothal and the wedding. The wedding ceremony itself was conducted with a wealth of ceremonials aiming to dispel all forms of unlucky results which might occur through this union of two distinct worlds. For all those who ever participated in a traditional Chinese wedding, it is clear that much of what happens has more to do with propitiation and purification than with a simple festive celebration.[44] Compare a marriage of well-to-do peasants in traditional China with their American counterparts and one sees that the latter are far more likely to indulge in what one might call "primitive behavior."

After the wedding the wife falls entirely under the authority of her mother-in-law, who governs her life in every respect, including sexual relations with her son. This is not necessarily felt as an abuse of power. Matrimonial exchanges between clans in rural areas are such that mother- and daughter-in-law often come from the same family. They are like allies within their husbands' family. Let us note that the bed is part of the dowry and remains in the wife's possession after the marriage. It is her exclusive domain. She sleeps there, with her children, and her husband is allowed there more or less as a guest. The open love and sexual play described in the manuals are not much a part of the picture.[45] Conjugal sex is more adequately characterized as *coitus furtivus*.

It is in the context of concealment and suppression that we must reconsider Chinese erotic literature, as well as that vast subculture of harems for the rich and prostitution for the less well-off. Even in modern China, the numerous brothels in townships and in the countryside are an everyday reality. Along with the above-mentioned sexual handbooks, it is probably these latter institutions which have most contributed to China's image as a sexual paradise in the eyes of its Western visitors.

The aim of the "bedroom manuals" is first and foremost to reassure the male reader, to give him courage, and to justify his behavior:

The Yellow Emperor asked the White Maiden: "What might be the result if I remained now for a long time without sexual relations?" The White Maiden answered: "Very bad! Heaven and Earth have their successive phases; *yin* and *yang* merge and are involved with each other. The human being should follow their example and conform to the law of nature. If you do not make love, your vital forces will become obstructed and *yin* and *yang* will be blocked. In that case, there will be no easy remedy! . . . If your jade shaft [penis] does not move, it will waste away. . . . You should therefore use it regularly and give it exercise."[46]

"Shouldn't a man of sixty keep his semen held in and remain alone?"
"No. A man should not remain without woman, because if that is the case, he becomes nervous and his spirit wears out, and this in turn will result in a shortening of his life."[47]

To make love is considered very healthy; that much is made clear by these manuals. But in reading them carefully, it also becomes obvious that this attitude is not really so positive. Love is also frightening, because it is also thought that women can be vampires who may take away a man's essence (semen). There are even hints that it was in this way that the Mother of the West, that great goddess, attained immortality.

The Mother, Queen of the West, obtained the Tao by nurturing her feminine forces. Such a woman has only to mate once with a man for him to fall ill from exhaustion, while her complexion becomes radiant, and she no longer has any use for cosmetics. . . . The Holy Mother has no husband. She likes to make love with young men. But one should certainly not divulge publicly the real nature of the Mother![48]

The fundamental imbalance between male and female power causes anguish. The manuals therefore devote much space to all kinds of methods to overcome impotence, for instance by eroticizing the women (whose positive response to the man's advances appears to be taken for granted!), by spacing out intercourse and, last but not least, by *compensating* for the initial inequality through a show of endurance, so as to convince oneself (and hopefully also one's partner) that one is invincible in love. In order to increase one's chances in this heavy competition with the Mother, an appropriate psychological preparation is of course much needed. As one of the "bedroom manuals" puts it:

When you have intercourse, think of your partner as a worthless pot of clay and of yourself as a precious object. When the semen is beginning to announce itself, leave the land quickly! Sleeping with a woman is like mounting a galloping horse with rotted reins, like walking along the edge of a deep chasm whose depths bristle with swords and where one fears to fall. Save your semen so that your life will not end![49]

The handbooks on the "Art of the Bedroom" contain yet other "tactics" so that men may try to collect the woman's "seminal essence" and thus beat her at her own game (the authors of these manuals are incapable of telling us what the female's "seminal essence" consists of, but that is not important. Those men who must at any cost be the stronger, and who therefore exert themselves in having intercourse with several women in a row without coming to orgasm, are supposed to be capable of "nurturing the *yang* with the *yin*." The idea of shared pleasure is herewith entirely forgotten. This kind of glorified male vampirism is, alas, the most redundant fantasy one encounters in Chinese erotic literature.[50] Thanks to various so-called Taoist secret tricks, the supermen know how "keep going" an ever increasing number of women: ten, one hundred, several thousand! "The Yellow Emperor lay with twelve hundred women and became Immortal; common folk have but one wife but destroy their lives. To know or not to know, that is the difference!"[51]

But this difference consists only of a mixed bag of tricks, some rather funny, but in general frankly morbid.[52] Whatever the case, the erotic literature and handbooks on the Art of the Bedroom speak of sex solely as it is experienced by the male, while in fact everything appears to depend entirely on the woman. She is the *other*: she must be beautiful, warm, welcoming, passionate, without body odor or too much individuality, or anything else that might disturb the male's obsessive dream.

This kind of literature, which continues to be very popular, in China as in the West, does now and then contain some aspects of Taoism.

Certain practices, such as breathing techniques and the circulation of energies (*tao-yin*), are here misused so as to boost the image the male imagines he has to convey of himself.

All this is not true Taoism. It is a mistake to look for Taoism in the idea of "nourishing *yang* at the expense of *yin*"; Taoism moves on an entirely different level. To illustrate the difference between the image of the Yellow Emperor as it is given in the erotic texts and the true Taoist concept of this mythical ruler, let me quote Chuang Tzu. These are the words that a master (in fact *the master,* since tradition views him here as the incarnation of Lao Tzu) spoke to the Yellow Emperor:

I tell you the supreme Tao. This is the essence of the supreme Tao: Confused! Obscure! This is the principle of the supreme Tao: Chaotic! Silent! No sight, no hearing; in silence embrace your spirits and your body will become spontaneously sound. Be calm, be pure, do not overburden your body, do not stir up your seminal essences, and you will enjoy Long Life! . . . I Keep the One so as to remain in harmony! [53]

Here, Keeping the One means to realize one's female nature, and sex—here explicitly evoked—receives a completely different meaning from the one it has in the Art of the Bedroom. The Master reminds us first of the primordial Chaos, a theme which—now that we have read in the *Book of the Yellow Court* about the organization as well as the disorganization of the Inner World—is fundamental to the understanding of the Taoist Body. Chaos is the theme of the words of Chuang Tzu quoted at the beginning of this book: "We can think of nothingness as his head, of life as his spine, of death as his buttocks?"

The text also specifies clearly where and how the transformation can take place: "No sight, no hearing; in silence embrace your spirits [this, as we have seen, corresponds to the preliminary stage of Keeping the One] and your body will become spontaneously sound [and find its equilibrium]. . . . Do not overburden your body, do not stir up your seminal essences." The meaning of this warning is: "Do not use your body to follow your passions. Do not let yourself be carried away by your senses, giving yourself over to 'things'; do not pursue your dream fantasies at the expense of your inner unity." The fact that sexuality is so *explicitly* referred to also implies this: "Let us seriously occupy ourselves with sex, so that we can then forget it."

It is not a question of repressing sexuality, but rather of being wary of its outer appearance, of eroticism and seduction or, as the Chinese say, of its "color" (*ssu*). Eroticism is not only dangerous, it is unworthy. One does not vanquish it by heroic feats in the bedroom, so as to prevent it from enslaving us, we must learn to keep ourselves together. "If it were simply a matter of not ejaculating, every eunuch would become immortal," remarks one Taoist author sarcastically.

Sex has to be learned and the first thing to acquire is self-control. Whatever may contribute in sexual practice to this self-control and ultimate equilibrium is justified. As explained by the Master-Who-Embraces-Simplicity, sex is extremely important, but it remains one of the *preliminaries*. He therefore classifies the sexual arts with physical exercises, breathing exercises, dietary restrictions, and medicine. In spite of its paramount importance, sex alone under no circumstances suffices to maintain the equilibrium of the body![54] And he, along with all true Taoists, vigorously denounces the practices of "nurturing the *yang* at the expense of the *yin*."[55]

Taoist masters, men and women, are generally married (though not necessarily to each other). Some modern schools (such as the Ch'üan-chen school mentioned in the first chapter) have advocated celibacy and monasticism, following the example of Buddhism, but that has never become the rule and involves only a small part of the clergy. The great majority of Taoists live within local communities where marriage is a condition for their priesthood.

In earlier times, the school of the Heavenly Master conferred the highest level of initiation—the quality of Master—not on individual adepts, but on couples. During the ritual of ordination they were supposed to unite their registers, that is, their respective spiritual forces. It is important to note that these registers, without distinguishing the sex of their owner, did comprise the names and symbols of *yin* and *yang* energies. This showed that each human being possessed both masculine and feminine elements. The ritual of ordination of the union of *ch'i* was carried out by the couple under the direction of a senior master.[56] The text of this ritual still exists, and thus we have a fairly good idea of how it was done. The ceremony began with a preliminary fast in a pure room. There, through meditation, cosmic powers were invoked. These invocations were accompanied by breathing exercises and visualizations of the Inner World. During these rites, the gods of the sexagenary cycle (the sixty-day period) were particularly important.[57]

When the cosmic energies were all there, the adepts would undress and loosen their hair (in ancient China, both men and women had long hair worn in a knot). The couples, facing each other, were first seated on floor mats. Later, the rites continued in a standing position and finally the partners moved about together in a very elaborate choreography modeled after the magic square. Each stage and every movement was accompanied by a meditation, which accomplished the corresponding structure inside of the body. In a slow dance the partners, holding and touching each other in precisely prescribed ways, moved from one point of the magic square to another, invoking each time the *ch'i* corresponding to the Eight Trigrams and the Center. With their joined fingers, the partners would indicate the numerological value of each direction: six for the northwest, nine for the south, five for the center, and so on.

Then even more difficult movements and gestures began. Taking turns, one of the two partners would lie down, while the other performed a dance around him or her and massaged (with the foot) precise points on the body. Again, this kind of acupressure was performed while visualizing and invoking the gods of the Inner World. At certain moments the sexual organs were involved and there were short moments of rhythmic intercourse without, however, interrupting the meditation. During the final part of the ritual, the participants would again invoke the gods of time, of the sexagenary cycle, but this time in a regressive order.

The ritual of the union of *ch'i* involved all the physical and spiritual faculties of the partners.

The different parts of the ritual had meaningful titles, such as Meditation on the Palace of the One, Spontaneous Conduct (of Energies), invocation of the Heavenly Cycle, Numbers of the Terrestrial Cycle, Return of the Gods, the Royal *Ch'i*, the Child who Turns Around, Sectioning Death, Crossing towards Life, Thanking Life.

The ritual was performed in a perfectly symmetrical manner. Each prayer, each gesture by the man found its symmetrical counterpart in a gesture and prayer by the woman. There was no such thing as one active and one passive partner. The text of the ritual, as it has come down to us in a version from the early Middle Ages (fourth century A.D.), is very beautiful and the execution of the ritual must have been an extraordinary event. The union of *ch'i*—certainly, in some ways, a continuation of the ancient peasant orgies Granet speaks of—must have required that the participants have perfect mastery of their bodies.

In this context, the first goal of sexuality is to bring order and equilibrium to the body. The same thing is also true on the social level. The *tao-shih* are simple citizens within local society and refuse to be set apart.

This integration, without any sectarianism,[58] in the natural group, as well as the leading of a perfectly ordered life, are the very conditions for surpassing the everyday religion and for experiencing the return to Chaos, the source of creation and renewal.

To my knowledge, the initiatory rites of the Union of *Ch'i* have not been preserved in modern China.[59] But the rites of hierogamy have continued in the body techniques of the, still very widespread, Inner Alchemy (*nei-tan*). *Nei-tan* does not, in fact, differ substantially from the methods of the *Book of the Yellow Court* or the ritual of the Union of *Ch'i*. Inner Alchemy is an individual practice, but it is a synthesis of all earlier rituals and is also integrated into liturgy as part of the meditation of the Great Master.

For this reason, I will use Inner Alchemy to illustrate what this fusion leading to chaos implies. Let me first introduce one of the most basic texts of the *nei-tan,* the *Transmission of the Tao to Lü Tung-pin,* a work attributed to Lü Tung-pin's master Chung-li Ch'üan, and in all probability dating from the eleventh century. Although in this book the preparatory exercises, such as breathing techniques, are also reviewed, it is mainly concerned with alchemical theory. The ingredients used to accomplish the Great Transmutation, such as cinnabar and mercury, as well as the different stages of the alchemical process, are all related to the body's energies, organs, and functions. The process of transmutation, minutely regulated in time, also includes mental images. In this system, the elixir of immortality corresponds to the child, the immortal embryo of the earlier methods, such as that of the *Book of the Yellow Court.* This elixir is produced though the hierogamy, the union of the antithetical elements Water and Fire, coming from the kidneys and the heart. These elements can be mentally represented in many different ways:

Yang which goes up can be pictured as a young boy, a dragon, fire, the sky, clouds, the sun, a horse, smoke, dawn, a harnessed cart, a flower . . . whereas *yin* which descends is often represented as a girl, a tiger, water, the earth, rain, a tortoise, the moon, an ox, a spring, mud, a ship, a petal . . . Since there are names, it follows that there are also symbols. These are the Five Sacred Mountains, the Eight Divisions (of the compass), the Four Seas, the Three Islands, the Golden Lad, the Jade Maiden . . . There are too many metaphors of this kind to mention them all. Without exception, these are symbols set up in the void as a means of support for our consciousness. As long as the fish has not yet been caught, one cannot do without a net? One cart following another necessarily follows the trail of the first. The accomplished work is the model for work performed later.[60]

In other words, in inner contemplation, one cannot do without imagi-
native representations, but the goal must be *to surpass them*. In conclusion, the same text says: "In the beginning, to establish the foundations
and create a basis, one must continually progress, and at this stage meditation is very useful. But once one reaches the Tao, one should abandon and again abandon[61] so as to enter the domain where there is
neither sight nor hearing, and thereby eliminate inner vision entirely."

I will speak later of this *return*,[62] which is the third stage of the
practice of Keeping the One. But let us first see, in Inner Alchemy, how
the union which leads toward fusion in chaos is accomplished:

In meditation, we see, inside ourselves, the Father of the Tao who leads upward
a young boy dressed in red, while the Mother of the Tao brings a young girl
dressed in black downward. They meet in front of a yellow cottage. Here they
are welcomed by an old woman dressed in yellow. She introduces the two
young ones to each other, according to the rites of betrothal of the world. Now
comes a hidden moment. When the great joy is achieved, boy and girl continue
their separate paths, she going upward, and he going downward, after they
have first taken leave of each other according to the customs of the world. Then
we see again the Old Yellow Woman, now carrying something that looks like
an orange in her arms. She places it in the yellow cottage, on a golden plate.[63]

An orange on a golden plate, a pearl in the incense burner, a point in
the middle of a circle: the same images found over and over again in
the iconography of Inner Alchemy are also those used in cosmology. Is
this to say that in the modern practice of Inner Alchemy the rites of
sexual union have become purely ideal and abstract? Is "chaos" still a
bodily experience? It is, to a certain degree, because in Taoism the spiritual must always be in harmony with real life.

A story known to all those who study Taoism in China today describes the teaching of patriarch Wang Ch'ung-yang (twelfth century),
founder of the modern movement of Ch'üan-chen (Total Perfection).[64]
When the patriarch had to explain the methods of Inner Alchemy to his
disciple, Lady Sun Pu-erh, he started by drawing a circle (image of the
matrix and the world of chaos, and then put a dot in the middle to
represent *T'ai-chi*, the Great Summit, the One, the Being who manifests
himself in the heart of Non-Being.

Having received this rather abstract lesson, the lady retired to her
apartments to practice meditation on the point in the circle, adopting a
strict purifying discipline. After having done so for a few weeks, she
quite unexpectedly saw the patriarch enter her room. He smiled at her,
winked, and said: "Come on! All methods are equally good, everything

comes down to the same thing, let's go, let's be spontaneous . . . You here in this cold room all alone sitting to meditate—what's the point? Don't you know that *yin* alone cannot give life, that *yang* by itself cannot reach its Center? The way you're going about it, all by yourself, *yin* and *yang* will never meet! How will you become pregnant and carry the child? Believe me, this thing here cannot be without that thing there, and that thing very much needs this thing!"

At these words, the lady blushed all over with shame and anger. In the end, however, she got to understand the true meaning of the patriarch's words: the condition for putting order in the body is to follow the world and not go against nature. The very goal of the preparatory stage is to adapt oneself to one's physical being and natural surroundings. Everyone should first learn to loosen up and to abandon oneself. Once this is achieved, it becomes possible to transcend the environment and to reach the *chaotic order* and, through it, involution ("the return") and regeneration.

The story tells us further that Lady Sun Pu-erh did indeed achieve this chaotic order. She did so through a carefully adjusted amount of lunacy, the reality of which no one was ever certain. This enabled her to enjoy a privilege rarely allowed to woman in her time: to live alone in a big city without being in the slightest inconvenienced and to work freely at her personal salvation. When the lady's husband afterwards questioned Wang Ch'ung-yang concerning his wife's insanity, the patriarch simply said: "Who can become immortal without a touch of madness?"[65]

Inner Alchemy puts sex at the center of its practice, just as it locates sex in the very center of the body, in the yellow cottage (the Yellow Court of yore). There, Fire from the heart (represented by a young girl, i.e., *yin* being born from *yang*) and Water from the kidneys (a boy, *yang* born from extreme *yin*) meet. Sex is no longer concentrated, or confined, to the genital organs, nor is it a matter of the heart or of the mind; it is *united at the Center* and from this Center it radiates and spreads through the whole body. Love thus engages the body as a whole, merging all the organs and all the functions. "One breathes with one's heels" says Chuang Tzu.[66] All the faculties of the senses: our eyes, nose, breasts, hands, come together in total participation. It then becomes possible to surpass orgasm, something many women already know, but which is much less frequent in male experience.

The rhythm of the pulsions which were harmonized during the preliminary stage now become like a stream of music flowing through the whole being. This joyful delight is the experience of Chaos; in the hidden moment of the great confusion, the One appears and is born. The moment of chaotic order is an enclosed whole, rounded like an egg, a time of union as well as transformation and pregnancy. Then the One is accomplished: intercourse becomes pregnancy.

The practice of Long Life is, as we saw earlier, called *hsiu-yang*, literally "to put in order and nurture." These are the two stages of Keeping the One: the preliminary stage and the union through intercourse. The first stage demands strict discipline and regularization, a point by point harmonizing, as though a harp with ten thousand strings were being tuned. Then follows the playing, a flood of sounds which sweep us like a wave, a moment of utter passion, an extreme tension that comes apart in abandon, a fall toward the origin of things.

The Return

The union of being and non-being is achieved in the breaking up and the disintegration of the conceptual system. According to the first chapter of the *Tao-te ching*, therein lies the Obscure or the Mystery. The vision of chaotic order in the Yellow Court, the sounds of cosmic music that vibrate through the body, can be compared to the *True Writs* in liturgy: these images, sounds, and signs mark a moment in time. The forces liberated during this privileged moment should not be exploited, say the masters. When existence is reduced to essence, when the universe is condensed into signs and images, *it is dangerous to try make use of them.* This is explained in the book consulted earlier, *The Transmission of the Tao to Lü Tung-pin:*

The representations of ecstatic inner vision correspond to a necessary stage, but they ought not to be maintained continuously. True thought is the absence of thought. When the entire inner land is gathered at the hearing with the True One, the great transformation leads us first through the confusion of chaos and then onto the gradual path of liberation. In the beginning, to establish the foundations, one must continually progress, and at this stage meditation is very useful. But once one reaches the Tao, one should abandon and again abandon so as to enter the domain where there is neither sight nor hearing, and thereby eliminate inner vision entirely.[67]

These remarks hold true for all of Taoism; finding the obscure mystery is only a stage. "Mystery" (the "Obscure," *hsüan*) remains a concept. As the first chapter of the *Tao-te ching* says, not the obscure but "that which is obscure in this obscurity itself (*hsüan chih yu hsüan*) is the 'door to all marvels.' "[68]

To find the Tao through "union" implies a return, an involution, and this return is part of the dynamics of mastered time. As shown above, out of the gap of the "hidden period" and the eclipse of time, a counter cycle is put into motion. The theories of calendar computation establish that these periods of eclipse form a kind of deviant cycle which moves by retrogression. By having the body enter this particular time of conception and gestation, the circulation of energies (*ch'i*) in the organism is also reversed. The generative succession of the Five Phases— Water produces Wood which produces Fire, et cetera—is now carried out in the opposite direction.[69] The cycle of creation moves in reverse as well.

Our bodies, as we have seen, are formed through the coagulation of energies (*ch'i*), and this coagulation obeys a transformational dynamic inscribed in time. The *ch'i,* still floating and free during childhood, become more and more fixed; they pile up and begin to secrete their essences. When the individual grows up, seminal essence, whose generative power transcends the individual, is distilled from the Original Breath. Chinese physiology often insists on the limited quantity of seminal essence our bodies are able to produce. Our desire to use our physical and psychic faculties to materialize this precious quintessence—which we are destined to lose in order to create life elsewhere or, even worse, to simply lose—leads us inexorably to exhaustion. To slide downward following our human inclinations, without offering resistance to the attraction of the earth, brings us ever further along the path of death, whereas the return leads us towards life.[70]

These fundamental ideas concerning seminal essence (which, in Taoist thought, is also associated with menstrual blood) are part of a whole complex that pervades the daily sexual life of individuals. It is very much present in medical theory—the famous theoretical treaty *Huang-ti nei-ching* begins with a chapter on the economy of sexual energy—as well as in mythology and in popular literature where the themes of vampires, succubi, incubi, and other monsters avid for sperm abound. The strength of these negative representations is such that they may lead to morbid and even pathological symptoms.[71]

Even in the sexuality advocated by Taoism, recentered, depolarized, and diffused through the entire body, we encounter this complex. It is connected with the practice of "the return of the spermatic essence" (*huang-ching pu-nao*) and with that of "embryonic breathing." One of the oldest texts on the techniques of "circulation of energies in the body" (*tao-yin*) says: "What causes the human being to be born is cinnabar [the quintessence conferring immortality, here equivalent to the spermatic essence], but what saves the human being is the return."[72] To reverse the course of the energy cycle consists first of all in reversing the course of the spermatic essence which, instead of running downward, must travel back up through the body to the top (i.e., the brain) and then stabilize itself in the center (i.e., the belly).

This return and its imagery are variously described and give rise to the most diverse speculations.[73] What remains constant, however, is the physical practice of involution. Retreating to an isolated room to lie on one's back (in the past some adepts seem even to have suspended themselves, head down),[74] fists clenched around the thumbs (like a newborn baby), tongue curved back toward the palate, eyes half closed but rolled back, one identifies with a fetus to return to the mother's womb. In this position, one proceeds to Embryonic Breathing.[75] From a technical point of view, this is not essentially different from the process of swallowing breath, but it does constitute a more advanced stage.

Inhale slowly and deeply through the nose, when your mouth is full [with saliva] swallow [the breath], then exhale all at once. Try to decrease progressively [the amount of air] exhaled and to increase the amount inhaled. In fact, this method of swallowing the breath is called Embryonic Breathing. This means that this breathing is like that of the embryo in his mother's womb. For ten (moon) months he goes without eating and yet during this long period, he is fed and becomes whole. "His bones are soft, his tendons weak, but he tightly clenches his fists."[76] Keeping the One implies no more thinking, no more reflecting.[77]

These are the very same breathing practices that first establish equilibrium and harmony, and then make one return toward the state of the child.[78]

Whether this method of holding the breath does ultimately induce a trance I do not know.[79] As described here, retention corresponds to inner breathing, as opposed to outer breathing—an interiorization that signifies a reversal of the exhalation process, the latter being synonymous with the progression towards death. Embryonic Breathing, the third stage of Keeping the One, is further characterized by a suppression of all images and thoughts—which are really also "external things"— in order to find a completely concrete existence. *No more "spirituality"*! To return to the spontaneity of the child is to do away with the crutches and aids of systems of correspondence, symbols, concepts in general, as well as with masters. Only one thought, that of the union of *yin* and *yang* and of the great cosmic landscape, has now taken possession of the adept, and no other could possibly match this vision.

"If you see the Master, dismiss him from your mind," says *The Transmission of the Tao to Lü Tung-pin*.[80] Visions are but a *means* of reaching reality. Reality, however, goes beyond these visions and makes them obsolete and worthless. The Immortal Embryo is "my True Self." It is pure, undifferentiated matter, and thus as inconceivable as the Tao.

There are various theories of involution and different ways of envisioning and analyzing it. For the adepts of Inner Alchemy, regression towards ataraxia corresponds to sublimation. The reversal of the cyclic motion entails a reversal of the aging process. The seminal essence, a materialization due to the compression of our energies, is again etherealized and becomes breath; this breath—whose dynamics, unlike that of the essence, are ascending—goes back up the chain of the functional organs and phases of the body to become the lightest and clearest of the energies, the *shen*, "godhead."[81] Once this *shen* has been stripped of its identity, it returns into the undifferentiated, that is, the Tao. This is how the words of the *Tao-te ching* are fulfilled: "The movement of the Tao is to return."[82]

This return, or involution, can also be conceived of as a sacrifice.[83] Let us look at the different stages again: first equilibrium, cosmic order, is reestablished; then comes the movement towards chaotic order, total union in the Center; and, as a final image, the vision of the Ultimate Principle (*t'ai-chi*). In one fleeting moment, we then are given to contemplate the divine Work of the Tao. This moment of light and of total consciousness, this ecstatic vision, must then be abandoned, sacrificed. The child has fulfilled its task, its time has come, so let us be free of him! At each return, each regression, we recover a little more of our freedom.

The process of return can be experienced as a sublimation or an oblation of the divine image, as a regression of our knowledge towards the state of non-knowledge, and in many other ways as well. Already the first stage, the one that seeks equilibrium, can, according to one's surroundings, be approached in different ways. The exceptional moment of Union can also be found almost anywhere. "The Tao has ten thousand gates," say the masters, and it is up to each of us to find our own.

Keeping the One is above all a *creative process* realized in the freeing of our energies from the shackles of concepts. The fusion of *yin* and *yang* at the Center comes in a moment of self-mastery, in love or in artistic creation; one may find it in calligraphy, in poetry, dance, or in all other forms of art.[84] Once accomplished, this oneness is abandoned as a sacrifice, and subliminated. The fist relaxes, the chaotic structure comes undone. To master this process, to accomplish within oneself the passage from clarity to obscurity, from concentration to diffusion, to know, from the moment of exaltation, how to find the path of return, to become again "useless," to take life "as it is," all this is the secret, stolen from time. Those who master this process are Masters of Time. Taoism calls them Immortals.

9

The Immortals

Do try to recognize them, because wherever they are, there is celebration! Their portraits, embroidered or simply cut out of paper, decorate the long red banners which are hung over the gates of houses and temples at marriages, anniversaries, and other festivities, great or small. They are eight in all, each one on a fantastic mount. Gay and funny, each of them has his or her own emblem: a fan, a flower, an iron staff, and so on. Their proverbial drunkenness has a profound meaning: it corresponds to the state of chaotic confusion which leads across the threshold dividing the ordinary world from the sphere of the sacred festivals.

Who does not know the Eight Immortals? We find them, as liminary figures, in a short but obligatory ritual playlet at the beginning of all theater performances, which shows their prancing dances and jolly libations (*tsui pa-hsien*). Their laughing portraits are embroidered on the hems of women's clothes, on bed curtains, on temple gates and roofs, on children's bonnets. An unending stream of stories tell about their *kung-fu,* their mastery in the arts of the body, which enable them to perform all kinds of feats.

The most famous among them is certainly Lü Tung-pin, Lü "the Host of the Caverns." He is the carefree dropout, the gay character who prefers a life of wandering in the mountains to an official career. His legend says that once upon a time, returning from a visit to the capital (where he failed to succeed at the examinations), he happened to meet an old man in an inn who invited him for a drink.[1] While his host was having the wine warmed, the young student took a nap. He dreamt that he was an official with important responsibilities, enjoying a life of glory and prosperity. For fifty years his star kept rising, he had several wives and many children and grandchildren, when suddenly he became implicated in a scandal. His family was executed or scattered, and he himself was exiled. Abandoned and miserable, he was bemoaning the vicissitudes of human fate, when suddenly he awoke: the wine was not yet warm. "That entire eventual life lasted only a few instants," said the old man laughing. Lü then realized that it was his host who made him have this dream and he recognized in him a Master.

Indeed, the man behind the dream was none other than Chung-li Ch'üan, a famous immortal who at that time was already six hundred years old. Lü fell at his feet and begged him to accept him as his disciple. Chung-li Ch'üan then said: "To become an Immortal, you must first perform many good deeds. When you have accomplished three thousand of them, I will begin to teach you.[2] But in order to help you, there is an alchemical formula for transmuting ordinary stones into gold. By giving this gold to those who really need it, you will be able to do much good."

"Will this artificial gold ever lose its value?" asked Lü.

"Ah! Yes," said the old man, "everything that has been transformed one day returns to its origin. Alchemical gold turns back into stone after several thousand years."

"So, my good deeds of today are very likely to bring harm to people of later times," cried Lü. "I don't want that recipe!"

"Good, said the old man, your answer shows that your kindness already extends to future generations. Thus, your three thousand good deeds may be considered accomplished now and I may begin to instruct you right away."[3]

Instead of outer alchemy (the art of making gold), Chung-li Ch'üan taught Lü Tung-pin Inner Alchemy (*nei-tan*). The book to which I have already referred several times, *The Transmission of the Tao to Lü Tung-pin,* is supposed to contain this teaching.

Lü became Chung-li's companion in his wanderings about the world. While they led a life free of worry and obligations, they sometimes would put people to the test to see if they might find any worthy of their help. Thus, for a time, Lü became an oil merchant in order to spot those of his clients who would ask no more than their due. It was almost a complete waste of time, for after a full year there was only one old lady who had accepted without argument the amount of oil she had been given for her penny. As a reward, Lü conferred on her the miraculous power to change water into wine. Now she not only could become very wealthy, but could also get drunk whenever she felt like it!

But more than a jester or good fellow. Lü stands out among the Immortals as a poet. Along his wanderings, he liked to write on walls or on stones his own simple poems, which were in fact profound and full of meaning:

> I came alone,
> I sit alone,
> Without regrets that people know me not.
> Only the ghost of that old tree,
> To the south of the city,
> Happens to know that I am an Immortal,
> Passing through.[4]

For many people, Lü Tung-pin is still living. He is nowadays more than a thousand years old, but he still travels the world to heal the sick—especially the poor and lonely—and to pass on his teachings to those able to receive it.[5]

Legends abound about him and his companions, who form together the merry band of Eight Immortals. Besides Lü Tung-pin and Chung-li Ch'üan, the group consists of six other rather eccentric people. Lan Ts'ai-ho, for instance, the troubadour of the band, is a young person of indeterminate sex. He (or she) plays a flute or sings popular songs. When someone gives her (him) money, she immediately donates it in turn to the poor so that they can buy wine. A refrain from one of his (her) songs goes: "I am pregnant, all year long!"

Also very popular is Li T'ieh-kuai (Li with the Iron Staff). Once upon a time, after a long ecstatic journey outside his body, Li wanted to return to it, but found it dead and already decomposed. So right away he found himself another body, which turned out to be that of a beggar who had just died. Not very handsome according to the usual criteria—lame, untidy, and shaggy, with bulging eyes—this new body was rather perfect for moving about unencumbered in the world. Li now walks with the aid of an iron stick (*t'ieh-kuai*) to which he has attached a gourd. During the day he wanders about, but at night he retires into the gourd. There he rests in another world, far from men.

Han Hsiang-tzu is yet another ambiguous character. A beautiful small boy and a special friend of Lü Tung-pin, he once wanted to imitate the Monkey-God who climbed the Queen Mother of the West's tree to steal the peaches of immortality. Instead of getting at the peaches, he fell out of the tree and, miraculously, that great fall made him into a real Immortal.

Chang Kuo-lao used to be an eminent statesman, an adviser of emperors, until one day he left the court to become a hermit. In the course of events he began to ride his mule backward, facing the animal's tail. When he didn't need his mount, he would transform it into a paper *image* of a mule, which he then could fold up and put in his pocket. To reanimate the dear animal, all he had to do was sprinkle it with purifying water.

Ho Hsien-ku (the Immortal Maiden Ho) was born as the daughter of a druggist. She was a model child, full of wisdom and piety, and, just like Ma-tsu, she wanted to remain pure and unmarried. But Lü Tung-pin was looking for a disciple to form a group of eight Immortals so that he could cut a nice figure at the Queen Mother of the West's forthcoming banquet of peaches. He thus resolved to seduce the druggist's daughter. He began by asking her for all sorts of drugs which were not stored in her father's pots and drawers, but rather referred to her sweet young female body. Despite her pure and chaste countenance, White Peony (as the future Immortal was called) very well understood Lü Tung-pin's intentions. She agreed to his desire and together they went to a mountain. There for three days and nights they made love passionately, but Lü did not ejaculate a single time. Determined to win, the young woman took the advice of Lü's companions, Lan Ts'ai-ho and Li T'ieh-kuai, who also were in the vicinity. They told her the secret points of her lover's body which she was to press at the right moment. The next time White Poeny and Lü were together, the young lady applied this secret pressure and, indeed, the Immortal released his precious seminal essences. There were naturally very pure and very concentrated *yang,* and therefore, for her who received them, a very powerful drug of immortality. In this way it happened that the young woman was victorious in the battle of love and, at the same time, fulfilled Lü's desire by allowing him to recruit the Immortal he needed to complete his band.[6]

The eight Immortals—including one last figure, Ts'ao Kuo-chiu, a renowned geomancer—travel the world in a constant state of inebriety. They are invisible and, as a group do not receive formal worship. Lü Tung-pin is honored as a patriach and as a saint, not as an Immortal.[7] There exist countless humorous anecdotes and proverbial sayings about the Eight Immortals, and they are depicted everywhere: on screens, on vases and plates, on paintings, in miniature gardens, et cetera. As indicated above, a banner with their pictures has to be hung above the entrances of all places where a ritual feast is taking place, for they are gods of passage.

They share many of their attributes with other Immortals, the thousands of extraordinary beings who succeeded in becoming one with the Tao. The *Taoist Canon* has several large collections with the biographies of Immortals of all times. Certain of these biographies are about purely legendary figures, but others—the vast majority—are about historical persons. Each biography tells us something about the method which she or he used to obtain the Tao and these methods are never completely the same. There are as many ways to become immortal as there are Immortals, and there is nothing systematic about it.

The word *hsien,* which we translate as "Immortal," is written in Chinese with a character that contains two elements: "human being" and "mountain." The meaning is thus simply: "the human being of the mountain," or alternately, "human mountain." The two explanations are appropriate to these beings: they haunt the holy mountains, while also embodying nature. Phonologically, the word *hsien* derives from the root meaning "to change, evolve, go up," or even "to dance." This recalls the themes of transformation, of ascension to heaven, and of dance which, in the ritual, allows one to take possession of a sacred space.

Fundamental as they may seem, these themes which are expressed by the etymology and the writing of the word *hsien* remain superficial and general. Who are these Immortals? There is no precise way to define them, no method is error-free, no ecclesiastical institution or tradition has ever confirmed their quality, no official canonization has ever distinguished the true Immortals from the false ones. Their stories do not allow a distillation of an exact doctrine, for there is no dogma defining how the body can become one with Tao. Every human being, whether big or small, humble or great, young woman or old man, musician, herbalist, clown, or scholar, may—on the sole condition of finding his or her own mountain—quit the treadmill of progress towards death and discover the return towards life. It is not even necessary to act intentionally: luck and a certain predisposition may sometimes be the only needed conditions, but nothing is guaranteed. It is necessary, however, to at all times be open and prepared to recognize, at a given moment of one's life, the mountain or the initiating Immortal, which some day is to be found on everyone's life path. It is in this readiness and openness that we find all possible latitude for individual free will and faith.

The obstacles to be overcome lie within us. The earlier mentioned patriarch Wang Ch'ung-yang had to live for seven years as a beggar at Lady Sun Pu-erh's door before she recognized him and realized that she needed him. Others, on the contrary, are able to find immortality by themselves and without any difficulty. The young shepherd Huang Ch'u-p'ing, for instance, completely disappeared one day with his little herd of sheep in the mountain. For forty years his elder brother looked all over for him. Finally he met a master, who said that during his wanderings he had seen the little boy and told the elder brother where he was. When the brother found the young Ch'u-p'ing, the first thing he asked was: "What has become of our sheep?" "They are there on the eastern slope of the mountain," the little shepherd answered. The brother went to look, but all he could see was a lot of white rocks. He returned disappointed, but Ch'u-p'ing assured him: "Yes, they are there; you're just unable to see them." They went together to the eastern slope and the young boy cried out: "Come on! Hurry up!" and on the spot the rocks changed into tens of thousands of sheep. The big brother understood then that his little brother had become an Immortal. He left the sheep where they were and remained in the mountain, adopting a diet of pine nuts and mushrooms, like his younger brother. At the end of ten years, he had recovered a youthful appearance. He no longer had a shadow and could appear or disappear at will. The two brothers had decided to visit their family in their native village. But the passage of time in the mountain is not the same as that of the exterior world. Many centuries had elapsed in the meantime and none of their family survived. So the brothers left once more to become forever one with nature.

This story has a very simple moral: anyone can become immortal. One has only to get rid of the trouble of keeping those sheep—these animals multiply perfectly well on their own—and to live from the mountain. The little brother became Immortal spontaneously, whereas the big brother was changed thanks to his faithfulness and brotherly love. The two Huang brothers blended into the landscape so well that in the long run they became themselves gods of the vegetation. They now preside over the ecological cycle of the mountain, and it is they who cause the forests to burn and the rain to fall. They have been absorbed into nature and "no one knows where to find them."[8]

The same holds true for the other legendary and historical Immortals: they simply left. Some met an apparent death by transforming themselves into a corpse—it is always recommended that one respect to some degree the order of the world—and then escaped (*shih-chieh*). Their mortal body was only an empty cocoon: or sometimes, when the coffin was opened, it was found that the body had been replaced by a familiar object belonging to the deceased: a pair of shoes, a walking stick, et cetera. Their true body was elsewhere, somewhere in liberty, or as Chuang Tzu says: "After a thousand years they had enough of the world and left. They rose up to the heavens on a white cloud."[9]

The Immortals are just the opposite of the gods of the people, whose temples (*miao*) are in many respects funerary monuments.[10] Indeed, the point of origin of their worship is often a tomb or mausoleum of the saint or the deity. The first temple built to Ma-tsu, in her native village on the island of Mei-chou, used to hold the relic of her mummified body (it was destroyed during the Cultural Revolution). The men who killed Lord Kuan built him a tomb, which became the first place of worship. The gods are linked to particular places and, as we have seen, their cults define communities in political and administrative terms. Moreover, the gods of the people are often considered collective ancestors ("Ma-tsu" means "grandmother").

All of this contrasts sharply then with the Immortals (*hsien*), those liberated elves who, like the Old Child (Lao Tzu), know neither parents nor children, neither lineage, nor country. They have no tomb nor holy relics. They do not fit into any system and it is impossible to place them into any framework whatsoever. The Immortals are unapproachable; nothing is guaranteed to make them answer the prayers of the adepts. They eat no human food and no sacrifice could ever force them to manifest themselves.

Let us recall once more the passage Chuang Tzu wrote on the Immortals:

In the distant mountains of Ku-yeh live divine beings. Their skin is cool like frosted snow and they are delicate and shy like virgins. They eat no cereals, only breathe wind and drink dew. They mount clouds of *ch'i* and ride winged dragons to wander beyond the Four Seas [the limits of the world]. By concentrating their minds, they can protect all beings from the plague and ripen the crops. . . . These beings! What power! They embrace the Ten Thousand Beings, making them into a single one. The men of this world may beg them to bring order but why would they tire themselves with the concerns of this world?[11]

The Abstinence from Grains

One of the most recurrent themes in the legends of the Immortals is that they do not eat grains. This cutting off (the term is *tuan-ku,* "cutting oneself off from grains") is related to a whole complex of concepts and attitudes concerning different aspects of the body. Not to eat grains is, as we have already seen, tied to the ideas about the powers of corruption and death within our bodies. The Three Worms, or Three Cadavers, feed on cereals, and the cutting off weakens them to the point where they can be eliminated, for example, with the help of certain drugs (especially alchemical ones, and cinnabar in particular).[12]

One can advance positive explanations for this belief, and the practice that derives from it, if one thinks, for example, of the relative abundance of feces produced by cereals as compared to that produced by a diet of meat. The conclusion of recent studies on the harmful effect of excessive amounts of carbohydrates in the form of sugar and bread, have led some to see the Taoist abstinence from cereals as the result of an ancient empiricism in matters of diet.

Mythology may contribute another explanation. The Immortals do not eat any cereals, but they are nonetheless the ones who assist in ripening the harvests. This belief is mentioned several times by Chuang Tzu and also occurs in other ancient texts.[13] From Antiquity on, one also finds the expression *ku-hsien,* "Immortal of grains," and this might well refer to this same belief.[14] Perhaps the *hsien,* spirits of the forests, also incarnated the divine forces which allowed crops to be grown according to the slash and burn agricultural techniques that were common in ancient China. One might then posit a sort of taboo based on the fact that the spirits who help the cereals grow do not themselves partake of these foods. But this hypothesis is not confirmed by any of our sources.

Taoism has developed another explanation for this fundamental interdict by linking it to the question of alternative foods. In the third century B.C., in the western and central provinces of China (especially Szechwan, Kiangsi, and the region of the lower Yang-tse) a highly perfected irrigation system was introduced which enabled a great agricultural development at the expense of the breeding of livestock. During the first empires (Ch'in and Han), at approximately the same time as Taoism became a mass movement, this technique spread and gave rise to those intensive cultivation methods which have remained typical of rural China up until the present day: wherever possible, land was converted into rice fields, irrigated or dry, with two or more harvests a year. As a consequence, not only hunting but also herding disappeared. Meat was almost exclusively provided by raising poultry and pork. The peasants depended entirely on agriculture and were forever tied to their land through all kinds of fiscal and administrative measures. As a result, the rural communities became an easy prey to all the ills of sedentary civilization: ever higher taxes, enslavement to the government through corvée labor and military draft, epidemics, periodic shortages and famines, and wars and raids by non-Chinese tribes from across the borders.

Whenever such calamities of natural or human origin occurred, the peasants had in general no other alternative than to flee. They took their refuge in nonarable areas—essentially hills and mountains where the natural vegetation had remained intact—and these became their sanctuaries. It is unlikely that there ever existed in China any of the "sacred village places" where Granet locates the places of worship of the gods of nature and of the souls of the ancestors; but it is true that the mountain sanctuaries were all that and much more.

The dioceses of the early organization of the Heavenly Masters were almost always located in the mountains, but close to the cultivated plains. The population gathered several times a year at these dioceses for its festivals, which at the same time were meetings of its regional assemblies. Military exercises of the peasant militia were undoubtedly part of the program.

The dioceses could accommodate great crowds which came not only to the celebrations but also to seek refuge from the cataclysms which occurred regularly in rural areas. The Chinese recognized already in ancient times the imminent danger of plague when they saw rats die at the beginning of the hot season. At an early stage, too, they realized that maintaining the natural environment of the mountains was the best way to avoid floods and preserve the vitally necessary sanctuaries. Hence the ecological rules which the leaders of religious groups were asked to obey: do not cut down trees, nor kill the birds, nor pollute the springs and streams.[15]

How did the people survive in the mountains? They were sustained by survival diets without grains, about which the Master-Who-Embraces-Simplicity has much to tell. Answering an inquiry about the abstinence from cereals, he says: "Whenever there is a famine, one can take refuge in the mountain and thereby escape death from hunger.

[One has to train for this beforehand and] not make an abrupt break from cereals."[16] The best remedies against hunger, according to the author, are alchemical drugs, but, he says, the ordinary man can also survive on a diet of pine nuts and roots, especially a sort called *shu* which resembles our burdock. This diet in the long run even causes better health and the possibility for a longer life. There are, of course, many other plants to fill out the diet of those who, like the Immortals, live in the mountains. Besides Taoist recipes, there also exist complete herbaria devoted to survival foods in times of famine, the oldest known versions of which go back to the early Middle Ages.[17]

Elsewhere in his book, the Master-Who-Embraces-Simplicity tells the story of a woman who had become a hermit in spite of herself and who, because of circumstances, had to give up cereals:

During the reign of emperor Ch'eng [32–6 B.C.], hunters in the Chung-Nan mountains [near present day Hsi-an] caught sight of a naked creature whose body was covered with black hair. The hunters tried to capture it and pursued it, but it jumped over crevices and ravines as though it had wings, and they were unable to catch up with it. By hiding and then encircling it, they did catch it. Then they saw they were dealing with a woman, who said to them: "I am a servant at the court of the Ch'in (221–207 B.C.). When I learned that rebel troops from east of the Pass were coming, that the heir to the empire had capitulated and I saw the palace in flames, I fled in fright to these mountains. I was famished and had nothing to eat. I was on the verge of dying of hunger when an old man taught me to eat the needles and nuts of the pine tree. In the beginning, I found all that very bitter and not to my taste, but little by little, I got used to it. As a result, I was never hungry or thirsty. In winter, I did not suffer from the cold, nor from the heat in summer."

It was clear that this woman was more than two hundred years old! Afterwards they brought her back [to the capital] and gave her cereals to eat. In the beginning, the odor of the cereals made her vomit, but after a few days she got used to it. At the end of two years, however, all her hair had fallen out and she had aged. Then she died. If she had not been captured, she would probably have become Immortal!

The same was true of the grandfather of the Wen family of Nan-yang, who fled to the mountains during the disturbances that marked the end of the Han period . . . He lived on burdock.[18]

In addition to the question of *survival* from the calamities befalling the world—and from those that will befall it in the future, for this theme also has its eschatological aspects—we also find the idea of an increase in *mobility* for one who is able to abstain from cereals. Such a person can live from what the environment has to offer. He also always carries with him a few pieces of dried meat and a gourd full of wine to survive in times of need. Light as a feather, he can travel great distances in a short time. Add to that the magic of the Hidden Period (*tun-chia*) which the adepts of immortality know how to practice, and we see that for them distance is abolished. Some *tun-chia* practices even have the Six Jade Maidens of the Ting Period bringing meals to the adepts during their travels.[19]

The Taoist ideal of the free wanderer, who no longer needs cereals for food, brings us back to the subject of agriculture. The "cutting off" of grains, which were the basic staple food for the peasants, was also a rejection of their sedentary life and the peasant condition as such. This refusal should not solely be interpreted in the light of the miseries endured by farmers, but also in a much more fundamental way. Agriculture has occasioned, since neolithic times, a radical break with the way of life that prevailed for almost the entire prehistory of humankind. Agriculture has also been the main culprit of the imbalances of human civilization over the last ten thousand years or so: the systematic destruction of the natural environment, overpopulation, capitalization, and other evils that result from sedentariness.

The legends of the Immortals often touch on these socioeconomic problems. One story, for instance, tells about an adept who got caught in the nets of agriculture. He retired to a mountain to live there as a hermit, and the people in the valley gave him a goat so that he could have milk. But a goat needs grass, so the hermit cleared part of the forest. And so it went, and in a few years he had become a peasant, enmeshed in his possessions and duties, and bore no resemblance to what he had to set out to become. In the practice of abstinence from cereals, we can see how myth and ritual merge with reality. Survival diets based on wild plants are still known in China today. At the same time, at the festive banquets at religious festivals—which are called "meals of happiness and Long Life"—rice is always excluded. Indeed, temples are also mountains, and mountains forever remain places where humans can survive.

Mountains

"All those who wish to practice the Tao, make the elixirs of immortality, escape disturbances, and live a secluded life should go into the mountains," says the Master-Who-Embraces-Simplicity in a chapter devoted to mountaineering. He continues by saying:

But whoever does not know how to take on the mountain risks death. That is why a proverb says: "At the foot of Hua-shan [sacred mountain of the West], there are piles of white bones!" [of those who sought immortality]. These skeletons belong to those who knew only one method and were ignorant of the rest. If this is the case, even with the most excellent resolve, one will meet a cruel death. . . . Those who do not know the right technique . . . will fall ill or injure themselves. They will be frightened constantly, will see lights, and hear strange sounds. Across their path, without their being any wind, tall trees will crash down; rocks will begin to roll for no reason at all and will strike and crush the passerby. Sometimes they [these unschooled adepts] will go mad and throw themselves into ravines; or still again they will meet tigers, wolves, venomous snakes. Never enter lightly into the mountains.[20]

Then the author gives indications on the days one should not visit the mountains, for, according to their orientation, the mountains are open or closed at certain periods of the year. It is also absolutely necessary, before going, into the mountains, to observe a purifying fast for a period of seven days. There are other precautions to be taken as well:

Know that all things, as they age, become capable of taking on human forms and manage thereby to deceive the human eye. In this guise they are continuously taking people in. It is only in mirrors that they reveal their true form. This is why, since ancient times, Taoists who go into the mountains always carry a nine-inch mirror (a solar number) on their backs; in this way, the ghosts of old things dare not go near them. If by chance they come to provoke the adepts, the latter will have only to turn around and look into the mirror: if they are Immortals or true mountain gods, they will keep their human aspect even in the mirror; but if they are perverse animals or ghosts of old things, then the mirror will reflect their true appearance.[21]

Thanks to the magic of the mirror the *true form* of things is revealed. We saw earlier, with respect to the Inner Land, that the light of the two eyes (the sun and the moon) must be concentrated in a point located between the two eyebrows, where there is a mirror reflecting this light and directing it below. In this way, one can then perceive the Infant, the True One, or, as the Master-Who-Embraces-Simplicity puts it: "the true form of Lao Tzu."[22] Other texts describe a method of ecstatic meditation, which consist of staring into a mirror for a long time. This allows one to see the gods of the body, the jade maidens, and even Lao Tzu himself and his *nine inner transformations*[23] Here the mirror is not the spiritual mirror, so dear to Buddhists and Christian mystics, a symbol of the soul and conscience, whose clear reflection materializes the emptiness and absence of passions. It is instead a typical Taoist instrument of transformation, of return towards the origin and the essence of things.

Inner vision is called in Taoism: *"the returned view"* (*fan-kuang*); the light is reflected, the mirror reverses the flow of energies. The "old things" have progressed in time and thus achieved a transcendent power; the *reflection* of the mirror effects a return towards their original identity. In the same way, the inner-directed look allows us to discover our original and essential self, our true form.

The old bronze mirrors of the Han period, which nowadays can be found in many museums, are in this respect especially meaningful. The front surface is silvered and polished, whereas the reverse side shows a rich relief design with labyrinthine meanders, stylized mountains, clouds, dragons, tigers, and other wild animals. Often there are also human beings with long hair or feathers covering their bodies; these are the Immortals. Some mirrors show the Queen Mother of the West playing the lute. The accompanying inscriptions say, for instance:

This is a beautiful mirror, carefully made. One can see the Immortals who know nothing of age. When they thirst, they drink at the Jade Fountain; when they hunger, they eat wild fruits, such as jujubes. They wander and play wherever they go and fly above the four oceans. They are as old as gold and stones; they protect the land.

When you go up on T'ai shan [the most important of all sacred mountains], you can see the Immortals; they feed on the Light of Jade and drink at the fountain of liqueurs. They mount dragons and white clouds.[24]

The mirrors are round, and the decoration not only consists of the above mentioned elements but often also of magic squares and compass rings inscribed with the cyclic signs of time. Mirrors thus show *the reverse side* of the original and fundamental image of the universe which, through an involution toward the origin of things, we are supposed to perceive by looking *through* the mirror.

Like the incense burners mentioned earlier (chap. 1), the decorations on the bronze mirrors of the Han period represent some of the earliest examples of landscape art in China. Carried by adepts on their backs, these mirrors are talismans and tokens identifying the adept as initiated into the true form of the mountain.

This idea is once more confirmed by the Master-Who-Embraces-Simplicity: "The higher adepts who climb mountains must procure for themselves the *Esoteric Signs of the Three Sovereigns* and the *Map of the True Form of the Five Sacred Mountains*." These are very famous and ancient talismans. The first consists of a graphic representation of the True Names of the first sovereigns of the world, the second one is based on the relief ("the geological writing") of the great sacred mountains, which are the guardians of spatial order. These sacred and spontaneously revealed writings of the hidden structures of the natural universe look—especially in the case of the second talisman mentioned—like a sort of map of the labyrinth of the mountain, which allows the adept to be recognized as initiate to the gods and Immortals. And, as we might expect, there are mirrors that also have on their reverse side the *Map of the True Form of the Five Sacred Mountains*.

These talismans are signs, writings, and as such their strange figures are supposed to reveal the *secret names* of the divine beings. That is why the Master-Who-Embraces-Simplicity says that they enable one to call upon the gods of the mountain. Another holy document, called the *Register of Demons,* enables the adept to communicate with the Earth God and the other guardian spirits (the censors) of the sacred places. They then may let him in, on the condition that he also knows the *times* of the mountain.

First there are the rules and interdictions of a structural nature: in *spring* one should not disturb a mountain by approaching it from the east; in *summer* not from the south, et cetera. But it is also absolutely necessary to understand the secrets of the Hidden Periods (*tun-chia;* see chap. 8). Without this knowledge, the adept will not be able to overcome the resistance of the mountain and this world will remain closed to him forever; the primordial universe of the mountain will end up rejecting the foreign body. Thanks to the knowledge of the Hidden Periods, the adept will be able to find the opening in the shield, slip inside, and be totally absorbed so as to become invisible, that is to say, to become part of the landscape.

The Master-Who-Embraces-Simplicity tells us that one must dance along the path leading from the *yang* world to the realm of *yin* inside the mountain.[25] Thus, inside the labyrinth the adept progresses, dancing the Step of Yü, from the Palace of Light and the Star of Fire down to the depths of the dark regions of water. This reflects mythology, where Yü, the great demiurge, recovered the world for humankind through his lame dance following the great deluge.[26] The Master teaches us how to dance this step: hop from the left foot to the right, one time *yin,* one time *yang*. The tracks left behind look like two Trigrams, *li* and *k'an,* the powers of Heaven and Earth.[27] With each step forward, one also has to hold one's breath.[28]

Without the talismans (secret maps of geomantic structures), without the names of the essences, without knowledge of the periods, and without the concentration of the dance and the breathing exercises, the sought-for medicine remains hidden.

The Taoist mountaineer looks in the first place for ordinary medicinal plants, in order to heal and to feed himself.[29] But the final goal is the mushroom of immortality, the Marvellous Fungus (*ling-chih*), which can take all kinds of extraordinary forms, and depending on whether the person approaching it is an initiate or not, appear or disappear.

The Marvellous Fungus is generally considered to be a token of good luck. At certain periods, its presence in the palace courtyards was heralded as a lucky omen for the reigning dynasty. The Marvellous Fungus can mostly be identified as the *Ganoderma lucidum,* a beautiful woody mushroom that grows in dark and secluded places and often takes on a strange form resembling deer antlers.[30] The mushroom itself has no particular medicinal value; it is the stag antlers that are considered auspicious. For the Master-Who-Embraces-Simplicity, however, these mushrooms are endowed with immortalizing properties, for they are the product of the sublimation of precious minerals lying under the ground, notably gold and the divine cinnabar.[31] Mushrooms are, so to speak, natural alchemical products, comparable to the great elixir, the quintessence derived from the transmutation of these very minerals. For the Master-Who-Embraces-Simplicity, alchemy is the supreme art and the most powerful weapon against death. "Indeed, vegetable drugs, as well as the practices undertaken to nourish the Vital Principle," he says, "can prolong human life, but only alchemy can confer complete immortality." As a consequence, the transmutation "nine times reversed" of cinnabar is the summit of all Taoist research.

Alchemy

Chinese alchemy is supposedly the oldest in the world. According to some modern scholars, the word *alchemy* itself—-from the Arab word *al-kimiya* and from which our words *chemistry, chemical,* et cetera are derived—is originally of Chinese (and Taoist) origin.[32] Chinese alchemy is not at all at variance with the methods of Keeping the One and with its underlying ideas; rather alchemy perpetuates these same ideas in the area of physics by seeking to reproduce the work of time and the secrets of life in laboratory experiments. Alchemy was very popular all through the Chinese Middle Ages (third to eleventh centuries A.D.), and it gave rise to some extraordinary technical developments. Alchemical experiments produced a number of discoveries—such as the invention of gunpowder—and greatly contributed to Chinese pharmaceutical research. The *Taoist Canon* has preserved a number of texts related to alchemy, which are of great interest to the history of science and which are today studied extensively.[33]

Towards the beginning of modern times (that is, around the eleventh century A.D., for China), laboratory alchemy gave way to Taoist research to the study of Inner Alchemy (*nei-tan*). This is, as we have seen, a form of Keeping the One which uses the theory and vocabulary of ordinary alchemy as a theoretical basis for the sublimation of the body's energies. But the main aim of alchemy, spiritual or laboratory, remains the search for immortality.

The Chinese word for alchemy is *chin-tan,* literally "gold-cinnabar," or simply *tan,* "cinnabar." One also finds *huang-pai,* that is: "yellow and white," in reference to two of the most basic alchemical ingredients, gold and mercury. All these names emphasize the fundamental role of minerals and base metals. In Chinese physics, these minerals and metals are the products of the interaction of cosmic energies and time and thus constitute the quintessence of our planet.

The aim of Taoist alchemy is not so much to make gold, but rather to refine raw ingredients found in nature and thus to discover the ultimate and fundamental element, the seminal essence of the world, which, once absorbed within our bodies, might confer immortality. In some way, this same idea is related to abstinence from cereals. Already during antiquity, the "eating of stones," which were to confer on the body their durability, was in opposition with the "eating of cereals," which were a putrescible food.[34]

Another Chinese tradition that contributed to the development of alchemical experiments was that of bronze and iron technology. Chinese civilization brought bronze smelting and casting to a very high level of development—as is evident in the magnificent archaic bronzes in many museums in China and the West. The myths of the heroes of Chinese culture, the founders of the legendary dynasties, abound in stories about the sacred art of fusing metals and the casting of royal treasures.[35]

It is to Great Yü, who also drilled through the mountains, that the work of casting the *nine* cauldrons of the Hsia [dynasty] is attributed. Metal was brought from the faraway lands and offered to him in tribute by the nine shepherds. Symbols of all beings were represented on the cauldrons. The faraway lands had devised these emblems. Since all beings were thus [represented] together, the Chinese were able to distinguish the divine from the impure things and thus could go on rivers and into marshes, into mountains and into forests without ever encouraging hostile beings or being attacked by the *ch'ih-mei* and the *wang-liang* [ghosts of old beings]. Thus the union of the High and the Low was assured, and the favor of Heaven reigned. . . . The magic cauldrons of the Hsia were said to have been cast at Kun-wu.[36]

In this way, following classical texts, Granet summarized the different legends concerning the Nine Cauldrons (or Tripods), the royal treasures and sacrificial vessels of Great Yü. The land of Kun-wu, where the cauldrons were cast, is a mythical region, far from the human world. There reigned a potter king, who also was called Kun-wu. In this land, pots were made in the shape of gourds, and these vessels were equally called *kun-wu*. This constantly repeated name is etymologically related to *hun-tun*, "matrix" or "chaos."

It is significant that one of the first events reported in historical records about alchemy concerns the making of artificial gold. An important part of the procedure was a sacrifice made to the furnace. The artificial gold was meant to make ritual vessels that would confer immortalizing powers on the food that was put in them.[37] The main concern was thus to make a container, an enveloping body, that would be thoroughly pure, owing to the noble substance made according to symbolic, ritual proceedings. This vessel was then supposed to confer spiritual force to its contents.

Instead of sacrificial food, Chinese alchemy fills its vessels with mineral "food"—especially cinnabar, which is considered to be the quintessence of the earth, the most powerful *yang* energy of nature, and which for this reason is compared to the sun. Found in the depths of the earth's crust, cinnabar is, so to speak, a highly concentrated form of solar energy which makes all things live and can heal any form of decay. As we saw above, Taoists who live in the mountains detect the presence of cinnabar in the earth through the marvellous mushrooms that grow at that spot (and that even shine at night).

The relation between gold and cinnabar is, according to ancient belief, based on the idea that, in the long run, gold is transformed naturally into cinnabar. Deposits of cinnabar are found beneath lodes of gold. Alchemy, by *reverting* this cyclical process, proposes to transform cinnabar into gold. This idea is strengthened by the fact that cinnabar can be sublimated to produce mercury, a liquid metal that can be used to gilt certain metals. The transmutation of cinnabar into mercury and vice versa is the cornerstone of alchemical theory and practice:

Plants, when burnt, turn into ashes. But cinnabar, when heated, becomes quicksilver and then, after repeated transformations, cinnabar again. This is very different then from ordinary herbs and this is why cinnabar is able to confer to us Long Life. Only the divine Immortals understand this reasoning, . . . as men of this world know but little and are easily astonished. Some do not even know that quicksilver comes from cinnabar, and if they are told about it, they do not believe it. They say: "Cinnabar is all red; how can it become white?" And in the end they simply refuse to believe us. But if we speak in vain, how is that the Nine Transformations and the Nine Returns can be accomplished in just a few days? Is it not thanks to the method? . . . It is true that the things of this world have ten thousand different aspects and that those concerning the arts of the Tao are the most difficult to understand.[38]

Thus spoke the Master-Who-Embraces-Simplicity. He reveals that he has in his possession a work entitled *The Book of the Divine Cinnabar of Nine Cauldrons*.[39] In this book it is written that, in order to accomplish the alchemical work, the adept must first go to a holy mountain, then enter a long fast and purify himself, and that the fusion of nine times returned cinnabar must be accompanied by a sacrificial ritual. Following are the nine successive phases undergone by cinnabar in the alchemical vessel:

At the first transmutation, it is called *Cinnabar Flower*. Heated in a sealed reaction-vessel for thirty-six days, this cinnabar, mixed with mercury, can be turned into gold.

At the second transmutation, it is called *Divine Talisman*. If one coats the soles of his feet with this cinnabar, he can walk on water or cross through fire. It expels worms from the body and heals all illness.

At the third transmutation, it is called *Divine Cinnabar*. It protects against wounds from swords. A hundred days after the adept takes it, Immortals, jade maidens, and mountain gods come to serve him or her.

At the fourth transmutation, it is called *Returned Cinnabar*. He who takes this drug will see red birds and phoenixes fly above him. . . . If it is put on the eyelids and eyebrows of an ordinary man, no demon will dare attack him.

At the fifth transmutation, it is called *Delicious Cinnabar*. After thirty days come jade maidens and gods.

At the sixth transmutation, it is called *Refined Cinnabar*. Now the gods come after ten days.

At the seventh transmutation, it is called *Weak Cinnabar* [like the *Infant*]. After one hundred days, one becomes immortal. Even those who are ninety years old can beget children.

At the eighth transmutation, it is called *Hidden Cinnabar*. One becomes immortal on the same day.

At the ninth transmutation, it is called *Cold Cinnabar*. One can fly, even without wings.[40]

The Master-Who-Embraces-Simplicity gives no other explanation regarding the nine times returned cinnabar. But for those who have followed the nine transformations of the embryo, the nine inner phases of the One, and also the dynamics of *return,* the terms used here speak for themselves. The "flower," which is a kind of projection (like the mushrooms), comes before the "return" and the "absorption"; these in turn lead to the "weakness of the child," to the "hidden," and to the "coldness" of *yin.* As the backward cycle progresses inside the matrix of the sealed vessel, turning into quicksilver nine times by sublimation, the raw cinnabar is purified and spiritualized.

Following the example of ritual vessels such as the nine cauldrons of the mythical sovereigns, the alchemical instruments should be pure, perfect, and made in the image of the universe. Illustrations in the manuals show a round reaction-vessel on a square furnace and the dimensions, as well as the decorations, are all chosen for their cosmic symbolism: the Eight Trigrams, the different emblematic numbers, the "Ten Thousand Beings," et cetera. The method of transmutation itself should be performed according to very strict ritual rules. The temperature at which the reaction-vessel is heated should be made to correspond to the temperature curve of the four seasons and the twenty-four calendar periods. Another frequently used model of a *yin-yang* cycle of growth and decline is that of the sixty-four hexagrams of the *I-ching.* So as to conduct this process in a perfectly controlled way, the amount of combustibles must be very carefully measured.[41]

One speaks here of the "fire phases" (*huo-hou*). They represent the positive cycle, the march of time in the world. To this progressive action there corresponds a retrograde or negative reaction of this *returned cinnabar* inside the alchemical vessel. In this respect, let me also note that an alchemical laboratory always has a *mirror* next to the reaction-vessel.

Thus conceived, alchemy is a great play of metaphors, or, as the Master-Who-Embraces-Simplicity said, a symbolic means to accomplish in a few days the cosmic process of returning to the True. This implies making a fabulous voyage in time, inasmuch as the same process would require millions of years in the macrocosm. By participating in a ritual manner in the transformation accomplished in the laboratory—

through purification, meditation, prayers, and by having a mirror present—the adept can "live" a period of time infinitely longer than that of an ordinary person. And if one takes into account the fact that this period of the nine returns corresponds to a *gestation,* a pregnancy, and thus an inner life, one sees that for the adept the outer life after the making (the birth) of the elixir should be, like that of Lao Tzu, virtually endless.

It is clear that laboratory alchemy of this kind has been developed following the paradigm of Keeping the One. Between laboratory alchemy (sometimes called "outer alchemy" *wai-tan*) and inner or "spiritual" alchemy (*nei-tan*), which I have already discussed, there is much overlapping. There is so much similarity between the two, in terms of vocabulary and procedure, that it is often difficult to determine whether a given manual relates to laboratory experiments or to physiological practice. Indeed, the homology does not start with the theories of inner alchemy, developed much later historically. Even ancient texts, such as *The Book of the Center* and the *Book of the Yellow Court,* made use of alchemical terminology (e.g., Cinnabar Field and the True Person Cinnabar-of-the-North) to describe the gestation of the immortal embryo. In fact, everything here seems to be connected, since even for laboratory alchemy the taking of the drug was often not the most important part. Ritual participation in the transmutation was itself a guarantee for Long Life.

It did of course also happen that the elixir produced by the alchemical reaction was consumed. This solar medicine was supposed to expel forever the worms or cadavers from the body and transform the adept into a being of light who casts no shadow. He could then fly to the heavens and merge with the subtle energies, the Immortals, the gods and the jade maidens, whose bodies were of the very same essences he had just absorbed.[42] Often, these essences did not only consist of cinnabar and mercury, but included realgar (orange-colored arsenic sulfide) and orpiment (yellow-colored arsenic trisulfide), sulphur, mica, alum, and stalactite milk (calcium).

Were the Taoists aware that a preparation composed of these ingredients was highly poisonous?[43] In fact, they were. The texts clearly describe the symptoms of poisoning. The drug was to be taken in very small doses, at regular intervals and with certain antidotes, while observing a special diet. A "medicine" composed of "stones" was thought to have many virtues. It had a sedative effect (owing to the cinnabar), heated up the body, strengthened the growth of hair, helped breathing, and was an antidote for snake bites (effects all due to arsenic, found—in oxidized forms—in realgar and orpiment). To this one might add a notable increase in sexual energy and in aesthetic sensitivity, which might even lead to the point of hallucination. Another important side effect was the preservation of the body's tissues; indeed, the corpse of someone who had died of an alchemical overdose decomposed more slowly than that of someone who had died of natural causes. The lifelike appearance of the corpse, with its supple skin and ruddy complexion, created an illusion of physical immortality.

Suicide by alchemical drugs was possibly not very frequent in Taoism. For the most part, the ingredients were very expensive. The Master-Who-Embraces-Simplicity, at the time he was writing his book, lamented that he was too poor to buy any cinnabar. Laboratory experiments must not have been within the reach of very many people. One might, therefore, easily dismiss the suicidal aspect of the search for immortality, if the following elements did not throw a different light on the question.

Alchemical research in medieval China produced many different drugs. One of these became very popular among the nobles and scholars of those times. It was called Eat-Cold Powder (*han-shih san*), or alternately, Five-Stone Powder (*wu-shih san*) and was made of stalactite milk and quartz, along with some realgar and orpiment, as well as a mixture of circulation-increasing medicinal plants like ginseng and ginger.[44] One of the immediate effects of this drug was a sharp elevation in the body's temperature, forcing the user to drink a lot and to eat cold things; hence its name.

Among the beneficial effects of this drug, the most frequently mentioned are sedation, an increase in aesthetic sensitivity, vision, and sexual energy, and greater physical resistance. The drug may also have been hallucinogenic. Aside from the immoderate rise in body temperature, other disadvantages included a gradual decrease in intellectual capacity, partial paralysis, aches and inflammation of the joints, ulcers, intercostal pains, and, over time, a general deterioration of the body. It was extremely important to follow the prescriptions regarding when and how much of the drug was to be taken. The powder was mixed with warm wine and had, like opium and heroin, an immediate effect. But if one made a mistake in the dose or the timing, or if one was not in a good psychological frame of mind (that is, too nervous, worried, sad, et cetera), the drug "rose" too fast, bringing on not only a depression, but also intolerable pains.

The final effects of taking the Eat-Cold Powder drug were all too well-known. An author from the third century A.D., himself an addict, who had written a work on the methods of countering certain second-ary effects of the drug, says of himself: "The longest one can hope to live when taking the drug is ten years or so; for some, it is only five or six. Even though I myself can still see and breathe, my words resemble the loud laugh of someone who is presently drowning."

We should view this rage to do away with oneself through an addic-tion to mineral drugs as a kind of subculture within Taoism. In this respect, it is rather comparable to the arts of the bedroom. Taoism can not be held responsible for developments in society which are in fact a distortion and misuse of its practice. But, as the Taoists themselves say, the deviations necessarily point to something basic and important, which, in the present case, is the choice of the moment of death in the search for freedom, and this aspect is indeed present in Taoism.

When Lady Sun Pu-erh wanted to throw herself into an adventurous and haphazard search for the place of her perfection, the patriarch Wang Ch'ung-yang said to her: "In this way you will die before attaining your goal. Death must be good for something; it should be positive. What is the point of sacrificing your destiny for nothing in return?" He then taught her the advantages of lunacy, so that she might live in peace and practice the Tao (see chap. 8). But some time later, he himself decided to die, so as to rid the little group of disciples he had trained of the superficial, worthless adepts who had also attached themselves to him. First he decided to fall ill: his body became covered with nauseating, pus-filled ulcers. The bad disciples said to themselves, "He wants to teach us immortality, but he is unable to keep himself in good health!" and they left. The patriarch then shook off his illness long enough to give the last instructions to his disciples. He handed over a collection of poems, gave them a wide, beautiful smile, and died. At that time he was only about forty years old.[45]

Here is another example of a way of committing suicide, this time from Taoist institutions: During the T'ang period, the different schools and traditions of Taoism were brought together and a classification of the degrees of initiation was adopted, giving preeminence to the Mao-shan school of the Great Purity (Shang-ch'ing) tradition. This highest stage was itself subdivided into several levels. The highest initiation, following completion of all the schools and systems, was called "The Register of Accomplishment of the Tao and Return of the Carriage." "Return of the Carriage" referred to the practice of taking the adept by carriage to a holy mountain and leaving him there alone never to return, while the carriage returned empty to the world.[46] This good death reminds us of the final line in so many of the biographies of Immortals: ". . . and no one knows what became of him."

The Master-Who-Embraces-Simplicity was in daily life called Ko Hung.[47] He lived from 383 to 443 and acquired in his middle age a certain fame based on his literary renown and his military exploits. He was therefore pressed into accepting a position in the civil service. As a last resort, he asked to be named prefect of Chiu-lou, a region which corresponds to present-day North Vietnam, in the hope of finding cinnabar there for his experiments. His request was granted and Ko Hung set off, but was stopped on the way by a despotic governor in the region of Canton who wanted to keep him at his provincial court. Forced to remain in Canton, Ko Hung retired to live as a hermit in the Luo-fu mountains (about forty miles from the present city of Canton), where he dedicated himself to Taoist practices. One day, he wrote his officious jailer, saying that he was preparing a special surprise for him. The latter hastened to the sage with a large retinue. As the cortege reached his gate, Ko Hung, absorbed in meditation position, smiled and died. At the burial, it was noticed that the coffin held only his clothes: the sage himself had escaped from the world "by means of his corpse," (*shih-chieh*), and obtained immortality.[48]

All these different elements from history and legend, from myth and ritual, converge to bring us to an unexpected conclusion: the final act of the Taoist search for immortality may very well imply suicide. Should we look at this suicide as if it were a sacrifice, an oblation of the image of the universe, as elaborated in the alchemical laboratory as well as in the practices of the physical body? Is it a final sacrifice to the furnace, to the mountain? The final destruction of the order of the universe in a movement of return, a regressive transcendence? These are but theoretical questions, which risk obscuring the essential.

The Immortals, creatures of light, are like the mirrors that guide us in the labyrinth of the mountain, which show us the way through the world of death and resurrection. They are the ferrymen, the guides who come to our aide by revealing to us the secret structure of our own body. The secret of the Immortals is indeed that of knowing how to die when one wants to, when one should. Beyond myths, history, and theories, they teach us in concrete terms how to live and how to pass from one world to the other, smiling, drunk, dancing to the rhythm of nature.

10
Teaching without Words

When Lao Tzu was about to leave [this world], he crossed, on his way to mount K'un-lun, the mountain pass that leads towards the West. The Guardian of the pass, a certain Yin Hsi, having probed the winds and the clouds, concluded that a divine person was soon to pass through. So Yin Hsi went to greet him, sweeping the road to be taken by him who was to come. He swept the road over a distance of forty miles, when finally he saw Lao Tzu and realized that he was the one (he was waiting for). Now Lao Tzu, while he was in China, had not yet transmitted anything to anyone at all. He knew, however, that Yin Hsi was to become one with the Tao and therefore he stopped in the middle of the mountain pass. . . .

Yin Hsi asked to receive his teachings. Lao Tzu then spoke the Five Thousand Words. Yin Hsi withdrew and wrote them down. This text is called the *Tao-te ching*.[1]

This is the well-known legend of the origin of the *Book of the Way and Its Virtue* (*Tao-te ching*) "in five thousand words" (quoted here in the words of the Master-Who-Embraces-Simplicity). The same story already figures in the biography of Lao Tzu by the great historian Ssu-ma Ch'ien (145–86 B.C.).[2] For Ssu-ma Ch'ien, as for most of Chinese literati, the *Tao-te ching* is the only book revealed by the Old Master and also the only essential book of Taoism. The Taoists themselves are only in partial disagreement with this view, as it is undeniable that "The Book in Five Thousand Words"[3] indeed encompasses all the traditions of the Mysteries.[4] In the treaties on the art of Keeping the One, as well as in the liturgical manuals, the *Tao-te ching* is always quoted as being the most authoritative source, as well as the sum of Taoist thought on the physical body and the social body. In Taoist legend, however, this comprehensive work presents itself as being not the first, but the second revelation. The first Taoist revelation remains that of Mother Li to her Old Child. Lao Tzu's *birth* comprises the teaching of Nurturing the Vital Principle, whereas the transmission of the *Tao-te ching* intervenes on the moment of passage to the land of *death* (the West), the return to K'un-lun and Chaos.

The teachings of the Mother, when she reveals the mysteries of her body, carry the seal of the occult and are fraught with interdictions. They are to be transmitted only to initiates. By contrast, the transmission of the *Tao-te ching* to Yin Hsi marks the beginning of the spread of Taoism throughout the world, and thus is known to outsiders. The guardian of the Pass is Lao Tzu's first disciple, the Heir of the Writings. The Guardian's watchtower, the observatory from which he searched the sky to learn the time of the sage's coming, is the first Taoist sanctuary.[5] The *Tao-te ching* is not an esoteric book, although certain passages do allude to concepts and practices that must have belonged to the spheres of initiation. It does not contain any instructions restricting its transmission to a small group of adepts. Its message is meant for all.

The *Tao-te ching* is a philosophical text. As we have already seen, at least two centuries stand between the time when, according to legend, Confucius as well as Lao Tzu lived in this world (tradition places his birth around 602 B.C. and the crossing of the mountain pass at 488) and the moment when the *Tao-te ching* was edited into its present form.[6] The present text dates, according to the great majority of modern scholars, from the beginning of the third century B.C. That brings us to just a few decades before the beginning of the reign of Ch'in Shih-huang-ti, the unifier of China and the founder of the first imperial dynasty (in 221 B.C.). Many passages of the *Tao-te ching* betray the influence of the philosophical schools of this late classical period, in particular that of the Legalists (*fa-chia*) and of the Logicians (*ming-chia*).

Why then is the book attributed to the Old Master? One should not see in this an attempt at falsification. It was very common, in classical China, for authors and editors to sign their works with the name of the founder of the school to which they belonged, rather than to use their own names. This form of euhemerism occurs in many ancient texts and not only for the *Lao-Tzu*, as the *Tao-te ching* was originally called. Those who wrote the *Tao-te ching*—we do not know their names, but does that matter?—wanted to give a comprehensive summing up of the thought which tradition attributed to the Old Master, but in a version purified of mythical elements and detached from its historical context.[7] The *Tao-te ching* contains no proper names, no historical references, no signature. It says only the essential and the universal.

The book of the Old Master does not belong to any particular "school." Indeed, the term *Taoist* was introduced only after China had become an empire.[8] In classical Chinese philosophy, the term *tao* does not necessarily refer to the Mysteries. All the schools, Confucian, Mohist, Legalist, et cetera, spoke of their *tao,* their own way and specific doctrine, which was at the center of their system,[9] whereas the school of thought to which the name "Taoist" was later given maintained, on the contrary, that the true Tao, the permanent one which eternally endures and survives, is not a *tao,* that is, not a doctrine or a system.[10]

It is most likely that the tradition which produced, over a number of centuries, the aphorisms of the *Tao-te ching* was not that of "philosophers," but rather reflects the wisdom which originated among the diviners and the astrologers, the scribes and the annalists. The background of the book of the Old Master is not with the schools of the young noblemen of feudal China, as other ancient texts may be. Even if the present version of the *Tao-te ching* was written at a relatively late date, the book is nevertheless the final result of a long development. It contains a series of sayings and aphorisms, often in rhyme, many of which appear in other, much older texts. In these ancient texts, these early quotations are either presented anonymously or put in the mouth of the Old Master or the Yellow Emperor, the mythical ruler who is the creator of Chinese civilization.[11] This shows that a good part of the *Tao-te ching* comes from an ancient oral tradition.

The sayings are full of paradoxes: "My words are very easy to understand and easy to practice, but no one in the world is able to understand them or to practice them. Yet my words have an 'ancestor' and my practice, a 'lord.' It is precisely because they are not known that *I* am not known."[12] This kind of statement from the *Tao-te ching* must have been even more disconcerting for people in ancient China than it is for us today. Indeed, to a large degree, the aphorisms directly derive from proverbs and sayings of popular wisdom. But in the *Tao-te ching,* these ancient bywords are skillfully transformed in such a way as to have them say the opposite of the truths they were originally meant to convey. For example, the second chapter starts with the well known saying, "Everyone knows what is beautiful." Hereto the *Tao-te ching* adds, with subtlety: "Hence the idea of ugliness," thereby demonstrating that people will never agree on what is beautiful and what is ugly, nor on what is good and what is evil, but that everything is relative, and that as a conclusion, "the Sage sticks to Non-Action and professes a teaching without words."[13]

"When the Great (Royal) Way triumphs, benevolence and justice will reign." This is undoubtedly an adage from some classical discourse on the art of good government. In the *Tao-te ching* the word *triumphs* has simply been replaced by *declines,* and hereby "benevolence and justice" are suddenly denounced as false virtues.[14] The *Tao-te ching* systematically uses the method of literary subversion in order to break the tyranny of established ideas and prejudices.[15]

The text of the *Tao-te ching* is, in itself, not very difficult. The vocabulary and syntax are even rather simple, although the style is extremely concise. The *Tao-te ching* is apparently intended for the general reader. Only a few passages refer to the Mysteries, such as: "The spirit of the valley never dies. It is called the Obscure Female."[16] or "Be the valley of the world and the highest power will never fail you as you return to the state of the newborn child,"[17] or again: "I alone am feeding from the mother."[18] These passages are like signatures attesting to the original inspiration, the "ancestor" of the book.

On the whole, there are few formal difficulties in understanding the *Tao-te ching*. The problem is rather one of meaning. One might ask, as one of the most renowned Western translators has done: "What is all this about?"[19] What is the *Tao-te ching* talking about, exactly? Strategy? This, at one time, was the official interpretation sanctioned by Mao Tse-tung, during the recent Cultural Revolution. Politics? Certainly, but, as we shall soon see, politics from a rather particular angle. Morality? Doubtless this as well, but not quite the morality of everyone. The spirit? This is, finally, the most widely held opinion. It was first advanced by the Confucian commentary of Wang Pi (226–249), an interpretation which is very widespread among non-Taoists in China. Wang Pi's commentary has also influenced almost all translations of the *Tao-te ching* into Western languages.[20] The *Tao-te ching* actually speaks of all kinds of things at the same time. It detaches these things from their immediate context in order to create an essential and universal form of expression that will apply to all situations. The meaning of the book is to be found on several levels simultaneously.[21]

The constant use of paradoxes is indeed primarily intended to detach us from any general idea or prejudice. But one may well ask whether these paradoxes do not have a higher meaning which reaches beyond rhetoric and continually refers to another dimension, to something surpassing our common knowledge and our normal ideas. What if, generally speaking, the style of writing of the *Tao-te ching* sought to convey something about the conflict between our consciousness and that which is unknowable within ourselves (the two, however, being linked together in the body)?

Even though we do not always understand them, the words of the *Tao-te ching* have a certain ring of familiarity; the paradoxes echo a personal but inexpressible situation. "Very easy to understand"—although no one understands them. The antidiscourse of the Old Master refers us to a teaching without words.

The Kingdom of Humpty-Dumpty

Notwithstanding its background, the *Tao-te ching* presents itself as a philosophical text which, like almost all the writings from the different schools of thought of its period, considers the human being in his role as sovereign. The aphorisms take on the appearance of prescriptions in the art of government.

The *Tao-te ching* is divided into two parts: the Book of the Tao and the Book of the Te ("power," or "action"). The second part deals with the application of the principles found in the first part, and it is this second part in particular that seems—on the surface—to be the one most devoted to politics, with all sorts of recommendations for rulers.[22] But when one looks closer at the text, one cannot fail to ask what kind of government this could be when the subjects do not know the name of the ruler ("the greatest ruler is the one who is simply known to exist [somewhere]"),[23] where there is no law, no obligation, and where, for this very reason, the people live in harmony ("the more laws, the more robbers and bandits there will be").[24] "Let the government avert its eyes, let it be nearsighted, and the people will be pure."[25] "In the times of yore, those who knew how to practice the Tao did not seek to enlighten the people, but sought instead to keep them ignorant."[26]

This kind of "ignorance" is nothing other than a healthy mistrust of all established ideas and prejudices, a way of introducing a strong relativity into all that men pretend to know something about. Indeed, nothing can be more dangerous for a country than intelligent, brilliant people: "Knowledge about the future may be [for some] the flower of the Way, in fact it is the beginning of folly."²⁷ In consequence, the *Tao-te ching* advises kings to:

> Stop Wisdom, throw out Knowledge,
> And the people will be a hundred times better off.
> Stop Benevolence, throw out Rightness,
> And the people will rediscover the (natural) familial virtues.
> Stop Cleverness, throw out Profit,
> And there will be no more robbers and brigands.
> Something is missing from these three pieces of advice;
> Therefore let us add the following:
> Appear unadorned,
> Keep your native simplicity,
> Reduce your egotism and your desires.
> Stop learning, so as to live without worries.²⁸

The *Tao-te ching* is not only anti-intellectual—"when intellectuals arose, great artifices began," says chapter 18—but also antimilitaristic. Arms are disastrous things (chap. 31). The best course for a big country is to allow itself to be dominated by a small one (chap. 61). The sages conduct everything with great prudence: "To govern a great kingdom is like frying little fish" (chap. 60), meaning that it is best to handle things as little as possible. Only to him *who views the world as his body* and cares for it as such can the world be entrusted (chap. 13). Not only should the country be treated as though it were one's own body, but the ruler must also concern himself with the physical well-being of his subjects, and not worry about their minds. "The Sage rules by emptying the hearts of the people and filling their bellies, weakening their wills and strengthening their bones, so that they remain without knowledge or desire" (chap. 3).

This kind of action, the same chapter continues, is Non-Action. It will cause "all things to be well-ordered" according to the political principles of the kingdom of the Tao, land of simplicity. "When the world possesses the Tao, the post-horses are unharnessed and are kept only for their manure." What need is there for communication, when there is total communication in chaos? The ideal of the autonomy of the individual body is translated into a vision of an independent and self-contained local society as the fundamental political unit of the world of the Great Peace (*T'ai-p'ing*):

> A small country, with few inhabitants.
> Where, though there might be tools requiring ten times, even a hundred
>   times less work, the people would not use them.

Where the people would prefer to die twice, rather than emigrate.

Where, though there were boats and carriages, no one would use them.

Where, though there were armors and weapons, no one would ever see them.

Where the people would have gone back to the use of knotted cords.

Where all would be contented with their food, happy with their clothing, satisfied with their homes, and take pleasure in their local customs.

Where the neighboring lands would be so near that one would hear the cocks crowing, the dogs barking [from one land to the other], but where the people would grow old and die without ever having visited each other.[29]

The country of the Tao, closed and perfect like an egg, is the kingdom of Humpty-Dumpty (*hun-tun*), the land of natural anarchy and inner harmony.

This image, which is a projection of the human body on society, expresses a teaching without words, a teaching to which the *Tao-te ching* simply refers by way of the term: *this here*. The *this here* is the belly, the empty center, the seat of an intuitive and inner perception. "One can only take [possession of] the world by remaining in inaction," says chapter 57. It continues by asking: "How do I know it is so?" And then answers: "By this here."

This here is the foundation of all true knowledge:

Just as through one's own body one may contemplate the body,
So through one's family one may contemplate the family,
And through one's country contemplate the country,
And through one's world contemplate the world.
How do I know the world is so [as I see it in myself]?
By this here! (chap. 54)

The same is said in the chapter describing the genesis of heaven and earth:

The manifestations of the (cosmic) powers proceed from the Tao alone.
The Tao's way of being is imperceptible, indiscernible (*huang! hu!*)
Hidden within it are Images . . .
How do I know that the multitude of beginnings was thus?
By this here![30]

Opposed to *this here,* to what is closest—the ancestor, the belly, intuitive perception—is *that there,* the exterior, fragmented view of things:

The five colors confuse the eye,
The five sounds dull the ear,
The five tastes spoil the palate,

Hurrying and chasing make the mind go mad.
Things hard to get impede one's freedom of action.
That is why the Sage holds to his belly and not his eye;
Truly, he rejects "that there" but keeps "this here"![31]

Everything proceeds from the *this here*. The vision of the State is based on the *individual* body. Each time the word *me* or *I* occurs in the *Tao-te ching*, it refers to the situation of the adept, who looks at the world from the point of view of the Tao. The *I* knows how to contemplate not only the process of the creation and the evolution of the world, but also its involution:

Having arrived at the ultimate void,
Keeping complete calmness,
The Ten Thousand Things arise together.
I watch their return!
Yes! There are beings in great abundance,
Yet each one returns and goes back to its roots.[32]

This passage can be compared to the description that the *Tao-te ching* gives of the situation of the Taoist in the world:

While all the others celebrate, whether at a great sacrifice, or when climbing the towers in the spring, I alone remain inert, giving no sign, like a new-born child that has not yet smiled. I am like a homeless wretch. While others have more than enough, I alone seem to have lost everything. How stupid I seem! How dull! How the common people shine! I alone am an idiot. How sure of themselves the others are! I alone am in the dark. Restless as the ocean, but spread as wide, without shores! All men have their use. I alone am intractable as a boor. I alone am different from others in that I feed from the Mother.[33]

The evocation of the child and the mother in this chapter are not the only instances where the *Tao-te ching* recalls the practices of Keeping the One:

Can you keep the unquiet *p'o,* prevent them from leaving?
Embrace the One so that it will never quit?
Concentrate your breathing and make it soft, like that of a child?
Purify your vision of the Mystery and render it undistorted?
Watch over the people and rule the (inner) land through non-action?
In opening and shutting your natural gates (at the right moment), be a
    woman?
With the white light illuminate all the areas of the [inner] space, in the not-
    knowing?[34]

So many other passages, some of which I have quoted in earlier chapters, prove that the *Tao-te ching,* as a whole, was developed in a *religious* context. We know about this context from many sources. These sources, however, have come down to us in writings that are generally from a period several centuries later than the present version of the *Tao-te ching.* This fact has prompted many scholars to consider religious Taoism as a later, bastardized development of a "pure" mystical philosophy supposed to be that of the *Tao-te ching.* The whole philosophy of this book of the Old Master—and in this respect the work is entirely different from the other classical philosophies—is borne out of the situation of the adept of the Mysteries, and of his search for Long Life: religion here precedes mysticism. Mysticism and the related philosophy of power generally advocate freeing oneself of the physical body and of its daily, functional contingencies. The chapters of the *Tao-te ching,* on the contrary, do refer to real body practices. This is shown not only in the passages I have just quoted but also in all ancient commentaries. The commentators' aim was to fill in, wherever necessary, the space left open by mysticism and politics by equating each precept with a physical technique.

Let me take, for example, an excerpt from chapter 3, which says: "It is by not exalting men of talent that we avoid jealousies among the people; by not prizing rare goods that we avoid thefts; by not showing off things that excite desire that we avoid disturbing the minds of others. Therefore, when the Sage rules the country, he empties the hearts of the people and fills their bellies, he weakens their wills and strengthens their bones; he sees that they remain without knowledge or desire."[35]

An anonymous commentator, only known by his surname as Old Man of the Riverside (Ho-shang kung; dates unknown, but undoubtedly from the Han period) explained this political message in these terms: "The Sage's rule over the country corresponds to the rule over the body; cast away desires and worries, hold fast to the Tao, embrace the One, keep the gods of the Five (Viscera). . . . By being careful with one's semen, restricting its emission, the marrow will increase and the bones will be strengthened."[36]

Another anonymous commentary, under the pseudonym of one Hsiang Erh and probably dating from the same period, remarks on the phrase "filling their bellies": "The belly is the skin of the Tao wherein all the *ch'i* must be concentrated."[37]

A third gloss on the same passage, from a work known under the title of *Analytic Explanations* (*Chieh-chieh*), states categorically: "By 'ruling the country' we must understand 'ruling the body.' 'Emptying their hearts' means for them not to have harmful thoughts, and 'filling their bellies' means for them to hold their breath and nurture their semen."[38]

These ancient commentaries have often been ridiculed as being nothing but erroneous and even absurd extrapolations. Such a negative appraisal has led many to view Taoism's philosophical thought as something quite separate from its religious practice and even to view them as two distinct historical and social realities! This opinion is nowadays so widespread that it is important to consider it here, especially since the so-called opposition of the "two Taoisms" has for a long time been an argument in the campaigns against China's own religion, with the terrible results we know.

From among all the glosses of the *Tao-te ching*—and there are several hundred—the official culture of China has retained only the "philosophical" ones. This, as we have seen, is by no means the most ancient tradition. It goes back to a commentary written by the scholar Wang Pi (226–249). As I mentioned above, this commentary was used by almost all Western translators. Wang Pi was indeed a scholar of genius who, before dying at the age of twenty-three, had not only written his famous exegesis of the *Tao-te ching*, but also an equally successful commentary on the *Book of Changes* (*I-ching*).

But Wang Pi was not a Taoist. His thinking was even quite removed from what we have come to recognize as the background of the Old Master's aphorisms, that is: the mystery-religion of ancient China. Wang Pi belongs entirely to the intellectual currents of his time which developed after the fall of the great Han empire. The Confucian orthodoxy, which had reigned supreme over the minds of the literati, was abandoned, and the disillusioned intellectuals turned, as has been the case recently in the West, to the spiritual and the mystical. They referred to this new current as the "Science of the Mystery" (*hsüan-hsüeh*).[39] The movement towards spiritual renewal was reinforced by the spread of Buddhism, whose propagation was also facilitated by the fall of the ancient order.

The ancient cosmology of the *I-ching*, along with the new Buddhist ontology (new, that is, for China), together contributed to the development of a metaphysical interpretation by Wang Pi of the *Tao-te ching*. By way of example, Wang Pi explains the famous first sentence of chapter 6, "The spirit of the valley never dies; it is called the Obscure Female," by saying: "The spirit of the valley is the Non-Being found in the center of a valley. The Non-Being has neither form, nor shadow [substance]; it conforms completely [to what surrounds it]. . . . Its form is invisible: it is the Supreme Being."

With this, we find ourselves in the midst of all possible speculations on the subject of Being, the Void, Emptiness, without ever having had that most important term "Obscure Female" properly explained. Wang Pi's commentary is equally silent about such key notions as "the teaching without words" (*Tao-te ching,* chap. 2) or "knowing the white and keeping the black" (chap. 28). Very often, his rationalizing explanations completely miss the point of the paradoxes. For example, when it comes to explaining chapter 70, "My words are very easy to understand, although no one understands them," this inability to understand is simply attributed to the bad moral disposition of "some people." In other words, Wang Pi, that brilliant scholar, does not wish to associate himself at all with those "who do not understand!"[40]

In reading Wang Pi's commentary, we see how his insistence on the "empty" nature of the Tao leads him to conceive of the Tao as a kind of god. This is especially clear in his commentary on chapter 42 ("The Tao gave birth to the One, the One to the Two, the Two to Three, . . ."), where Wang Pi simply identifies the Tao with Non-Being (*wu*): "The One comes from the Non-Being. Non-Being produced the One. One can thus say that the One is the Non-Being and that, to the extent that the Non-Being is already the One, how could it be wordless? Where there is the word, there is the being of the One." Wang Pi—this at least is clear—thinks in terms of a dualistic system, in which Being and Non-Being form two opposite poles and in which the Tao is identified with Non-Being. But, we may ask, if it was Non-Being that produced the One and the Ten Thousand Things, what has then become of the Mother, the Chaos and the Obscure Female, who, in the *Tao-te ching* represent the creative functions? They have no place in Wang Pi's system. He either does not mention them or gives completely contradictory statements. Having decided to make the Tao a *concept,* he refuses to abandon the logical structures of thought and to let himself be guided by the fundamental indefinable nature of the body in this world. Wang Pi misses the fundamental meaning of the *Tao-te ching,* and instead of clarifying the text, his commentary makes it more difficult to understand.

The philosophical speculations of this brilliant scholar did, however, greatly impress his contemporaries and gained widespread acceptance, whereas the earlier commentaries mentioned above were forgotten. For the Chinese literati, the philosophical interpretation of the *Tao-te ching* became the only acceptable one, and from then on they claimed to have the only true key to the text. This key—and here the influence of Buddhism is perceptible—is the separation between mind and body, something which was to have a marked cultural, and later also a political, backlash.[41] From then on, following Wang Pi's exegesis, the literati made the famous distinction between a "philosophical" Taoism that they claimed was noble and pure, and a "religious" Taoism that was supposedly vulgar and materialistic, that is, the Taoism of the people. The latter corresponds, actually, to that of the ancient commentaries on the *Tao-te ching* as well as to all the other traditions I have discussed here. These traditions stand condemned because of a so-called lack of philosophy. This measly quarrel is but one of the many aspects of the separation in China between the class of the literati—who call themselves Confucians (and sometimes Buddhists, or in later times, Christians or Marxists)—and the *real country*.

It is here that we find the society of the ancient commentators. Legend makes of the Old Man of the Riverside a sage who lived hidden—that is, who refused to collaborate with the government. When the Han emperor Ching (157–140 B.C.) went to visit him, he asked the sage to bow before him, being "his subject." At this, the master quickly rose up into the air and, from up there, asked: "And here, am I still your subject?" The biography of Ho-shang kung, the oldest known commentator of the *Tao-te ching*, contains little else besides this story.[42]

We know even less about the second most ancient commentary, the one known by the name Hsiang-erh. But, who was Hsiang-erh? Is this the name of a person? Some scholars think this name refers to one of the first Heavenly Masters, the leaders of the liturgical Taoism from the second century A.D. But this is not certain and I am personally inclined to date this commentary from a slightly earlier period. What is certain, however, is that it was known to—and used by—the Heavenly Master movement. And we now know to what extent the role of the Heavenly Masters was essential to the development of the liturgical tradition of Taoism. We are therefore justified in thinking that the Hsiang-erh commentary does correspond to the vision of the world inherent to this tradition.

Lack of space forbids other translations of the ancient commentaries then those given above. In short, they all emphasize that the notions of "country," "to govern," "people," and so forth, which appear in the *Tao-te ching*, must be considered as metaphors and refer in fact to the human body. The famous adage, "the human body is the image of a country," can also be turned around: the land is the image of the body.

The ancient commentaries speak about many body techniques, such as breathing exercises and sexual practices, in order fill out the abstract thought of the *Tao-te ching* with concrete elements. This physical dimension, moreover, remains constantly of central significance, as it is from this very dimension—and this is confirmed time and again by the text itself—that the political begins. In other words: it is the way of perceiving the physical body that determines the vision of the social body. The autonomy of each individual ("I alone . . .") is reflected in the unity of each village, a world closed in on itself but also a social unit, similar and equal to all other units. Together these ideal village communities are a vast network of alliances, of natural confederations, modeled on the great cosmic systems.

This form of decentralized, almost democratic, nation was the one which the liturgical movement of the Heavenly Masters always sought to create. It is thus not surprising that the *Tao-te ching*, as explained by the Hsiang-erh commentary, was their bible. It is also evident that this interpretation and use of the political thought of the Old Master was forever unacceptable to the Confucians. As a consequence, the ancient commentaries were banned. The *Tao-te ching* continued to be cited as an authority on the practice of the physical exercises of Keeping the One, as well as on the meaning of ritual.[43] It was only with the persecution of Taoism in contemporary China that the tradition of the Taoist body was destroyed and that, like Humpty-Dumpty, once fallen, "all the king's horses and all the king's men couldn't put it together again."[44]

The Fast of the Heart

The source of the Old Master's thought springs from the religion of the body. The ancient commentaries show this and, in its own way, so does Chuang Tzu.

The *Tao-te ching* sounds as a single voice, the book of Chuang Tzu ("Master Chuang") as an orchestra. An impressive sequence of pieces, now grave, now light, long improvisations, suites of themes and variations make this immortal work into a symphony and even a festival of the Taoist genius.

It is unlikely that this text, made up of thirty-three long chapters, was written by a single man, and yet the "Book of Master Chuang" is a work of personal style.[45] About the "author," virtually all we know is his name, Chuang Chou. He is supposed to have lived in North China, in the kingdom of Wei or Sung, towards the end of the fourth century B.C., and a large part of the book—though scholars are not exactly agreed on which part this is—is certainly from this same period. Chuang Tzu presents the wisdom of Lao Tzu through anecdotes and philosophical notes. The text contains many quotations also found in the *Tao-te ching*. This poses a problem of chronology. How can a text of the fourth century B.C. quote a book of the third? The truth of the matter is simple: before being included in the *Tao-te ching*, the comprehensive sum of Taoist thought, the maxims of the Old Master must have constituted an oral tradition known to the authors of Chuang Tzu. Their book is thus to some degree a commentary, before the fact, on the words and ideas found in the *Tao-te ching*.

This is confirmed in the last chapter of the book of Chuang Tzu, an epilogue of sorts, which presents different trends of thought in ancient China and their relation to Taoism. In speaking of Lao Tzu, the author quotes these words: "To know the male and yet keep the female is to become the valley of the world."[46] The passage continues by saying that those, like Lao Tzu, who know how to remain peaceful and alone "dwell with the light of the divine mind." They "possess the arts of the Tao of ancient times." The text also speaks of Chuang Tzu himself. It says that he "had heard these ideas [of Lao Tzu] and liked them. Thus it was that with bizarre, extravagant stories, words meant to provoke laughter, sentences without rules or structure, he rendered these words as they came to him, without taking sides, without any partisan viewpoint."[47] In this way, the editor of the book of Chuang Tzu defined the work, its inspiration, and its style.

Let us look at an example of how the book of Chuang Tzu elaborates on the ancient Taoist maxims. Chapter 80 of the *Tao-te ching*, quoted above, describes the primitive society "where, though there might be tools requiring ten times, even a hundred times less work, the people would not use them." This idea is illustrated by Chuang Tzu in the following story:

Tzu-kung [a disciple of Confucius] travelled south to the land of Ch'u. On his way back, he passed through Chin and along the south bank of the Han river. There he saw an old man going to plant his field. He had dug a [diagonal] tunnel to reach the water down in a well. He entered this tunnel clutching a large jug and then came out again to bring water for irrigating his field. It was a hard job which required much effort for a meager result. Tzu-kung said to the gardener: "There's a tool for this kind of work; in a day you could irrigate a hundred fields. It demands but little effort for a big result. Wouldn't you like to have one?"

The Gardener looked up and squinted at the speaker, saying: "What is it?"

"All you need is some wood with holes drilled in it and then assembled like a machine [a lever] that is heavy on one side, light on the other. By moving it up and down, you can draw up water in a constantly flowing stream. It is called a wellsweep. At these words, the gardener turned red with anger and said with a laugh: "I have heard my master say that where there are machines, there will be the problems of machines, and these problems will produce people with hearts like machines. With a heart like a machine in your breast, there will be a lacking in pure whiteness. The gods of life [of the body] will be disturbed and there will no longer be a place there for the Tao to dwell. It is not that I do not know your machine. I should be ashamed to use it!" . . .

When Tzu-kung told this story to Confucius, Confucius said: "That fellow must be one of those who follow the Arts of Sire Chaos!"[48]

In this story which Chuang Tzu invented around a Taoist precept, the thoughts of the Old Master must have been transformed into a message which appears as very real. The unbridled extension of our body's abilities, through a proliferating and almost tentacular technology, has made us aware that this technology does not always free humanity, but makes it more and more dependent on it. In Taoist terms, this means that when the force of *yang* is allowed to expand without the necessary counterweight of the regressive dynamics of *yin,* natural equilibrium is destroyed. The useful chases away what is not useful, and what Chuang Tzu calls "the great utility of the useless" is relegated to leisure activities. The fascination with unlimited knowledge makes us lose sight not only of the very real limits of human abilities, but also of the obscurity in which the sources of being lie. Yet it is from this obscurity, this not-knowing, that springs "pure whiteness," the flaming pearl of vital energy.

These themes are developed time and again in Chuang Tzu, which is more concerned with the position of the individual in the world than with the concept of the State. Freedom, the real leitmotif of the book, cannot be realized except in the individual being itself, through the return to the source, to the beginning and to the child.

The famous words of the *Tao-te ching* concerning the newborn child and the fullness of his strength are also found in the book of Chuang Tzu, in the conclusion to a story about a disciple who failed. The story sets out by presenting a certain master Keng-sang, a disciple of Lao Tzu who was unable to hide his capacities. As a result he attracted pupils, and among them even an old scholar by the name of Nan-jung Ch'u. Once the old literatus asked the master how he might practice the teachings of the Tao. Master Keng-sang answered:

> Make your body whole,
> Hold on to your vital spirits,
> Let no plans or calculations intrude on your thoughts.
> Keep this up for three years and you may attain your goal.

But Nan-jung Ch'u, not grasping what the master meant by the "whole body," asked:

> The eyes are certainly part of the body—I have never thought of them in any other way—yet blind men cannot see with them (in other words: the blind have a body but it does not allow them to see).
> The ears are part of the body—I've never known them to be otherwise—yet deaf men cannot hear.
> The heart [seat of the intellect] is part of the body—I've never thought of it any other way—yet fools cannot use theirs.
> So the body and the body must also be very close [i.e., the body of the senses, which perceives and thinks, and the whole body, to which the master refers, must belong together]. But hasn't something come between them? Is that why the two seek each other without finding each other [in vain the senses seek one's real body]? You are telling me to make my body whole, to hold fast my vital spirits, to let no plans or calculations intrude on my thoughts, but these words go no farther than my ears!

Master Keng-sang had no reply to this and suggested that Nan-jung Ch'u go and see Lao Tzu, who lived in the wild regions of the South. The old scholar set off and was so eager to reach his goal that he walked for seven days and seven nights, without stopping, until he arrived.

When Lao Tzu saw him appear, he said to him: "You've come from master Keng-sang, haven't you?"

"Yes," answered Nan-jung Ch'u.

"Why then bring this crowd with you?"

Nan-jung Ch'u looked around in alarm but saw nobody.

"You do not understand what I mean [that you have come here with a crowd of problems and ready-made ideas, instead of coming "empty," after a purifying fast]," said Lao Tzu.

Contrite, Nan-yung Ch'u looked down and sighed: "Since I've answered poorly, I surely no longer have the right to ask you my question . . . ?"

"What question?" asked Lao Tzu.

"If I keep myself ignorant [that is: "pure"], the others call me stupid.

If I am full of knowledge, I injure my body. If I am not charitable, I injure others; if I am, I injure myself. Without justice, I harm others; full of justice, I bring affliction to myself. How do I get out of this dilemma? I have come walking all this way to ask your advice."

Lao Tzu understood in what a poor state his confused guest was: "You are like someone who has lost his parents and now looks for them with a pole in the middle of the ocean." Then he allowed him to stay at his home, and advised him to think only of the things he liked and not to let any unpleasant thoughts intrude on him. But Nan-yung Ch'u was unable to follow this rule, however simple. At the end of ten days, he gave up this mental discipline and asked Lao Tzu to "simply teach him the basic rules for keeping oneself in good health."

"The rules for preserving good health? Here they are," said Lao Tzu. "Can you Keep the One? Never lose it? Know good and bad fortune without divination? Stop? End? Leave others alone and seek it in yourself? Can you be without ties? Follow quietly? Can you be as a child, like an infant? The newborn cries all day long without getting hoarse, and that is the perfection of harmony [*Tao-te ching,* chap. 55]. It will clench its fists all day, without holding a thing, and that is the ultimate in strength. It will gaze all day long without moving its eyes, for nothing outside interests it. It progresses without knowing where, it rests without knowing what it does. It unconsciously mingles with all things, adapting itself to the pulse [of life]. These are the basic rules for preserving good health."

"Such a person must have the force of an exceptional being!"

"No," said Lao Tzu. "That is only the beginning, the first thaw. Can you do it? Afterwards, to become a superior human being, you should join with others to share the food of the Earth, and mingle with others to find the happiness of Heaven, having no relations based on profit and loss, no rivalries . . . These too are fundamental rules for keeping in good health."

"Is that all?" asked the disciple.

"Not yet," said Lao Tzu. I will ask you once more: Can you be as a child, a newborn who moves without knowing what it does, who moves without knowing where it goes? Its body is like dried-out wood, its heart like dead ashes. Thus, no good or evil fortune can touch it. What human suffering—insensitive as the Infant is to whatever reversals of fortune there may be—would it endure?[49]

We see that Lao Tzu answers here, indirectly, the question the old scholar had put to master Keng-sang earlier (i.e., "The body and the body must be very close, but hasn't something come between them? How does one find the body with the body?"). The solution lies in Keeping the One. The real body corresponds to that of a child, but a child about whom it is said, surprisingly: "Its body is like dried-out wood, its heart like dead ashes." Images of old age and death!

This bold juxtaposition of figures—of a newborn child and an old, dying person—is full of meaning. We recognize the image of the Old Child, but the expression "body like dead wood, heart like dead ashes" also describes the physical appearance of someone lost in trance, making a spiritual journey. In chapter 7 we saw Lao Tzu meditating and Confucius saying: "Dare I believe my eyes? A moment ago, master, your body seemed *dried-out as dead wood,* as if you had abandoned all things and left the world of men for solitude!" Lao-tan replied: "I let my heart revel [in the realm] where [all] things had their beginning." One may harrow one's mind, yet remain unable to understand; open one's mouth, yet be unable to express what [this experience] means."

Elsewhere in Chuang Tzu, there is a story about two sages, Nieh-chüeh (Toothless) and P'i-i (Shabbily-Dressed). It begins with P'i-i saying to Nieh-chüeh:

Set your body straight [and pure],
See everything as one,
And natural harmony will be with you.
Bundle your knowledge,
Unify your behavior [the same in all situations],
and the gods will dwell within you.
Virtue will be your beauty,
The Tao your dwelling,
And, stupid as a newborn calf,
You will never ask "why"!

He had not yet finished speaking when Nieh-chüeh fell asleep. Much pleased, P'i-i went away singing:

Body of dry bones,
Heart of dead ashes!
How true, his real knowledge;
He no longer seeks to know the causes.
Obscure! Obscure! Dark! Dark!
He does not think any more,
You cannot speak with him.
What a person is he![50]

This final exclamation reminds us of Chuang Tzu speaking about the immortals of Ku-yeh (see above, chaps. 1 and 9): "These men!" The human being who renounces intelligence and discernment, who follows the "fast of the heart," as Chuang Tzu calls it, begins a process of transformation. He reaches *beyond* concepts; he *survives* the breakdown of values.

Both for Chuang Tzu and for the *Tao-te ching,* to grasp the relativity of all established ideas and judgments of value is the first step in the search for freedom. Chuang Tzu begins his book with a description of fabulous and mythical beings, an enormous bird and a gigantic fish. Despite their strength, they are both dependent on exceptional circumstances—a strong wind for the bird, a very deep sea for the fish—before they can move around freely. Their situation is ultimately less ideal than that of the sparrow or the cicada who take up less space and are thus everywhere at home. Likewise, a magician who can ride about on the wind is not really a free being since he always needs a small breeze to carry him. Chuang Tzu concludes: "If only he knew how to mount the regulating [energies] of Heaven and Earth and ride the Six *Ch'i* [see above, chap. 8] so as to wander in that which is without end, then he would no longer need any *support.*"[51] In this way, Chuang Tzu shows how myths can be surpassed.

Another important theme is the relativity of time. How long does a fly live? A lifetime. And P'eng-tsu, the oldest man in the world? Also a lifetime. It is all the same and it is no use to make any distinctions. The arbitrary side of our preferences, desires, tastes, codes of behavior and social status allows Chuang Tzu to show his gift for satire:

To tire out one's divine spirit (*shen-ming*) in the search for Unity, while ignoring that it is all the same, is called "three in the morning." What does this mean? Once there was a keeper of monkeys who fed them chestnuts. He told them: You'll have three in the morning, four in the evening. The monkeys were furious. All right, said the keeper, then you'll four in the morning and three in the evening. The monkeys were content.[52]

The point that Chuang Tzu makes here is that it is impossible to find the absolute in the mind.

Freedom from the constraints of concepts is what Lao Tzu called "the thaw." But this is just a first step. The fourth chapter of the book of Chuang Tzu is called "In the Human World," and it contains a long passage on the life of the individual in society. Here the role of initiator falls not to Lao Tzu but to Confucius, a wise Confucius who has drawn the inevitable lesson from a political career full of failures. His favorite disciple, Yen Hui, is about to make the same mistakes as the master had in his youth. Yen Hui has heard of a tyrannical, perverse prince and wants to convert him to the principles of Benevolence and Justice (that is to say, Confucianism).

"You will only succeed in getting yourself killed," Confucius says to him. "Trying to convince people by getting mixed up in their affairs is not only dangerous, it requires that you make of your mind your master, which is contrary to the nature of things." Now Yen Hui no longer knows what to do. The sage then recommends that he fast (*chai*), to which Yen Hui replies: "My family is poor. For several months now I have had neither wine nor strong vegetables. Do I not fast enough already?"

"You are talking about the fast for a sacrifice, said Confucius, not the fast of the heart [the mind]."

"What then is this fast of the heart?" asks Yen Hui.

"Concentrate your will. Do not listen with your ears, but with your heart. Do not listen with your heart, but with your *ch'i*. . . . The *ch'i* are 'empty' and thus responsive to all beings. The Tao is found in that 'void' and that 'void' is the 'fast of the heart.' "

"A while ago, when you spoke to me," says the disciple, "I was still certain of me being Yen Hui. Now, there is no more Yen Hui. Is that the 'void'?"

"Yes," answers Confucius,

Without gate,
Without traces,
Your dwelling has become one,
You stick to the inevitable,
Then you will be close to it!
Not to walk is easy,
To walk without leaving a trace is harder!
Acting for others is easy,
To act in accordance with your nature is harder!
To fly with wings is one thing,
To know how to fly without wings is another!
There are many who seek knowledge with their minds,
Few are those who come to knowledge by non-knowledge.
Look! That dark space;
In the empty room a whiteness shines!
Happiness is there where all movement comes to an end.
Those who do not know how to stop,
Even when seated, continue to run around.

When hearing and vision communicate with the inside,
And mind and knowledge are banished to the outside,
The gods will come to dwell within you;
And human beings even more so!
This is called the transformation of the Ten Thousand Things.[53]

The term *dark space* in the text is written with a very rare character, which may mean "a well" or "a pool." This is the place of blackness from which, in the empty chamber of the heart, a white light shines. The same idea is expressed in a well-known passage of the *Tao-te ching:* "Know the white and keep the black: this is to be the valley of the world." This valley is the place where everything converges, where all is transformed.

Chuang Tzu translates this, in his own way, into an allegory:

Bright Light asked Non-Being: "Are you there or not?" Getting no answer, Bright Light looked carefully at the form [of the other]: nothing but dark emptiness! It looked all day without seeing anything, listened without hearing it, groped for it but could not seize it. Finally, Bright Light said: "This is the limit! Who can attain this? I can grasp Non-Being, but never will I be able to get at the Non-Being of Non-Being. This way he has of being the Being of Non-Being! Where does he come from to arrive at this?"[54]

"To sit and forget" (as opposed to being seated and continuing to run about) is the beginning of the fast of the heart. As we have seen, this fast must then be continued in daily life when one "joins with others to share the food of the Earth and the happiness of Heaven." The fast of the heart is a purification of the mind. It is performed as a rite. There is no mythology on this subject.

Bright light—the pure whiteness of which the gardener spoke, and the flaming pearl of the Great Master—is a phenomenon well known to mystics everywhere in the world and can be experienced by anyone who has seriously practiced meditation, yoga, *t'ai-chi ch'üan* or other techniques. In certain religions, the appearance of this light is considered to confer a state of grace or is seen as an illumination (*satori*). But Taoism does not attach the same importance to it and always locates it in relation to *something else*. For Taoism, the importance lies in the question: "And then?" As we saw in the story of Nan-jung Ch'u, spiritual purification is only the first stage among the "rules for preserving good health" and, if this "good health" seems to the old hero of the story only a last resort after his spiritual quest has failed ("I will content myself, for lack of anything better, with keeping my health"), it is the opposite for Lao Tzu: good health is one of the the highest goals of human life. The appearance of the white light is just the *sign* that all is well within, that all calculating thoughts have vanished; in itself, this sign has no spiritual value, and one certainly must not try to use it.

To "know the white" is a form of non-knowledge. All colors are contained in white, all opposition is abolished. This comes *first,* as a preliminary to the physical state of "keeping the black." The light—the spiritual mirror—is but an emanation from the source of our being, and thanks to this light we can pierce the darkness of chaos. "Keeping the black," which comes *after* illumination, is "nurturing what knowledge is not able to know," that is, the other, the true body.

The flaming pearl is an emblem which, in liturgy, is tied to the *name* of the master because the flame-shaped pin is given to him on his ordination, when he receives a new name. Similarly, the being of light, the One, constitutes the first of all the phenomena (*wu:* "things," "beings"). The One is only a passageway, a gate between the Ten Thousand Things and Anterior Heaven.

Let me emphasize once more that this obscurity, this unknowable from which the being of light emerges, is not the Tao. The dark, unfathomable dimension is considered to be the place where "the Tao resides"; it is perhaps even the privileged modality. But the attributes of "darkness" are not necessarily those of the Tao. The Tao is not just ineffable, mysterious, obscure—terms that would necessarily lead to a conception of the Tao as a spiritual force. The Tao is beyond duality and cannot be defined through oppositions like: expressible-inexpressible, systematic-chaotic. But to the extent that it does lie in the "permanent," it remains unknown and unknowable, like the body in which we live and which we nourish.

This not-thought-about body is substance, organic and living stuff, which is born, which grows, ages, and dies without our mind or understanding playing any essential role. The mind can, however, cause the organism to break down, destroy its spontaneous order. But it cannot perfect it, make it more *true* (*chen*) than it is. The white light comes from the purification of the mind; it is not the manifestation of the mind. It is only the spontaneous emanation of our vital strength, of the Original *Ch'i*. As a *sign* (*fu,* tessera), this light is the proof of total communication, the testament of the teaching without words.

One can go no further than to know that Heaven [nature] *is,* to know that the human being *is.* One cannot go further. What is Heaven? That which lets live.

What is the human being? To know what one knows, to nourish what our knowledge cannot know [the body], and thus complete the years of Heaven [conferred by destiny], without dying a premature death midway. This is the highest knowledge.

But there remains a problem, for our knowledge needs some kind of *support* [just as mythological creatures and magicians need the wind to be able to fly] in order to apply itself to something; and this support is never fixed and set. How are we then to be certain when [things are differentiated and that] what I call Heaven is not the human being, or what I call the human being is not Heaven? One must be a True Person (*chen-jen*) before having this true knowledge. What is the True Person? The True Person of ancient times . . . could enter water without getting wet, go through fire without being burned. . . . His breathing was deep! Deep! The True Person breathes through his heels, while ordinary men breathe only through the throat; humiliated (by endless debate), they vomit their words as though something were caught in their throats.[55]

Chuang Tzu does not fall into the trap of his own words. He does not attempt to denigrate the words of "ordinary men" in order to justify his own. Words, even those of the sage, mean nothing. "Those who know do not speak; those who speak do not know. The sage propagates a teaching without words."[56] Truth is not expressed in words or in silence. The highest discussion ignores them both. The speech of the sage is like the sound of a brook.

Do I say something? What I am saying surely must correspond to something. . . . Let me try: There is a beginning. And there is the beginning that has not yet begun. And there is the beginning that has not yet begun to begin.

Then there is being. And there is non-being. And not-yet-begun non-being. And the not-yet-begun of the again not-yet-begun of there being non-being. And suddenly, here is the being of non-being. But now I still do not know what this being and non-being do in fact consist of.

I have now just said something. But still I do not know if what I have said really means anything or not.[57]

All systems of thought only refer to themselves. They are worthless so long as they rest on what Chuang Tzu calls "a fixed support," that is: crutches. Their concepts prevent us from becoming conscious of the true body. This is the conclusion that appears at the end of a long story in the book of Chuang Tzu, a story which contains a great many of the themes encountered above, and which therefore can be seen as a kind of summing up of the previous arguments.

In the land of Cheng there was a shaman of the gods whose name was Chi-hsien. He could foretell a person's birth, death, destiny, fortune, or longevity, giving the person the exact date, to within a day, as if he were a god himself. Whenever they saw him coming along, the people of Cheng would leave their work and run away.[58] But Lieh Tzu[59] went to see him and his heart became as if drunken.[60] He returned home and spoke to his master Hu Tzu (Master Gourd) about him and said: "Master, I used to think your Tao was the best. But there I have found yet a better one!"[61]

Hu Tzu said to him: "Up to now I have given you only the outer appearance, not the real thing. Can you really say that you have obtained the Tao? Where there are only roosters and no hen, how can there be any eggs? By trying to measure your own Tao with that of the world, you have confronted it, which has enabled [the other] to get a hod on you and analyze you. Just try to bring (this shaman) here and show him to me."

The next day, Lieh Tzu and the shaman came to see master Hu Tzu. On leaving, the shaman said to Lieh Tzu: "Ah! Your master is a dead person! He will not live. He only has ten days or so left. I saw in him something strange, like dead ashes!"

Lieh Tzu went back in, crying so much that he soaked his sleeves, and told Hu Tzu everything. Hu Tzu said to him: "Just now I showed him the signs of the Earth, the sprouts. They are silent, but without being completely inert. It was that Modality of Hidden Power of mind that he must have perceived. Try to get him to come again."

The next day, Lieh Tzu and the shaman came a second time. On leaving, the shaman said: "Lucky your master has met me! He is already much better. He is full of life. I was able to see his hidden strength." When Lieh Tzu reported these words, Hu Tzu said: "I have just shown him the effect of Heaven on the Earth, a state in which there is neither name nor substance and in which the cycle rises from the heels.[62] He must have seen this Modality of Blessing of mine. Try to get him to come again."

The next day, Lieh Tzu and the shaman came [a third time]. On leaving, the shaman said: "Your master is not balanced. I cannot get hold of him to analyze him. Tell him to contain himself a little more, and I will analyze him again!" When Lieh Tzu had reported these words, Hu Tzu said: "I have just shown him the Great Center where nothing outweighs anything else. He must have seen my Modality of the Balance of *Ch'i*. There is a depth of swirling waters; there is a depth of calm water; there is a depth or running water. The depth has nine names.[63] The three [I have just mentioned] manifested themselves. Try to have [the shaman] come again."

The next day, Lieh Tzu and the shaman came [a fourth time]. They hadn't finished greeting each other when [the shaman] took off running. Hu Tzu said: "Catch him!" Lieh Tzu ran after him but wasn't able to catch him. He came back and said to Hu Tzu: "He has disappeared completely; I can't find him." Hu Tzu said: "Just now, I showed him the 'what-has-not-yet-emerged-from-the-ancestor.' I have myself to him empty and all mixed together, unconscious of anyone or anything; from there came a return and then something like a big wave. That was what made him flee."

Following these events, Lieh Tzu realized that he had not yet begun to learn. He returned home and for three years did not go out. He took his wife's place in the kitchen and fed the pigs in the same way he fed humans. He kept aloof from business concerns. He lost his polished appearance and returned to a state of uncarved simplicity. Like a clump of earth, he stood alone in his body. In the middle of the fragmentation [of the world], he kept himself sealed up, all One, till the end of his days.[64]

Four times the shaman measures himself against the Taoist. The story tells nothing about what they say to each other when they meet. Between the two masters, nothing of importance is communicated with *words*. The shaman, a great miracle worker, examines the body of Hu Tzu, "master-Gourd." In four days he is allowed to see four aspects of this body and all four are difficult to express in language.

It begins with *yin,* the first phase of the Fast of the Heart, which takes the form of complete ataraxia. Wet, burnt out ashes convey an image of death. The shaman, who can only see what the body "shows" him, is caught in the trap of the external aspect of things.

The second modality is that of nascent *yang,* the conception which is the result of the interaction of Heaven and Earth. The third modality is that of pregnancy, the transformation of the One. One is also the number symbolizing water and the text recalls here the Nine Depths and their successive alternations.

The three modalities are thus: *yin, yang,* and the fusion of the two into the One. Each time, the shaman takes them for localized symptoms, and his deductions, full of self-assurance ("It is fortunate that your master has met me!"), make us smile.

The fourth meeting is different. It is no longer a question of "modality"; we are confronted with the regression, with the vision of Chaos. There is at first a void, an indistinct swarming, and then something like a turning around and finally a wave rushing out to sweep away everything in its path.

Daily Life

The good people of Cheng flee as soon as they see the shaman coming. And he, in turn, flees at the sight of the work of the Tao. At the end of the story the circle is completed, when the Taoist adept returns amidst the people. Lieh Tzu understands that *"he had not yet begun to learn."* If we compare this expression with the passage quoted above on "what has not yet begun," we see that the real meaning here is: study with master Gourd concerns the domain of the "not yet begun"; in other words, Anterior Heaven, the pure, the closed in-on-itself to which the mind has no access. Lieh Tzu realizes that what he has to learn is precisely that which is buried deepest within himself, that which he carries within his body, and which he has always known without realizing it. In fact—that is to say *in truth*—he knows everything, for he has understood that he had not yet "learned." How fortunate to have a master Gourd who keeps you from learning and makes you go back towards what you already know!

Lieh Tzu goes to live the life of women. He cooks, feeds his small world, and looks after the daily life. All that is far more difficult and more essential than to concern oneself with the exceptional and the sensational. As a sage remarked so aptly on the subject of the "mastery of life": "When a traveller is killed on the road, people warn each other and do not venture outside their village without a good escort. This is very wise, of course. But what everyone should really concern himself with—namely, what happens in bed and at mealtime—is precisely what they are ignorant of, for which the do not know the precautions to take! What a mistake!"[65]

Those who do not know how to manage daily life, says Chuang Tzu, remind us of the hermit who led a saintly life in the mountains. At the age of seventy he still looked like a young person. But, unfortunately, one day he came upon a hungry tiger who ate him up. That brave hermit! He was so preoccupied with his inner being that he let the tiger eat his physical body![66] Both have to be taken care of.

After the "thaw," having unlearned our systems and judgments of value, one ought, says Chuang Tzu, to ally *with others* to find one's food from the Earth, one's joy in Heaven, keeping away from the rivalries, living in the middle of world and accepting the inevitable. Lieh Tzu is described as indifferent, as closed in on himself, like a lump of earth. "What a person that is!" Is he still a human being?

The philosopher Hui Tzu was an opponent, but also a good friend of Chuang Tzu. One day, Hui Tzu asked: "Can a human being really be without feelings?"

"Of course," answered Chuang Tzu.

"But a being without feelings, how can you call him human?"

"The Tao gave him his appearance, Nature his body; why then not give him this name?"

"To say that he is a human being, doesn't that imply that he has [human] feelings?"

"We are not speaking of the same thing," said Chuang Tzu. "When I say "without feelings," I mean that he doesn't let his tastes, his passions harm his body. He adapts and transforms himself according to how things are ["spontaneous," *tzu-jan*] and does not try to "add to life."

"How can he be himself if he does not add something to [naked] life?"

"The Tao gave him his appearance, Nature his body; he doesn't let his feelings undermine his body. That's all! Whereas you, you pull out your mind and tire your vital essences. You lean against a tree to recite texts and you fall asleep on your lute! You use the body Heaven gave you to hold forth on 'the hard and the white'!"[67]

Too often men define their personalities by their tastes. They are wont to say "I don't like this and I like that," so as to set themselves apart and to try to maintain a semblance of individuality. But this way of choosing, of cutting up existence into pieces, and using one's body in the search for some hypothetical satisfaction is fatal. This striving to "add something to life" reminds us of the proverbial farmer who started pulling on rice shoots to make them grow faster. All it brought them was death. There is no recipe for finding happiness and all teachings and precepts that say otherwise are falsehoods.

But isn't the person without feeling—or rather, without distinctive characteristics—a dangerous being? In the image of the True Person of Chuang Tzu, one could see the shadow of a mechanical, conformist, even fascist humanity. Indeed, this is not an imaginary danger, for it is true that Legalism (*fa-chia*), a current of thought in ancient China that produced the theoreticians of the totalitarian state, borrowed much from the Taoists in order to develop their plan for an inhuman, bureaucratic society. But it would be unjust to accuse Taoism of being at the origin of this monstrous deviation of its ideas. Chuang Tzu's True Person does have a conscience, something which is shown not only in his profound respect for nature and for all that lives, but also in the notion of "not-being-useful," that is: the refusal *to be used* for something. How many stories there are about old trees which, because their wood could no longer be used for anything, were spared by the woodcutters, or which, because of their venerable age, became objects of worship: a useless thing in itself but which protected them from being used as fuel. Their uselessness was finally very useful to them; this, says Chuang Tzu, is the great usefulness of the useless!

Not to be used *for* anything, not to use one's body for any particular aim: Chuang Tzu reminds us of what we have always known deep within ourselves, that one must know how to live alone in order to be able to survive among others. The desire to get involved with others and influence them betrays an imbalance in ourselves. The third chapter of the book of Chuang Tzu on the "Principle for Nourishing Life" begins this way:

Life has limits, whereas knowledge has no limits. To pursue what is limitless with what is limited is dangerous. Thus, to act according to knowledge brings disaster. Whatever one does, good or evil, one must keep away form fame as well as from condemnation. Take your spinal column as your regulating principle and you will preserve your body, make your vitality complete, nourish your kin, and complete the years [of your destiny].[68]

The phrase "take your spinal column as your regulating principle" is a free translation. The text says literally: "Follow the regulator and make it a rule of behavior." The word "regulator" can also have the meanings of "controller" and "assembler." But this same word has a special meaning as well since it is used as the name for the body's principal energy channel, the *tu-mai,* the central (and "empty") *ch'i* duct linking the upper and lower regions of our organism. This channel is located in the spinal column.

Kuo Hsiang, the classical commentator of the book of Chuang Tzu, explains the word "regulator" as "center" ("Follow the empty center as a rule of conduct"), but this abstract interpretation appears to be derived from the concrete meaning of "energy channel of control." Our proper domain, our inner and independent country, should indeed take as its central axis this channel which connects the different levels of our body. Concentrating and regulating our own energies (*ch'i*) enables us, like Lieh Tzu, to stand up and remain upright in ourselves, instead of having to lean against trees or on the crutches of systems and religious doctrines concocted by men, as does the intellectual Hui Tzu. Only by remaining independent, following the natural action of the spinal column, regulator of our vital energies, can we attain the goal of life: complete our share of years, nourish our kin.

Who exactly are these "kin" (Chinese: *ch'in*)? The first meaning that comes to mind is that of "family members," in particular the parents whom each individual is required by traditional Chinese morality to take care of. This is indeed the meaning usually given by the commentaries. But this idea would seem rather out of place in the context of the passage I have just translated. It is possible that the word *kin* does have another meaning here. In the second chapter of Chuang Tzu, titled "Discourse on the Equality of Things," we find the following passage:

The one hundred joints, the nine openings, the six receptacles, are all united and present [here in my body]. To which of these am I *closest* [same word in Chinese as "kin"]? Ought I to love them all the same? Or should some of them be especially dear to me? Are they all my servants? But then, not one of them commands another? Are they by turns master and servant? Does there exist among them a True Lord? Whatever the case, whether I seek and find the identity [of this True Lord] or not, it will neither increase nor diminish in any way his being *true*.[69]

The expression *kin* ("closest") can thus be applied to the organs of the body, organized according to a principle independent of the mind; Whether or not we are able to perceive it, this principle "truly" is. And our parents? Doesn't their presence in our existence belong to a similar, unknowable proximity? It is very possible that, from the perspective of Chuang Tzu, parents and organs of the body cover a similar immediate reality. Is it not true that, in the inner landscape, father and mother dwell in the kidneys? In other words: the free human being carries his heredity—his kinship and the family organization of which he is a part— within his own body. He looks after them by trusting the regulating principle of the energy channel of his spinal column, the pillar of his body, which enables him to stand upright and alone within his own vital space.

A partial and incomplete view of the body entails prejudiced feelings and an imbalance that destroys the harmonious vision of the world. The obstacles in inner communications result in incorrect perceptions, inhibitions of all kinds, and, finally, the irremediable loss of liberty. Chuang Tzu illustrates this state with a terrible image:

Having given birth in the middle of the night, the leper woman hastened to find a torch so that she could see her child, trembling for fear that it might resemble her! [70]

Only the Fast of the Heart can remove the obstacles (the "things") between the real body and conscious perception, and reestablish the unity between the interior and the exterior. Then all talk becomes superfluous. Our desire to talk—so long as it is not a ritual form of pure expression, like the words of the sage which are similar to the sound of a brook—is only due to the desperate desire to fill the gap between the perceived body and the real body. This calls to mind Lao Tzu's warning to the old scholar Nan-jung Ch'u: "You are like someone who has lost his parents and looks for them with a pole in the middle of the ocean!"

One day, Chuang Tzu and his friend the philosopher Hui Tzu were walking over a bridge of a stream. They saw some fish swimming. Chuang Tzu said: "To swim freely as they are doing is the joy of fish."

"You are not a fish," said Hui Tzu. "How do you know the joy of fish?"

"You are not me," answered Chuang Tzu. "How do you know that I do not know the joy of fish?"

"I am not you; it is therefore true that I cannot know what you know. But, [by the same reasoning] you are not a fish, and therefore you cannot know what makes the joy of fish!"

Chuang Tzu said: "Let's go back to the beginning, shall we? You were saying: '*How* can you know the joy of fish?' In other words, you already knew that I knew when you asked me that question. And I knew it when I stood here, on this bridge over the stream." [71]

Chuang Tzu is not an idealist. The Fast of the Heart does not improve the world as it is, but simply helps us to get rid of the obstacles that we ourselves put across the paths of freedom. As for the rest, we can only adapt to the inevitable, for there is no recipe for happiness. The true "art of the Tao" cannot be transmitted by precepts or sermons. The artisans, ordinary people, whom Chuang Tzu introduces to us, all say the same thing: the true craft, the hand of the master, the skill that enables one to make a perfect piece, is not passed on by word of mouth, still less in written form. It can be acquired only through long practice.

Duke Huan sat in his hall, reading out loud. Downstairs [in the courtyard] stood Pien the wheelwright, making a wheel. He put down his work and went up to ask the duke: "May I ask what are you reading there?"
"The words of the sages," answered the duke.
"Living sages?"
"No, these have died."
"So, what you are reading is just the refuse of men of former times?"
"What! A wheelwright ventures to judge what his prince is reading? Explain yourself or I will have your life!"
Pien the wheelwright said: "I look at this from the point of view of my craft. In making a wheel, if I go at it too carefully, it won't be round; if I go too fast, it won't be the right size. Neither too carefully, nor too fast; my hand knows how to do it in harmony with my heart [mind], but my mouth cannot explain how this is done. Between [the word and the gesture] there is an enormous distance. I cannot even instruct my own son [in my art], nor is he able to learn it from me. That is why at seventy I am still obliged to make wheels for carts. And this is also so for [the arts] of men of yesterday, [all the more so] now that they are dead. It is for this reason that what you are reading, lord, is nothing but refuse."[72]

Elsewhere in the book of Chuang Tzu, a butcher explains his art: In the beginning he concentrated on the object of his work to the point that all he saw were animals to cut up. At first he saw the animal as a whole, but after three years, he was able to see the innermost structures so well that when he cut into the animal his knife met no resistance and therefore was never blunted.[73]

This lesson teaches how "to nurture life," says Chuang Tzu. He who wishes to learn the art of the Tao must do as these craftsmen. Their approach is entirely concrete and practical: by concentrating and working on it day after day, we learn to hold our body in our grasp and not to use out our mind more then necessary. Knots come undone, barriers fall, the stream of energies flows freely and nature is rediscovered. Paradoxically, this spontaneity is the fruit of long, honest, and dedicated efforts, of ritual and rhythmical repetition of the same gestures, the same procedures. No discourse or sermon can take the place of this process of transformation.

Again, we see here the cultivation of self, *hsiu-yang*—"arranging and nourishing"—which I spoke about in chapter 3 with respect to the notion of the godhead. The practice of calligraphy offers one of the best examples of this daily training, gestures repeated a thousand times that lead to eventual mastery and enable one to create perfect forms without any apparent effort.

The same holds true for life itself. Our whole existence is nothing but a long apprenticeship to enable us to survive the disasters that come either from without or within us, until the quiet hours of the evening, the sunset, and the good death, for which, during this whole long life, we have been secretly prepared through the *return* within the advancing of time.

Thus, the goal is to enjoy "good health," so as to be able to live fully to and through this wonderful old age. Yet the masters of *T'ai-chi ch'üan,* that slow and soft form of martial art, warn their disciples against the tendency to mistake the sense of utter well-being they obtain from regular practice of this salutary form of exercise for the achievement of their goal. This satisfaction may be purely artificial and a source of error. Like the Fast of the Heart, practicing the martial arts is not just a pleasure; it should also remain a discipline, a daily, preliminary set of healthful practices to help one meet the inevitable. The same holds true, as we have seen, for the practices of "Keeping the One." Mediation on the inner landscape, described in the *Book of the Yellow Court,* long vigils of fasting, and psychosomatic exercises are a means for overcoming periods of crisis. For remaining alert, master of oneself, upright and lucid—to enter life with a firm step and to leave it with an equally firm step. All this contributes to making us—as much as possible—the artisans of our own destiny.

By referring constantly to the dimension of daily life, Chuang Tzu shows us the outcome of the many paths of Taoism. "Who can *join* with others without joining with *others?* Who can do something *with others* without *doing* something with others?" So as to follow the world in its daily course, he tells us: "To become a complete human being, one must join with others to find his nourishment from the Earth, mingle with others to find his joy in Heaven." Here we find again the rhythm of the seasons, the nutritional diet, the calendar of festivals of everyday religion see above, (see above, chap. 2). The alternation of *yin* and *yang,* the cycles of time and the systems of correspondence that are the very core of all Taoist practices—be they liturgy, physical exercise, or alchemical research—are also the foundation of our daily life. To follow nature, to become one with it, can one skip a single day?

It is in ordinary daily life that the harmony with cosmic rhythm becomes effective. The return to the source brings us back to the life at home and taking care of our kin. The perfect regularity required for the realization of Non-Action must take into account the phases of the physical body as well as those of the social body. Then the recovered equilibrium, in harmony with the current of time, will restore in us the silence, the "pure whiteness." In the midst of a word advancing towards death, a return is accomplished, a swerving towards *the other time*.

"The great perfection is like a defect," says the *Tao-te ching*. The mastery of time which belongs to him who knows how to shape his destiny allows him to find within himself the flow and drive of eternity. The passage through the break in the system, so simple and natural, follows no formula, no doctrine, no recipe, and requires nothing more than to live along with the times, whole, closed, sealed, and complete as a lump of earth, joining with others to seek our earthly foods and celestial joys.

When festivals are held to celebrate this joy, children gather at the local temple to sing ancient ballads. They sing the songs of the four seasons, of sowing and reaping, and of the hours of day and night. The repertoire invariably incudes a piece about the ten moons of pregnancy. It sings the transformations of the embryo and the food eaten by the pregnant mother. In the midst of this festival that marks the passing time, this song recalls that other time, the total, regressive time of the mother and her child in which the life of the world is transformed and renewed.

This is what must have inspired Chuang Tzu to describe Taoism as a religion without doctrine, without dogma or institutions, whose transmission is not inscribed in the history of the world. For him, the history of Taoism belongs to the *other time* and models itself—not surprisingly—on the phases of the mutation of the One, the nine transformations of the embryo in the womb, the successive stages of the cycle that go from the invisible to the visible, which he describes, of course, in *reverse* order.

It was Nü-chü, the woman-with-the-bump, who told this story of transformation: When asked, "Where did you hear about the Tao?" she replied:

I heard it from the descendant of Calligraphy,
Who had it from the child of Repeated Recitation,
Who in turn knew it from Vision of Light;

Vision of Light had it from Whispered Instructions,
Who in turn had gotten it from Hard Apprenticeship;
Hard Apprenticeship from Popular Song,
Popular Song from Obscurity,
Obscurity from Three-Void,
Who heard it from:
Perhaps a Beginning? [74]

Notes

1: Taoism

1. *Chuang-tzu,* chap. 6, p. 258. For a discussion of this book from the fourth century B.C., see "The Fast of the Heart" in chapter 10. The book *Chuang-tzu* is attributed to "master Chuang," Chuang Tzu, whose personal name was Chou. Very little else is known of him. It is most unlikely that the entire work in thirty-three chapters, bearing his name, is really his work. In general, only the first seven chapters (the so-called "Inner Chapters") are considered to be by Chuang Tzu himself, whereas the remaining twenty-six chapters must have been written later by his followers.

In keeping with Chinese tradition, and also for reasons of convenience, I will refer throughout to "Chuang Tzu" as the author of the entire work.

2. About this sentence, Ch'eng Hsüan-ying, a commentator of the book of Chuang Tzu from the sixth century, says: "like the members of a single body." (*Chuang-tzu,* chap. 6, p. 265.) See also the bibliography in this volume.

3. *Chuang-tzu,* 6 (*Chuang-tzu chi-shih,* p. 264).

4. Marcel Granet, 1934, p. 586.

5. The discussion here concerns the Tao as a religious and mystical concept. Other schools of thought in ancient China also spoke of the Tao, but for them it had a different meaning corresponding to a principle of order, a law, and *a doctrine*.

6. *Tao-te ching,* chap. 42. For the history of this work, see my discussion in chapter 10.

7. *Lao* means "old." *Tzu* has two meanings: "child" and "master philosopher." This double meaning was not, originally, a semantic pun, but it does play an important part in the myth of Lao Tzu's birth (see chap. 7).

8. In his "biography" of Lao Tzu, the great historiographer Ssu-ma Ch'ien (145–90 B.C.) admits that he was unable to separate myth from fact. See "Birth" in chapter 7.

9. In ancient China, as in China today, there existed shamanistic cults similar in type to those of today's Central Asia, Mongolia, and Siberia. In China, however, the practice of ecstasy and trance as part of religious services has a far wider scope and is used in ancestor worship and divination. Taoist practice has many forms of trance but Taoism does not admit possession by "external" spirits.

10. This mythical mountain (sometimes written Ku-shih) is also described in ancient mythology as being hollow in the center and having nine grottoes. This image recalls the mountain-shaped incense burners.

11. *Chuang-tzu,* chap. 1, p. 28.

12. Liu Hsiang (77–6 B.C.) has left us the following "Inscription on an incense burner":

> How elegant, this standing object, in the shape of a steep mountain!
> At the top it resembles the Hua-shan [a sacred mountain],
> At the bottom, it rests on a bronze bassin.
> Within burn aromatic herbs: red fire and black smoke;
> It is finely engraved on all sides and allows one communication with Heaven!
> I contemplate the ten thousand animals carved on the surface:
> Thus my sight surpasses Li Lo's [a legendary man with exceptional vision].
> ("Hsün-lu ming," Yi-wen lei-chü, 70.)

13. *Chuang-tzu,* chap. 1, p. 17. This quotation comes from the conclusion of a passage about the adept Lieh Tzu, who has acquired the art of riding the wind. According to Chuang Tzu, his apparent freedom is deceptive inasmuch as it requires "something on which to ride," be it only the wind (see also "The Fast of the Heart" in chap. 10).

14. In ancient Chinese mythology, the Yellow Emperor is supposed to have lived in the first half of the third millennium B.C. and to have invented civilization. He is the holy patron saint of many arts and crafts, metalworking being the first of these. His teacher was an old sage, considered to be one of the many incarnations of Lao Tzu. The ruler and his sage adviser form a pair which corresponds to the fundamental relationship in Chinese thought. This relationship is expressed in a number of metaphors, such as the puppet and the puppeteer, the medium and his master. On the philosophical level, this complementary structure is also found in the Tao and its "virtue" or strength (*Tao-te*).

We know virtually nothing about the history of the mystery cult of "the Way of Huang-lao," but the philosophers of the early empire all felt his influence to a greater or lesser degree.

15. Partially translated into French and English, this basic work on Chinese medicine, whose earliest passages date from the third century B.C., refers constantly to a Taoist background and to the rites and exercises of physical harmony. The main purpose of the book is, however, the establishment of a medical theory (see also chap. 6).

16. The expression *Tao-chia,* meaning "Taoist school," is used by the his-

toriographer Ssu-ma Ch'ien (see above, note 8), in the context of the search for immortality. During the same period of the Han, we also find the name *Tao-chiao*, "Taoist teaching," to refer to the Mysteries. Certain modern Chinese authors have seen in the two terms *Tao-chia* and *Tao-chiao* a differentiation between "philosophical Taoism" and "religious Taoism." But the Taoists themselves use the two terms interchangeably.

17. One of the first politicians who attempted to take advantage of a popular messianic movement is the "usurper" Wang Mang, who reigned from A.D. 9 to 24 (see Schipper, 1978a).

18. On the subject of the liturgical tradition of Taoism, see "The Register" in chapter 4. On the family of the Heavenly Masters, see note 31, hereunder.

19. Henri Maspero, "How Was Buddhism Introduced in China?" (Maspero, 1981 [translation]: pp. 249–262).

20. Zürcher, 1980.

21. On this important movement, see Strickmann, 1981.

22. See Kaltenmark, 1960. The term *ling-pao* is also an ancient, poetic name for *wu*, "shaman."

23. Lu Hsiu-ching (406–477), a Taoist patriarch whose contribution to the history of the Mysteries has been compared to that of Confucius for the Classical tradition. Lu collected, collated, and commented on the Taoist texts of his time and subdivided them into three "grottoes." The first grotto groups the texts of the Mao-shan revelations. These texts received the epithet of "supreme purity" (*shang-ch-ing*). The second grotto includes the texts of the *Ling-pao* (Sacred Jewel) tradition; and the third covers those of the ancient miracle-working practices of the South, (*San-huang wen*). This was the first *Taoist Canon*, the model for all later editions.

24. Among the most famous "saviors" are emperor T'ai-wu of the Wei (424–451) and emperor Wu of the Liang (502–550). In this respect, a given leader of contemporary China has not really invented anything new. According to the messianic expectations of the Chinese middle ages, the savior—the New Lao Tzu—would be named Li Hung. The imperial house of the T'ang Dynasty adopted the surname Li, presumably for reasons of religious propaganda.

25. Taoism have always remained exclusive. The revealed books were never put into general circulation. To this day the liturgical tradition is only transmitted in the form of handwritten (never printed) texts. Moreover, in Taoism there is no tradition of preaching.

26. Gernet, 1956.

27. At the beginning of the T'ang dynasty, the books of the Sacred Jewel (*Ling-pao*) tradition, which were texts to be recited, were very close to the Buddhist sutras. Some Taoist schools also adopted a monastic organization. But these short-lived innovations never enabled Taoism to seriously challenge Buddhism on its own territory.

28. See Demiéville, 1970.

29. Shao Yung (1011–1077), considered to be one of the founders of the new Confucian orthodoxy, was in fact a Taoist master. Other great literati of the period like, Ou-yang Hsiu (1007–1072), revealed their extensive knowl-

edge of Taoist culture in their writings. Nonetheless, the essential contribution made by Taoism to the renewal of thought during the Chinese "renaissance" of the Sung goes virtually unmentioned in modern historiography.

30. See Waley, 1931.

31. The authenticity of the hereditary tradition seems certain inasmuch as we find representatives of the Heavenly Masters in every period who occupied leading positions in the liturgical tradition. However, the institution of the Heavenly Masters has undergone many changes during the last two thousand years.

32. This copy, preserved at the White Cloud Temple in Peking, was reproduced in 1926 (thanks to the initiative of an association of bibliophiles) by a photolithographic process. It was only from that moment on that scientific research on the history of Taoism could begin.

33. In recent years the world has seen the development of a kind of fictitious Taoism which is propagated in popular *kung-fu* movies. There also is nowadays a form of purely theoretical Taoism adhered to by intellectuals, therapists, acupuncturists, and public service officials (serving on the "National Association of Taoism") of the Chinese government. But true Taoism is not merely a cult, nor a system, nor a therapeutic technique. It is, above all, the liturgical structure of local communities; it therefore belongs to the daily life of the people.

2: Everyday Religion

1. There is an excellent study of the institutions and practice of Buddhism in China before 1949 by Holmes Welch (Welch, 1966).

2. See Schipper, 1977.

3. These are concepts tied to the environment and to building sites of temples, houses, and tombs. These concepts and theories are generally called *feng-shui* (wind and water) or *ti-li* (geology). They assume that, in order for there to be harmony within the family or local groups, it is important for building sites to be completely integrated into their surroundings. From this point of view, the local temple, as the center and "mountain," is an important landmark. This system of "siting" is not a form of geomancy, but rather is related to the ideas of acupuncture.

4. This is one aspect of the problem of Christian missions in China. Not only in Western religion cheaper (it requires only a meager contribution on the part of the faithful for celebrations), but it is often established owing to the gifts of foreign communities, through the intermediary of specialized organizations. The construction of Christian churches in neogothic or imitation Chinese styles, without any concern for the harmony of the surroundings is one of the most striking manifestations of Western cultural imperialism in China.

5. The institution of a "master of the incense burner" remains the same for all forms of civil organizations, whether temples, guilds, or local communities

without sanctuaries. The folk community organizations have no permanent leaders but are governed democratically.

6. The house altar is usually located in the center of the dwelling, in the main building at the back of the first courtyard. One normally finds a long altar table on which is placed an incense burner flanked by a pair of candelabras and two flower vases. Behind the incense burner, images of the saints of the family are placed. The affiliation of this private form of worship with the community temples is accomplished by the "sharing of the incense" (*fen-hsiang*), in a way similar to that which joins the local sanctuaries to each other. The family altar is also the place where the tablets of the family's ancestors are found. A special incense burner with handles is placed before them. The arrangement of the altar, as well as its placement, varies greatly from region to region. The present period has seen the disappearance of the incense burners and other objects of worship, and their replacement by portraits of the political leaders. The sacred place, however, remains, and in recent years in traditional forms of worship are coming back.

7. *Ch'ing-ming* is one of the festivals to have most resisted the repression of the last decades, and many travellers to China have observed that the tombs have been cleaned up and decorated with sacrificial paper offerings for this festival. The reason for this resistance lies no doubt in the deep attachment to the dead—which is characteristic of the Chinese mentality—as well as in the importance of the *ch'ing-ming* as a calendrical marker in agricultural life. Archaic culture probably plays a role, too: "cold food" recalls the forest-clearing rituals before sedentary agriculture and the farming in irrigated rice fields.

8. The best study of the cycle of annual festives remains that of J. J. M. De Groot (de Groot, 1886). This work remains a valuable source for the study of contemporary creeds and customs of southern Fukien and of Taiwan.

9. Every year a votive inscription of four characters is glued to the door lintel. The most common inscription is *wu-fu lin-men:* "May the Five Forms of Happiness Come to This Door." Two parallel stanzas adorn the doorposts and these may be chosen from a great number of examples, usually according to the trade or social status of the inhabitants. These inscriptions are generally written by specialized calligraphers.

10. As is now well-known, a series of twelve animals corresponds to the cycle of twelve "terrestrial branches." According to this cycle, people speak of the year of "the cock," "the tiger," et cetera. This system of simple computation can in no way be compared to Western nor to Chinese astrology, which are far more complicated.

11. Marcel Granet (Granet 1926, p. 321) quotes the description of the feast of the fifteenth day of the first moon by a scholar of the sixth century:

"Every year, in the capital and elsewhere, during the night of the full moon of the first month, the streets and alleys are full of people. The noise of drum deafens Heaven and torches blind the Earth. Many people wear animal masks. Men dress up as women; singers and tumblers disguise themselves in strange costumes. Men and women go together to the show and find themselves assembled side by side and don't avoid each other. They waste their property, destroy their inheritance, and at these jousts, exhaust their household riches in an instant."

Lanterns, drums, joyful crowds, disguises and spectacles, games of chance and betting, all this was still the custom in modern times. Granet adds: "Everything in these festivals went against orthodoxy."

12. The third day of the third lunar month is today generally celebrated as being the anniversary of the High Emperor of the Dark Heaven (*Hsüan-tien shang-ti*). He is the personification of the purifying and exorcising energies of the North. He was also the divine protector of the Ming dynasty (1368–1644).

13. For more on these two characters, see "The Gods" in chapter 3.

14. A lack of personal discipline leads to a loss of vital energy. This, in turn, leads to illness, accidents, bad luck, and the need to have recourse to divine assistance; this is a sin. Penitents in the processions are therefore designated by the expression *yu-tsui-chih,* "sinners." Flagellating mediums belong in the same category (see chap. 4). Sin, however, is not considered to be irreducible (there is no "original sin"). Neither it is something that is solely and simply moral, but it is rather related to the equilibrium of the body.

15. About the *chiao,* "offerings," see chapter 5.

16. Following Rolf A. Stein's formulation (Stein, 1957).

17. Within each group—family, village, region—an unwritten law requires each individual to participate in the celebrations. The unity of the community at the time of the festival (a critical period; see chapter 8) is considered to be essential. It is therefore not rare to see the faithful of other religions, particularly Christians, defy the interdictions of their own churches to participate in the community festivals.

3: Divinity

1. Doré, 1911–1918. Despite the reservations one may have about Doré's work, his "researches" remain today an important source of documentation on Chinese religion.

2. The *I-ching* is best known in the West through R. Wilhelm's translation, *Das Buch der Wandlungen,* Jena, 1924, translated into English by Cary F. Baynes (with a famous foreword by C. G. Jung) and with a preface by Wilhelm's son Helmut (Princeton University Press, Bollingen Series 19, 1966).

The *I-ching,* one of Confucianism's "Classics," was originally a manual for divination, a purpose restored to it in the West by Wilhelm's translation and C. G. Jung's support. It is incorrect, however, to say, as Wilhelm suggests (English translation, p. XIV), that this use of the *I-ching* is Taoist. The works of the *Taoist Canon* retain only the cosmological aspect of the *I-ching.* As a rule, Taoism does not concern itself with the oracular arts (see chap. 10 in this volume for a quotation from *Tao-te ching,* chap. 38, concerning predictions). Today's Taoist masters are not fortune-tellers.

3. The *I-ching,* as well as the other Confucian Classics, do not speak of the Original Chaos, but mention only the One. The word *hun-tun* (see also the

next note) appears only in Taoist books. As we shall see, this fundamental concept is closely related to Taoist mythology and its religious practice.

4. The word *hun-tun* is what Marcel Granet, (1934, p. 39) has called a "descriptive auxilliary" or a "vocal emblem." *Hun-tun* resembles a kind of onomatopoeia, and comparable expressions can be found in other languages, as, for example *tohu ubohu,* meaning "chaos and confusion" (from the Hebrew *tohu wa bhohu:* "without form and void"). Or again, the English nursery rhyme's Humpty-Dumpty to designate the egg, and metaphorically, the simplicity of the natural order. In Chinese there are a great many correlates, the most important being *k'un-lun,* the mythical mountain, the dwelling of the Mother, the place of birth and death. There are many ways of writing *hun-tun,* all closely related. The principal meaning conveyed by the graphic character used to write *hun* is a cloud of insects or a luminous cloud; the predominant meaning of the character used for *tun* is obtuse, stupid, confused. The two signs generally come under the classifying element (the key) of water.

5. Chinese numerological series constitute a system to describe a continuous and ever-expanding universe. Individually, each mathematical series is applied to a complete spatiotemporal continuum within which operate the rules of mathematical games. (See also the chapter on numbers in Marcel Granet, 1934, livre 2, chap. 3: "Les Nombres."

6. See *T'ai-ch'ing fu-ch'i k'ou-chüeh.* F. 7b. This very ancient consecration formula is a call to the gods of the body for the protection and purification of the inner universe. It is still recited today for the consecration of the elders at the major offering (*chiao*) ceremonies. Here *hun* does not mean "chaos," but is, as we shall see hereunder, another word meaning one of the many kinds of human souls.

7. See Sivin, 1980.

8. Water is the first of the Five Agents (or Five Phases) and the initial phase of the transformation of energy matter (*ch'i*).

9. See Marcel Granet, 1934, livre 2, chap. 3: "Les Nombres."

10. *Ti-li,* literally "the structures of the earth," is the name given to Chinesegeology and the science of siting construction. See chapter 2, note 3.

11. See de Groot, 1892–1910: "On the Soul and Ancestral Worship."

12. See Schipper, 1971.

13. See Hou, 1975. The money offering, in all its forms, always represents a debt to be paid by someone for his or her sins, and never an attempt "to buy" the gods, as some Christian missionaries have unfortunately maintained.

14. There are many legends concerning the Earth God (see Schipper, 1977). The importance of the omnipresent tutelary *T'u-ti kung* (literally "Mr. Earth") is not confined to the limits of modern popular religion. His worship, as a representative of the celestial order on earth and symbol of local social unity, goes back to ancient times. Even today his cult is fundamental. Every community and all temples have an altar to the Earth God. Edouard Chavannes (Chavannes, 1910, "appendix") has studied the relationship between the ancient cult and contemporary observances.

15. On these mourning rites, see chapter 5.

16. Veneration of relics and of tombs belong to the popular cults of the

gods and not to Taoism proper, which believes that "True Men" and "Immortals" leave the world without a trace (see chap. 9).

17. In addition to the pantheon of the official religion (imperial sacrifices to Heaven, Earth, the Planets, and the dynastic Ancestors), each imperial dynasty recognized a variable number of local gods or saints. Thanks to this canonization, the latter also entered into the national public domain. In modern China (that is, since the ninth century A.D.), Taoism has played a role in the promotion of the local gods and their official canonization, while preserving a very clear distinction between the public pantheon and the Taoist pantheon proper, that of the Mysteries.

18. *T'ai-shang Lao-chün shuo T'ien-fei chiu-k'u ling-yen ching* ("Scripture of the Queen of Heaven Whose Miracles Save from Distress, Spoken by the Most High Old Lord"). Within Taoism and its pantheon, the gods of the public and popular cults enjoy a status comparable to that of our saints: subordinate intercessors each with his or her own particular domain. In the Taoist liturgy, Matsu is the patron saint of seamen, and the blessing of sailors falls within her liturgical domain. As a rule, the great gods of the people occupy a lower rank in the Taoist universe, which makes them dependent on the Masters and subject to their will.

4: The Masters of the Gods

1. See Sun, Kai-t'i, 1952.

2. The Queen Mother of the West, goddess of the mythical Mountain K'un-lun, has a marvellous orchard where the peaches of immortality ripen once every three thousand years. It is then that all the gods are invited to a great banquet. Once, the king of the monkeys, who had not been invited, stole all the peaches. He ate them and became immortal. This legend, among others, is part of the popular novel *The Journey to the West* (*Hsi-yu chi*); see Yü, 1977.

3. Tung Yung is one of the "Twenty-Four Examples of Filial Piety," one of the frequent themes in popular literature and art. His story tells us that he was so poor that at his father's death he had to sell himself into slavery in order to buy a coffin. This great filial love touched Heaven, which sent a young goddess to help him ransom himself. From their love was born the god of music, a little boy with braids. To ivoke this deity, one sings "tra-la-la" (in Chinese, *lo-li-lien*).

4. The Heavenly officer, *T'ien-kuan,* is in charge of distributing divine grace on earth. He appears on stage dressed as a mandarin, wearing a smiling mask. He performs a dance and then blesses the community, a sign that the offerings are pleasing and that Heaven and human beings are harmoniously joined.

5. See "The Gods" in chapter 3 for the story of Lord Kuan.

6. Mandarin is the language formerly used by the officials in the capital. Theater is usually performed in a regional language, such as Cantonese, Hokkien, Shanghai, and so forth, all very different from the official language. Literature and Taoist liturgy are always *in classical Chinese,* that is to say, the writ-

ten language of ancient literature (comparable to the use of Classical Latin in ancient Europe), very different from either Mandarin or the regional languages.

7. Literally, the word *fu* means "double." From this initial meaning derive those of a "sign corresponding to another," an "insignia in two parts" (like those carried by courriers and messengers so that they could identify themselves to their correspondent), a "*tessera*," an "identity card," a "token of faith," a "password," and so forth. The etymology of the character used to write the word *fu* corresponds to the original meaning of our word *symbol*.

The *fu* in Chinese religion appears as a written sign in sacred characters, different from those of ordinary writing, on a narrow strip of yellow or red paper. This writing conveys the initiatory *name* of a god who is thereby called on to manifest his power.

8. See Schipper, 1967.

9. See Elliot, 1955.

10. The training and initiation received by the young men of the community at the local temple is called, *shou-chin*, "keeping the interdicts" or "receiving the commandments." The community normally calls on a "red head" master to conduct the training. See also "The Barefoot Master and His Ritual" later in this chapter.

11. This is the proper meaning of *kung-fu*, the martial arts of China made famous by the films of Bruce Lee.

12. See Dunstheimer, 1964.

13. See Maspero, 1981, pp. 119–120. In addition, there are women's clubs founded in honor of one or several goddesses. These clubs offer to women of every social condition and status a bond of solidarity.

14. The Five Generals of the "Heavenly Armies" (*wu-ying*) are the guardians of sacred space: their presence is indicated by mounds and stelae or posts raised on the borders of a village as well as along the circumference of places of worship and theater stages. Here, they delimit and protect the sacred space of the human body.

15. Only psychosomatic techniques are used to obtain a state of trance, never drugs.

16. As known, the word "shaman" originally referred to the priests of Siberian peoples, especially the Tungus, a Mongol ethnic group of North Siberia. Today the term is used far more generally for specialists who, in traditional religions, enter into a relationship with the world of the gods so as to be able to heal illness. On the relationship between Chinese shamanism and Taoism, see Schipper, 1985a.

17. On the significance of this costume, see hereunder, note 27.

18. The text is quoted from a manuscript containing models of documents for the ordination of "red head" masters, used in Fukien province (author's collection). Note the intermediary role given to the Earth God.

19. The epic hymn which accompanies this ritual and which describes the journey has been translated from the Chinese by Hou, 1975.

20. "Ritual for Planting Flowers," a "red head" rite in the regional (Hokkien) language of South Fukien (liturgical manuscript from the author's collection).

21. This form of inspired writing—comparable to our planchette—is very common. There are religious associations dedicated almost exclusively to these practices which regularly publish the texts and messages they have received from the spirits. One special genre of this kind of literature is the account of sessions of the tribunals of the dead held in the underworld.

22. "Ritual to Call on All Gods" (liturgical manuscript from the author's collection).

23. These mourning rites are described in chapter 5.

24. The ballads also circulate in the form of little printed books which can be had for a few pennies in the market, or which are peddled by travelling salesmen. The repertoire of these popular ballads is extremely rich, but has not yet been studied.

25. As, for example, the Pekinese *ta-ku,* the Suchow *p'ing-t'an,* and the *koa-à-hi* of Fukien.

26. Van der Loon, 1977.

27. In order to illustrate and explain this relationship, the Masters tell the story of Hsü Chia: One day during his earthly existence, Lao Tzu saw the skeleton of a man. He resuscitated the dead man, who was called Hsü Chia and turned out to be a poor illiterate. To cover his naked body, Lao Tzu took the sleeves of his own inner garment and made him a smock. With a strip of his red coat, he tied a turban around the man's head. Then Hsü Chia became Lao Tzu's servant. When the Saint wanted to leave this world to return toward the West, to the paradise of K'un-lun, Hsü Chia could not follow him. To enable him to provide for himself, Lao Tzu taught him to write *fu* and gave him one of his buffalo horns to use as an instrument. The "red heads," barefoot masters, consider themselves to be Hsü Chia's descendants and worship him as their patron saint, "their own Lao Tzu." See Schipper, 1986a.

28. See "The History of Taoism" in chapter 1.

29. There used to be nine major Taoist establishments with a total of more than a thousand monks on Mount Luo-fou shan near Canton before 1949. Except for a single sanctuary with a few officially appointed "Taoists," nothing remains of these magnificent temples and monasteries.

30. See Welch, 1966.

31. See "The Register," further on in this chapter. According to Taoist belief, Lao Tzu appears in every period of history.

32. Most of the ritual texts, however, can be found in the Taoist Canon. But this collection of more than four thousand volumes, printed in 1444, was obviously accessible only in a few large monastic centers. Moreover, the internal organization of the Canon is conceived in such a way as to make these texts unusable for noninitiates. In any case, the layman never had access to the Canon, let alone to manuscript texts.

33. *Tai-t'ien hsing-hua; hua* means "to transform," but it also means "culture." The sentence can thus be translated: "to propagate culture as a delegate of Heaven" (that is, the natural order of the universe).

34. The Chinese word for "thing" or "phenomenon" is *wu.* The character corresponding to this word represents a flag, a signal.

35. "Old Lord," Lao-chün is the honorific title given to Lao Tzu in his

existence outside the world, as a being of Anterior Heaven. Lao-chün appears regularly on earth, according to the cosmic cycles, and his birth signals the coming of a new era.

36. That is: worship with bloody sacrifices to demoniacal gods.

37. *San-t'ien nei-chieh ching* ch. 1, f. b. The Pure Covenant (*ch'ing-yüeh*) whose terms are recalled here by the text marks the divide between Taoism and the popular forms of worship.

38. *Cheng-i fa-wen t'ien-shih chiao chieh-k'o ching*, p. 12a. We will see the cosmic Three Breaths and their colors again later, in ritual and in cosmological theories. White is the color of the Tao in its aspect of "non-knowledge" (see "Daily Life" in chap. 10). The color of Heaven is blue-black or blue-green (*ch'ing*). The text on the Three Breaths just quoted goes on to say (p. 14b) that:

in the year 142, the Tao revealed the Way of the Covenant with the Powers of the Orthodox One. Chang made a contract with Heaven and Earth, and established the twenty-Four dioceses. He "distributed" [*fen-pu*] the "Obscure, Primordial, and Initial" Energies (*ch'i*) to heal the people.

39. On these numerological categories, see Granet, 1934: "Les Nombres."

40. Chinese archeology has discovered a certain number of compasses from the period of the first Heavenly Master. See Ngo, 1976: fig. 1. These instruments were used for divination. Taoism itself scarcely ever practiced divination (see chapter 3, note 2 above for remarks on the *I-ching*) and the school of the Heavenly Masters was even opposed to any oracular practice. But the materialist cosmology developed by divination is also that of Taoism, and the numerological categories of computation used in Taoism provide the structure of its theology.

41. This could also be translated as "Great Equality." The ideal of an anarchistic society takes as its model primitive civilization, such as it might have existed before the Yellow Emperor. The expression *t'ai-p'ing* is found among the thinkers of the Han period and became the slogan of the peasant revolts at the end of the second century as well as all similar rebellions up to the modern period. The Taoist masters embody the equalizing force of the Orthodox (or "normative") One (*cheng-yi p'ing-ch'i*), an expression that was part of their ordination title.

42. *Chung-min,* the ancestors of a race of new human beings.

43. See Granet, 1962, p. 482f.

44. The *T'ai-hsüan tu-sheng;* compare the "Certificate of Immortality" quoted below in this chapter.

45. *Fen-pieh:* to distinguish, differentiate; to create "real" or "true" (*chen*) beings from the incoherent and sometimes contradictory forces dwelling within us.

46. *Fa-shih,* which we have translated as "magician" in the context of the barefoot masters, is also used for the *tao-shih.* In this case, it has the meaning of Master of the cosmological system (*fa*).

47. Here the name of the agent should be given, that is, the aspect of the Tao that corresponds to the fundamental Destiny in the Taoist cosmology.

48. That is, three (the Three Breaths, three levels of the Universe) times five (Five Phases, five cardinal points) times ten (One, with universal power).

49. The eight minor festivals (*pa-la*) belong to the agricultural calendar. The twenty-four *chieh-ch'i,* "Energy Nodes," correspond to the first and fifteenth day of each moon.

50. Traditionally, five bushels of rice. These five bushels were used to set out the sacred area, in the same way as, in popular religion, the camps of the guardian generals (*wu-ying*); see above, note 14). This practice was especially odious to the imperial officials who collected taxation in grain and considered this liturgical contribution by the faithful to be an encroachment on the rights of the ruler. Hence the nickname "Religion of the Five Bushels of Rice," *Wu-t- mi-tao,* given by the official chroniclers to the movement of the Heavenly Masters (and the epithet of "rice thieves" given to its leaders).

51. See also the Immortal's Certificate quoted below in this same chapter.

52. This reform was enacted under the influence of the famous K'ou Ch'ien-chih (365–448), a Taoist leader under the Northern Wei dynasty.

53. *Ling-pao wu-liang tu-jen shang-p'in ching,* a book of the nineteenth century which reveals the sacred names of the heavens as they were spoken at the creation of the universe.

54. *Ling-pao chiu-t'ien sheng-shen shang-ching.* This book of the fifth century deals with the birth of the gods in the human body and gives the text of the nine hymns which accompany the nine phases of the creative transformation.

55. *Tai-shang hsüan-ling pei-tou yen-sheng miao-ching.* This text is the most ·frequently recited in Taoism today. It describes the characteristics and attributes of the stars which rule human destiny. By reciting it one is able to recapture and activate one's vital forces.

56. Let us recall that earlier registers were *lists* of the gods and demons who served the Master. The transfer of these *lists* to the ordinand at his investiture reflected the passing on of sacred powers. Those documents are no longer in use, but the sacred books (which contain the names and attributes of the gods), handed down from generation to generation, are considered to have the same function as the former registers. Nowadays the Masters place a copy of a holy book (in the tradition I have studied, the *Yü-huang pen-hsing ching*), wrapped in yellow silk, on their altar and worship it daily.

57. This Initiation Master is called *tu-shih,* literally "the master of the passage."

58. See chapter 8 on "Keeping the One."

59. "True Heart," in Chinese is *chen-sin;* this expression is related to the notion of "non-knowledge."

60. Each individual, according to his day of birth, is related to one of the seven stars of the Big Dipper. The star, called the "Agent," rules over the person's Fundamental Destiny (*pen-ming*).

61. This means that the ordinand succeeds his ancestors, the latter having supposedly obtained in their time an initial transmission and initiation from an Eminent Master (ming-shih).

62. Although the costs involved in ordinations (banquets, offerings et cetera) are paid for by the families of the Masters, they could not take place with-

out the sponsorship of the leaders, the Elders, of the communities. This is another proof that Chinese religion, as a whole, is not a centralized ecclesiastical organization but remains the expression of local and social and political structures.

63. The text of this document is quoted from a liturgical manuscript from Ch'üan-chou (South Fukien) dating from the early nineteenth century (author's collection).

64. On these rites, see the first part of chapter 5.

65. *Fa-ming*. This name is chosen according to which generation of the Master's descendants (*fa-p'ai*) the ordinand belongs to.

66. See "The Altar" in Chapter 5.

67. See *Yü-yin fa-shih* (a book of hymns and formulas of the Sung period), ch. 3, p. 40b. The same formulas remain in use today.

68. See chapter 6 on the Cinnabar Field.

69. A formula recited while the ordinand is being dressed. See *Yü-yin fa-shih* (above, note 67).

70. "He who wears the ritual vestments is Master" is a common Taoist expression. The clothes express the *function*, and the function determines the individual in the liturgical structure. Already in early times, the rites of ordination were essentially dressing ceremonies. For a ritual of the twelfth century, see *T'ai-shang ch'u-chia chuan-tu i*.

71. In a rite of "opening the eyes" (*k'ai-kuang*) similar to the one used for the consecration of statues and tablets.

72. The pin is alternately called *hua* ("flower"), *yang* ("glory"), or *liu-chu* ("luminous pearl"). It is identical inform and meaning to the flaming pearl adorning the top of a temple (and comparable to a bishop's miter).

5. Ritual

1. "White, hulled rice" is written with the character *ching;* the same is used to write the word "essence."

2. *Pei-chi,* often translated as "polar star." Throughout the ages, a number of different stars have been identified as *pei-chi.*

3. *Tou* ("bushel") also signifies the wooden tub which receives the newborn child at birth (Chinese women habitually gave birth while squatting).

4. The sacred characters used to write *fu* talismans are considered to be materializations of energies or breaths (*ch'i;* see also hereunder, in this same chapter, the rite of the Five True Writs).

5. For example, if he were to see an American student come into his home.

6. These signs are drawn with the outstretched index and middle fingers of the right hand (as is done for the apostolic blessing of the Roman Catholic Pope).

"One" corresponds to "Water," whereas "heart" is "spirit"; hence the purifying force that revives the vitality of the child. This rite is in certain respects comparable to Christian baptism.

7. From time immemorial Taoists have been physicians.

8. With the exception of medicine, these methods (*shu*) do not generally fall within the domain of the Taoist Master, but are the concern of other specialists, often considered *Confucianists*.

9. The Masters are not supposed to perform the great community rituals for their own benefit, but only on the express (written) invitation of a community.

10. On these mourning rites, see de Groot, 1892–1910, vols. 1 and 2.

11. These services for the repose of the dead are independent of the mourning and burial rites which are carried out within the most closely related family.

12. The ritual (*k'o-i*) is always performed by a group of *tao-shih*. Its performance is of a dynamic and dramatic nature. Recitation of holy scriptures (*sung-ching*), on the other hand, is very staid.

13. See "Birth" in chapter 7.

14. Hence the name *yen-kung*, "to express merit," given to this offering.

15. See Hou, 1975.

16. This type of "literature" in the spoken language consists of ballads recited by a single person as well as dialogues and even small plays. The spoken texts are interspersed with songs. The accompanists—the drum and the gong player—may act as the chorus: their commentaries expand the words of the protagonists. The main text is interspersed with more or less improvised speech of a daring and erotic nature.

17. The legend of Mu-lien (Maudgalyâyana), who goes to the underworld to save his mother, is of Indian origin, but has become extremely popular in China.

18. This is an ancient epic describing the adventures of two young lovers. The young man is drafted to work on the construction of the Great Wall. After a while, his young bride goes on foot to take him some warm clothing. On arriving at the wall, she learns that her beloved one is dead. Her tears make the wall crumble and the bones of the dead workers, which were incorporated in it, appear. Men Chiang-nü now poors her own blood over the bones. Those which absorb it belong to her lover. Finally, he is restored to life.

19. In voluntary contributions to the community, notable for the construction or restoration of the temple, or to help the poor and the sick, et cetera. In no case do the donations of the faithful benefit the Taoist Masters or any ecclesiastical organization.

20. The Chinese word for "Enclosure of the Tao" is *tao-ch'ang*; see hereunder in this same chapter, the section on "The Sacrifice of Writings."

21. This ritual is called *ming-mo*, "the investiture of the demon."

22. These rites are called "hearings," *ch'ao*. On the surface they resemble court ceremonial in the imperial palace.

23. The *chiao* rites for the gods of epidemics remain important, even today, even where these diseases (plague, smallpox, et cetera) have long since disappeared. This shows that the Great Assemblies meet deeper social and political needs, which are independent of the apparent goal of the ceremonies.

24. On the concept of the "true form," see "Mountains" in chapter 9.

25. On the occasion of a *chiao,* the doorposts of sanctuaries and houses are often adorned with parallel stanzas (Chinese: *tui-lien*) which express in the most general way the avowed purpose of the celebration: "Harmonious winds and abundant rains, / Greatness of the land and peace for the people."

26. Buddhist liturgy also has the recitation of holy scriptures for the obtainment of religious merit, as well as the performance of *sujiang,* (ballads and plays in the vernacular). But it does not have the rites of The True Writs nor those of the installation and dispersal of the sacred space.

27. Traditional Chinese ideas tend to conceive orthodoxy as being the sum of all existing ways of thought, excluding no *one.* Orthodoxy tended thus to be *inclusive,* and not an *exclusive* faith, as in the West.

28. This custom is explained by the close relationship between the Taoists and the Earth God.

29. These "pure" services celebrate the covenant of the people with the gods and also the alliance *among* the gods themselves, that is, among the tutelary saints of the temples who represent the local communities.

30. The Master is the *guest* of the communities, and the remuneration for liturgical services is never discussed. We must remember that conducting a *chiao* is an exceptional event for the Master as well. The considerable sums that the Master may receive on this occasion—which in any case make up only a fraction of the community's overall expenses for the *chiao*—are never part of a regular salary.

31. Under normal circumstances, the families never exhibit the art objects or other treasures they might hold. For the *chiao,* the new leaders of the community are consecrated; they must win prestige; hence the public exhibition of their family's heirlooms.

32. This fact is one more example of the chasm in China between the state and local society.

33. Aside from utmost purity, the Master must show a perfect mastery of himself in every circumstance and speak as little as possible.

34. Although the rituals are written down, the Master must know everything by heart: the text, the movements, the secret formulas, and so forth. There are dozens of different rituals.

35. The Taoists are wont to tell all kinds of horrible stories about the harmful consequences of professional mistakes: amnesia, madness, even violent death following a lack of concentration or, worse, the usurpation of power. Above all the Taoist has to learn not to meddle in things which do not concern him. He should never perform overly strict exorcisms of evil influences, as the sufferings and diseases which these influences bring about may well represent a just revenge on behalf of wronged spirits.

36. Let me emphasize once more that the *chiao* require long preparation. Simply writing petitions, reports, and other necessary forms requires three months of work for a qualified scribe.

37. The *tao-shih* speak among themselves a secret language which is incomprehensible to ordinary people. The vocabulary of this language is made up of borrowings from several different areas: specialized words (names of rites, et

cetera), metaphoric words, coded words, and so on, pronounced in a way that is meant to correspond to the dialect of Kiangsi province, where the Mountain of the Dragon and the Tiger, home of the Heavenly Masters, is located.

38. The "wooden fish" or "temple block" not only indicates the beat but also conveys signals that indicate changes and new parts in the ritual.

39. Except for the dummer, who must be a *tao-shih,* the instrumentalists are laymen.

40. The principal scriptures recited during the *chiao* are *Yü-huang pen-hsing ching,* [The Book of the Fundamental Action of the Jade Emperor], *Pei-tou ching,* The Book of the Bushel] *San-kuan ching* [The Book of the Three Officials] and *Yü-shu ching* [The Book of the Jade Pivot]. At the services for the repose of the souls of the dead (*chai*), the *Ling-pao wu-liang tu-jen shang-p'in miao-ching* [The Book of the Immense Salvation of Mankind] is recited.

41. This gong, which resembles a large bowl, is called a *ch'ing* and is placed at the right hand of the reciter. Originally this *ch'ing* was a chime stone.

42. Each holy scripture is, in principle, a cosmic writing, created out of Chaos from spontaneous characters. The recitation corresponds to the reactivation of that moment of creation.

43. These dances enact the ascension of a mountain, that is, the altar, and the journey in the labyrinth of grottoes located inside this mountain (see "The Altar," further on in this chapter, "Mountains" in chapter 9.

44. The constellation (in general the Little Dipper) and the magic square corresponds to the symbolism of the altar itself. See also the remarks on the meaning of the bushel at the beginning of the present chapter.

45. These are called "seats of the spirits" (*shen-wei*), as are the ancestor tablets.

46. *Hai-ch'iung Bai zhen-jen yü lu,* ch. 1, f. 2a.

47. Although altars are installed in the temples or near the houses of the dead, they are essentially moveable and, in their move from one place to another, are supposed to be following the trajectory of the Dipper stars of Destiny.

48. This example illustrates the basic misunderstanding between laymen and *tao-shih.* The supreme gods of the faithful are just half-gods or demons in the eyes of the Masters. The *tao-shih* keep this understanding, which is part of their initiation, secret and do not reveal it to the common people.

49. An exhibition of Taoist liturgical paintings, the first of its kind, was held in 1980 in Marburg, Germany. See Kraatz et al., 1980.

50. This used to be done with a tendrill and some touchwood.

51. See Schipper, 1975a, plate 8.

52. This text is quoted from the *su-ch'i* (overnight prayer) ritual. See *Chin-lu su-ch'i k'o-i.*

53. Here again we find the five bushels of rice from the contribution of the faithful to the dioceses of the Heavenly Masters (see chap. 4, note 49).

54. The patriarchs are the Master initiators of times past, notably the Heavenly Masters, in whose name the current Masters perform the ritual.

55. The back wall of the sacred area is always "north."

56. By virtue of the contract concluded by the First Heavenly Master. This

Pure Contract between men and gods stipulates that "the gods neither eat nor drink [bloody sacrifices], the Masters receive no salary."

57. Today this rule is followed only for *Ling-pao wu-liang tu-jen shang-p'in miao-ching* [the Book of the Immense Salvation of Mankind].

58. The same word also means "civilization." See chapter 4, note 33. Note also the relation with the notion of *wu-hua,* the transformation of beings, in the *Chuang-tzu* as illustrated in chapter 7 of this volume.

59. Every Taoist ritual implies and represents a contraction of time. See the remarks on alchemy in chapter 9, and Schipper and Wang, 1986.

60. *Wu,* "things." The character used to write this word denotes a flag, a sign, et cetera.

61. Fire and water are opposed elements. In cosmology, they represent antithetical phases, similar to *yin* and *yang.*

62. See Tsiuen, 1962.

63. See Chavannes, 1910.

64. There is evidence, in the treatise devoted in the *shih-chi* to the *feng* sacrifice, that Taoists were instrumental in its introduction to the imperial court. See Chavannes, 1910, p. 160.

65. See Granet, 1919, p. 185.

66. See the text of the "Certificate of Immortality" in chapter 4 of this volume. The name of the Master's altar is determined by his date of birth from a list of thirty-six names.

67. Because of the refusal to discuss this kind of question with someone who is not initiated.

68. The paintings hung above on the north wall.

69. Of course, these gates are invisible to the normal eye.

70. The hand also is a map and a compass of the universe. With the thumb, the Master touches points located at the tips and on the sections of the fingers (see illustrations in Granet, 1934, p. 188), thereby activating the cosmic force corresponding to these points.

71. This is an incense burner with a handle, normally held by the first of the community leaders. This form of incense burner is derived from the mountain-shaped *po-shan lu* of antiquity.

72. This is a breathing exercise known as the "Six Breaths"; see "The Preliminary Stage" in Chapter 8.

73. This expression refers to a mystic, absorbed in meditation (see chap. 7 and chap. 10).

74. See *Hsüan-t'an mi-chüeh.*

75. The formula is taken from *Ling-pao wu-liang tu-jen shang-p'in miao-ching* [The Book of the Immense Salvation of Mankind] ch. 1, f. 66, adapted for the liturgy by Lu Hsiu-ching (see *Tai-shang tung-hsüan ling-pao chung-chien-wen* f. 3b). The lighting of the incense burner is one of the Taoist rites whose text has scarcely changed since the fourteenth century. The Master who performs this rite first calls on his Original Ch'i (*yuan-ch'i,*) his "Agent" of the Three Energies of the cosmic body of Lao Tzu. From these energies, he creates emissary gods, who are the manifestation of his role as sacrificer. Through the intermediary of the Earth God, these deities will carry the message, *transformed*

by the sacrifice, to the heavens. In answer, the heavens fill the Master's body with their cosmic energies so that it becomes "cosmic."

76. This concentration corresponds, for the Taoists, to "differentiating" (*fen-pieh*) the energies (*ch'i*) by giving them a name and a particular identity; see chapter 4, note 44.

77. By incorporating the cosmic energies, which make his body similar to the Old Lord's.

78. "*Ming shu Shang-ch'ing,*" that is, these merits are counted towards their promotion in the pantheon. This ennoblement is also that of the Master himself, for these are breaths from the Master's body and, through his role as intermediary, from the whole community.

79. The cauldron is a symbol of the matrix (see "Alchemy" in chap. 9) and the sword a representation of *yang*.

6: The Inner Landscape

1. *Huang-ti nei-ching su-wen* ch. 8, ff. 1a–1b.

2. This is so, for instance, in the works of the classical philosopher Hsaün Tzu (*Hsün-tzu*, chap. 17) and in *Chuang-tzu*, chap. p. 507.

3. *Huai-nan tzu,.* chap. 4. On this book, see chapter 7, note 14, of this volume.

4. Granet, 1934, p. 395.

5. *Ch'un-ch'iu Kung-yang chuan*, ch. 6, Chuang 4, p. 11b.

6. *Tao-te ching,* chap. 48.

7. This is a reference to the Fast of the Heart in *Chuang-tzu*, chap.4; see chapter 10 of this volume.

8. *Tz'u-chih t'ung-chien* ch. 210, p. 6670.

9. *Chuang-tzu*, chap 7. pp, 290–291.

10. It should be pointed out, in this respect, that traditional Chinese Cosmology recognizes a supreme reason (*li*), a great universal design giving meaning to the world.

11. See chapter 7 of the present book.

12. See the glosses on the *Huang-t'ing ching* [The Book of the Yellow Court] in chapter 8 of this volume.

13. It was during the Han period that the theories on *yin* and *yang* and the Five Phases were most highly developed. This scholasticism has provided the foundation for Granet's studies of Chinese thought.

14. See "Chaos," in chapter 8.

15. See Schipper, 1979.

16. Chinese physiology considers sight to be the result of the combination of light from the stars and the vital energy of the body.

17. These two instruments produce the sounds of Heaven and Earth. As mentioned earlier, today's gong has taken the place of the chimestone.

18. See Maspero, 1981, pp. 431–442, book 8, "How to Communicate with the Taoist Gods."

19. These numerological and systematizing categories, in accord with scholarly cosmology—which the text sets forth here concerning the Cinnabar Field—are interpretations only appropriate to the text quoted here. The passage in its entirety is an example of how scholasticism of the Han period was grafted onto the symbolic system of the old mythology.

20. *Lao-tzu chung-ching* (The Book of the Center of Lao-tzu), paragraph 17.

21. *Chuang-tzu,* chap. 17, p. 563.

22. *Lao-tzu chung-ching,* paragraph 14.

23. *Huang-t'ing ching.* This long poem in heptasyllabic verse dates from the second or third century A.D. It describes the inner landscape and the psycho-physiological practices (see "The Preliminary Stage" in chap. 8).

24. See the image of the Inner Landscape on page 000, where the lower Cinnabar Field (*hsia tan-t'ien*) is represented by an irrigated rice field being tilled by a young boy.

25. In the different handbooks of Taoist practices we see the same layering of successive contributions that has also taken place in the liturgical texts. But despite this superposition of different systems, the basic themes—the One, Chaos, and Regression—remain.

26. A work from the sixth century, the *Tung-hsüan ling-pao sheng-hsüan pu-hsü chang hsü-shu,* f. 4b, says: "the mountain is [as] the body" (*shan-chih, shen yeh.*)

27. On the upper portion of this painting, preserved in the Palace Collection (now in the Palace Museum in Taipei), there is a poem inscribed in the hand of the emperor Ch'ien-lung (1736–1796). It is a rather inept doggerel which identifies the subject of the painting as a "drunken immortal." The painting shows, however, such a striking similarity to ancient representations of Lao Tzu that there is no doubt as to the fact that this painting represents the great saint.

28. According to the words of Pierre Ryckmans on the painting of Liang K'ai in *Encyclopedia Universalis,* vol 9, p. 859. Paris 1968.

29. The expressionless face of the Immortal recalls that of a newborn infant. The skull has the shape of an egg. The big square cloak that covers his shoulders stands away from the body like wings. Both light and massive at the same time, the whole figure conveys a strong sense of interiority.

30. In the saying of the *Tao-te ching,* "to know the male but keep the female" (chap. 21), the word "male" literally means "male pheasant." Ancient representations of the mountains, in paintings as well as on incense burners *po-shan lu*), often place a bird (a cock, a phoenix, a crow) on the summit. This theme of the bird on the mountain is also found in mythology.

31. *Lao-tzu chung-ching,* paragraph 1.

32. The numbers nine and one remind us of the cycle of creation of the universe. See chapter 7, of this volume.

33. Compare Saussure, 1909, p. 428.

34. *Lao-tzu chung-ching,* paragraph 2. The Mud Pill, *ni-wan,* corresponds to the point between the eyebrows.

35. Here again, we find the Queen Mother of the West, *Hsi-wang mu.*

36. *Tzu-tan; tan* means "cinnabar" and *tzu,* "child"; but *tzu* is also the cyclical sign corresponding to the North. The term refers to the birth of *yang* from extreme *yin.*

37. *Lao-tzu chung-ching,* paragraph 12.

38. Ibid., paragraph 39.

39. Ibid., paragraph 5.

40. According to legend, one of the diagrams representing the position of the Five Phases (the *Luo-shu*) was revealed on the shell of a turtle to the Great Yü.

41. *Lao-tzu chung-ching,* paragraph 14.

42. On the Three Cadavers and the Nine (or Three) Worms, see chapter 8.

43. See Schipper, 1978a.

7: Lao Tzu

1. *Chuang-tzu,* chap. 21, pp. 711–712. In classical literature, Lao Tzu is often referred to as Lao-tan; historians like Ssu-ma Ch'ien treat Lao as a patronymic and consider Tan to be a first name. But here Tan certainly has an allegorical meaning: to have long ears is a sign of longevity.

2. Concerning "the Ancestor," see below in this chapter, the section, "Birth."

3. *Lao-tzu ming* (an inscription in honor of Lao-tzu), by Pien Chao and dated A.D. 165. See Seidel, 1969, p. 123.

4. *Lao-tzu pien-hua ching* [Book of the Transformation of Lao Tzu]. Probably dating from the second century A.D., the complete version of this text has been lost. An important fragment was found in the famous medieval manuscript library in Tun-huang. See Seidel, 1969, p. 61, and *Yün-chi ch'i-ch'ien,* ch. 102, f. 2b. On Mother Li, Lao Tzu's mother, see hereunder in this chapter, the section, "Birth."

5. *Hsiao-tao lun,* quoted in Maspero, 1981, p. 340. Note the similarities between this myth and the symbolic vision of the body, especially regarding the two kidneys.

6. *Shu i chi,* quoted in Maspero, 1981, p. 340.

7. *Chuang-tzu,* chap. 7, p. 309.

8. *Chuang-tzu,* chap. 13, p. 462.

9. *Chuang-tzu,* chap. 2, p. 112. The dream is comparable here to the movement of involution in the Fast of the Heart and in meditation. See Chapter 10.

10. *Lao-tzu pien-hua ching* (Seidel, 1969:61) and *Lao-tzu pien-hua wu-chi ching,* a work of the third century A.D. preserved in the *Taoist Canon.*

11. *Lao-tzu pien-hua ching.* See Seidel, 1969, p. 69. See also the "Hsiang Ehr" commentary on the *Tao-te ching* in Jao, 1956, p. 11.

12. Yin Wen-ts'ao (biographical author from the seventh century), quoted in *Hun-yüan sheng-chi* ch. 2, f. 37a–37b.

13. This is my personal interpretation of the nine names of Lao Tzu as they are given in *Lao-tzu pien-hua ching* (see Seidel, 1969, p. 65) and, with some variations, elsewhere as well. In general these names are not translated. The word *po*, which today means paternal uncle and which I translate here as "ancestor," once had the meaning of "leader" or "elder." *Po* is thus the opposite of *tzu* ("child") in the way that "senior" is opposed to "junior." But, I must admit that my translation is hypothetical. For similar lists of the names of Lao Tzu used in meditation, see Kaltenmark, 1974, p. 159.

14. *Huai-nan tzu,* chap. 7. Liu An, Prince of Huai-nan (179–122 B.C.) assembled at his court a great number of sages and asked them to write a philosophical summa of Taoism. The texts that survive from this collective enterprise have been collected into a book under the name of the prince. See Fung, 1952, vol. 1, p. 395.

15. *Lao-tzu pien-hua ching* (Seidel, 1969, p. 61).

16. *Hun-yüan huang-ti sheng-chi,* in *Yün-chi ch'i-ch'ien* ch. 102, f. 1a. Note the quotation from chapter 21 of the *Tao-te ching* ("no light, no image . . .") incorporated into this text. The name of Old Lord (Lao-chün) corresponds to the original aspect of the Old Master, "before" his birth into this world.

17. Concerning this ritual, see "The Altar," in chapter 5.

18. Compare the images related to Embryonic Breathing in the section titled "The Return," in chapter 8.

19. *Lao-tzu pien-hua ching;* see Seidel, 1969, p. 61.

20. Li, Lao Tzu's family name, means "plum tree." See the section, "Birth," further on in this same chapter. (Jade Maiden of Obscure Mystery) or Obscure Brightness) is the theological name of Lao Tzu's Mother in Taoist texts from the fourth century on.

21. Lao-chün, that is, Lao Tzu before conception.

22. The story teller's little phrase "one might say that" introduces a simplification of the myth for the audience. In reality, it is not an incarnation but a *transformation*.

23. *Kan-lu,* "sweet dew," is the Chinese name for ambrosia. Compare *Tao-te ching,* chap. 32: "When Heaven and Earth unite, sweet dew will fall."

24. The Northern Bushel, that is, the Big Dipper and the Pole Star, the One. See the beginning of chapter 5.

25. This detail in the story recalls the birth of Buddha who was born from his mother's right side. But ancient China was already familiar with this mythological theme regarding the birth of heroes.

26. "Lao Tzu"; here the storyteller repeated the name twice, the first time with a classical pronunciation, the second time, with the vernacular pronunciation, to emphasize the meaning of *child*. This tale was recorded in August of 1979, at Taipei. The storyteller, a Taoist Master whose family came from the An-ch'i district (in south Fukien province), was then seventy-four years old.

27. See "The Fast of the Heart" in chapter 10.

28. The name Li, meaning "plum tree," used for Lao Tzu, is found for the first time in Ssu-ma Ch'ien's *Shih-chi,* ch. 63. As the modern scholar Kao Heng

remarks (Kao, 1933, pp. 351–353), this family name did not exist before the end of the period of the Warring States.

29. See, for example, the tale of the plum tree and the hollow mulberry tree in *shou-shen chi*, ch. 1. Confucius was said to have been born from a hollow mulberry tree. See Granet, 1926, p. 428f.

30. *Shih-chi*, ch. 63.

31. *Hun-yüan sheng-chi*, ch. 1, f. 4a., quoting a *Ho-t'u tai-hsing chi* that is lost today. Chapter 29 of the *Chuang-tzu* (p. 995) says: "People of antiquity knew their mother, but not their father."

32. *San-t'ien nei-chieh ching*, ch. 1, ff. 3b–4a. This work probably dates from the fifth century. Following his birth, says the text, Lao Tzu created the world and men.

33. *Hun-yüan huang-ti sheng-chi*, ch. 2a.

34. *Huan-yüan sheng-chi*, ch. 2, ff. 39b–44a.

35. *Tao-te ching*, chap. 21.

36. Here, I use "ancestor" for the Chinese word *ti*, which originally meant "deified royal ancestor" in ancient China, but which has since taken on the meaning of "emperor." Aside from the Heavenly Worthies, those impersonal aspects of the Tao, theology is familiar with the *ti*, emperors or divine ancestors which correspond to specific roles in the pantheon.

37. See the legend on the Sage's departure from this world at the beginning of chapter 10.

38. This theme on the indebtedness to the vulgar gods, seen above in the context of the daily religion, is found repeatedly in the ancient texts denouncing the perverse, "lascivious" (*yin-ssu*) cults of the shaman masters (*wu-shih*).

39. The *Huang-ti nei-ching su-wen* introduces the Yellow Emperor's instructor in the medical arts, Chi Po, saying that he is a Heavenly Master (*t'ien-shih*). The book begins with a long passage recalling that the perfect body can only be realized by those who practice the Arts of Long Life.

40. The Art of the Bedchamber (*fang-chung chih shu*) belongs to the Taoist procedures for the search for immortality. Many texts handed down to us on this subject fall outside the domain of Taoism itself and belong more properly to that of erotic literature. See "Chaos" in chapter 8.

41. According to the legend, the Mysterious Maiden is supposed to have transmitted to the Yellow Emperor the manual of strategy called *Yin-fu ching*.

42. Poem by Chang Heng (78–139), quoted and translated in van Gulik, 1961, p. 73. Van Gulik translates as "Celestial Old Man" the word *t'ien-lao*, title of the god Kao-mei, that is, the Great Go-Between.

43. The hairpin which young girls used to receive when they reached nubility was intended to serve as an acupuncture needle (to insert in the *yin-hsüeh* point) in case their partner should experience an excessive discharge of sperm.

44. That is to say that these manuals reflect a rather good knowledge of female anatomy and reflexes. But, on the whole, they are centered around the male experience. See "Chaos" in chapter 8.

45. *Chuang-tzu*, chap. 7. See "The Fast of the Heart" in chapter 10 of this volume.

46. Jao, 1956, p. 9. See also "The Kingdom of Humpty-Dumpty" in chapter 10 of this volume.

47. See *Tai-shang Lao-chün ching-lü*, f. 1a.

48. Compare the *Tao-te ching*, chapter 10: "Can you return to the state of the infant?"

49. *Chuang-tzu*, chap. 33, p. 1095.

50. This point is brought to the fore by the fact that the Taoists consider women to be more apt than men to succeed in the search for Long Life. See *Nü chin-tan fa-yao:* "Kuan-hsin chai chi-wen" [Memories of the Kuang-hsin Studio], pp. 34b–35a.

51. *Lao-chün i-pai pa-shih chieh.* Reproduced in *Yün-chi ch'i-ch'ien*, ch. 39.

52. Sun, 1950, p. 36.

53. *Lü-tsu chih*, ch. 3, f. 9b.

54. Confucius is known for having scorned and detested women.

55. See the biographies of Chang Lu (in *San-kuo chih*, ch. 8) and of Kiu Yen (in *San-kuo chih*, ch. 31).

56. Strickmann, 1981, p. 142.

8. Keeping the One

1. The Anterior Heaven (Chinese: *hsien-t'ien*) is the potential state of the universe, its pure, diffuse structure, before it has taken shape. See Fung, 1952, part 2, p. 459ff. The term "Anterior Heaven" was not common until the Sung, but the idea it refers to is present in Taoist thought in every period.

2. Pao-p'u tzu (the Master-Who-Embraces-Simplicity) is the pseudonym of Ko Hung (283–343), a great scholar and philosopher of South China. Of his many medical, technical, historical, and theoretical works, only a part survives today. Only his great philosophical summa, *Pao-p'u tzu nei-p'ien* and *Pao-p'u tzu wai-p'ien* [The Book of the Master-Who-Embraces-Simplicity; Inner and Outer Chapters], is unquestionably authentic. The theme of the Esoteric Treaty is: "Immortality can be obtained through study and effort; why not try?"

3. *Tao-te ching*, chap. 39.

4. *Tao-te ching*, chap. 21.

5. *Pao-p'u tzu nei-p'ien*, chap. 18, p. 92.

6. Ibid.

7. Ibid., p. 94. A similar passage can be found in the encyclopedia *Wu-shang pi-yao*, ch. 5, ff. 6b–7a, quoting a now lost *Huang-jen ching*.

8. Ibid., p. 93.

9. See "The Register" in chapter 4.

10. *Pao-p'u tzu nei-p'ien*, ch. 18, p. 93.

11. This book exists in two versions. The oldest, with which we will be concerned here, goes back to the second century A.D. The second version, the

so-called *Huang-t'ing neiching ching,* is part of the Mao-shan revelations of the fourth century A.D. See Schipper, 1975b, introduction.

12. *Huang-t'ing ching,* verses 1 to 7. Compare Maspero, 1981:491–492.

13. *Yün-chi ch'i-ch'ien,* ch. 54, f. 7a.

14. See "The Abstinence from Cereals" in Chapter 9.

15. Excrements are considered a means by which the *p'o* souls can escape.

16. This is the "Pure Chamber." This space used to be furnished only with an incense burner and mats to sit on.

17. The rites of confession have an important place in Taoism, as much in private practices as in the collective liturgy. See Maspero, 1981, pp. 380–381.

18. According to Chinese etiquette no rice is served at meals when wine is served.

19. Introduction to the *Huang-t'ing ching* by Wu-ch'eng tzu, reproduced in *Yün-chi ch'i-ch'ien,* ch. 12, f. 28a.

20. Ibid.

21. *Tao-te ching,* chap. 6.

22. *T'ai-shang Lao-chün yang-sheng chüeh,* f. 4b.

23. These numbers also correspond to the values of the Five Phases in the system of computation called *tun-chia,* the "Hidden Periods." See the section on "Chaos," in this same chapter, and Schipper and Wang, 1986.

24. There are different traditions concerning the respiration of the Six Breaths and their vocalization.

25. See Despeux, 1981.

26. This system has been developed in the very famous but apocryphal text *Chou-i ts'an-t'ung ch'i* (the Concordance of the Three from the *I-ching* of the Chou [Dynasty]), attributed to the alchemist Wei Po-yang (second century), but in fact a text of the T'ang period.

27. *Tao-te ching,* chap. 10.

28. The energy cycles (*yün-ch'i*) play an important role in Chinese medicine, and a large part of the famous *Huang-ti nei-ching su-wen* is devoted to them. The fact that the *yün-ch'i* cycles receive hardly any attention in the Western practice of Chinese acupuncture is rather revealing as to the prejudices of Western civilization.

29. *Huang-t'ing ching,* verses 8 to 52.

30. See Schipper, 1978b.

31. See the commentary by Wu-ch'eng tzu to the *Huang-t'ing ching,* in *Yün-chi ch'i-ch'ien,* ch. 12, f. 36a.

32. See Schipper and Wang, 1986.

33. See Ngo, 1976, pp. 190–195.

34. *Pi-tsang t'ung-hsüan pien-hua liu-yin t'ung-wei tun-chia chen-ching,* ch. 2, f. 2b.

35. *Tao-te ching,* chap. 45.

36. *Huang-t'ing ching,* Part 3, f. 8b.

37. See "The Inhabitants" in chapter 6.

38. See *Hsüan-yüan pen-chi* (Biography of the Yellow Emperor), in *Yün-*

chi ch'i-ch'ien, ch. 100, p. 21a–21b. Thanks to the teachings of Jung-ch'eng tzu, Master of music—and author of books on the Arts of the Bedroom (*fang-chung chih shu*)—the White Maiden and the Yellow Emperor invented lutes and mouth organs to channel their desires.

39. *Huang-t'ing ching,* verses 13 and 19.

40. Ibid., verse 26.

41. Ibid., verse 63 with the commentary of Wu Cheng-tzu, in *Yün-chi ch'i-ch'ien,* ch. 12, f. 38b.

42. *Chen-kao* 2.1a–2.1b, quoted by Strickmann 1981, p. 183.

43. This remark by Granet was reported to me by his former students.

44. There is a popular novel called, *T'ao-hua nü tou-fa p'o chou-kung* [The Battle between the Duke of Chou and Miss Peach-Flower], which relates the story of the origin of the marriage ceremonies and their meaning. The Duke of Chou is the paragon of Confucian virtues, whereas Miss Peach Blossom is a Taoist witch.

45. Romanticism is considered to be dishonest. Until recently in the peasant society of South China, young married people were not supposed to smile at each other or hold hands in public.

46. *Su-nü ching,* f. 1b. Quoted in Maspero, 1981, p. 519.

47. Maspero, 1981, p. 520.

48. *Yü-fang pi-chüeh,* p. 1a.

49. *Su-nü ching,* p. 1b.

50. This tendency characterizes the erotic manuals as well as current pornographic literature in China.

51. *Yü-fang chih-yao,* f. 1a. Also quoted in Maspero 1981, p. 519.

52. See Schipper, 1969, pp. 23–30.

53. *Chuang-tzu,* chap. 11, p. 381.

54. *Pao-p'u tzu nei-p'ien,* chap. 8, p. 33.

55. See *Yüan-yang tzu fa-yü, Tao-tsang,* no. 1071, ch. 2, p. 2a: "How many young people of this world have been killed by [those who practice] the Art of the Bedchamber!"

56. Henri Maspero studied this ritual (Maspero, 1981, pp. 536–541), but without taking into account the text of the *Shang-ch'ing huang-shu kuo-tu i* (*Tao-tsang,* no. 1294), which corresponds to the original ritual. My description here is based on this text.

57. Among these deities, the Jade Maidens of the Six Ting Days are especially invoked.

58. Vows of ordination in modern times specify that the Master is not to belong to any faction, sect, or party.

59. Van Gulik (1961, p. 125) mentions, in regards to this, the rites of union of the modern sect called I-kuan tao. These rites do indeed exist, but their liturgical function is unknown.

60. *Ch'ung-Lü ch'uan-Tao chi,* ff. 17a–18a.

61. An allusion to *Tao-te ching,* chap. 48.

62. This has been termed variously, by different authors: "involution" (*ni*), "return" (*fan*), "turning back" (*huan*), or "come home" (*kuei*).

63. *Ch'ung-Lü ch'uan-Tao chi,* ff. 18a–18b.

64. This school originated towards the end of the twelfth century in North China under the educated elite. It became very influential thereafter. One of the early Ch'üan-chen patriarchs, named Ch'iu Ch'ang-ch'un, so impressed Genghis Khan that China was largely spared in the wholesale destruction by the Mongol invaders. See Waley, 1931.

65. This story is taken from the novel *Ch'i-chen yin-kuo chuan* [The Story of the Retribution of the Seven True Men], which presumably dates from the seventeenth century.

66. *Chuang-tzu,* chap. 6, p. 228.

67. *Ch'ung-Lü ch'uan-Tao chi,* f. 18a.

68. See Kaltenmark, 1965, pp. 40–45.

69. *Ch'ung-Lü ch'uan-Tao chi,* f. 23a.

70. This corresponds to the Taoist proverb: "to go with the stream is the way to death, to go against the stream is the way to life" (*hsün wei ssu, ni wei sheng*).

71. There is a voluminous literature, even today, on the harmful effects of nocturnal ejaculations and on the ways to prevent them. Masturbation is very severely suppressed if indeed it is every mentioned.

72. *Tai-shang tao-yin yang-sheng ching,* f. 6a.

73. The main theme remains: "to return of the essence to repair the brain." See Maspero, 1981, p. 522.

74. Kaltenmark, 1953, introduction.

75. On this method see Maspero, 1981, pp. 459–484. It must be noted that embryonic breathing is not a late development in the breathing exercises, but has always existed under different names.

76. "His bones are soft . . ." is a quotation of *Tao-te ching,* chap. 55.

77. *T'ai-ch'ing tiao-ch'i ching,* f. 2a.

78. That is to say that they correspond to the three stages outlined above in text; preliminary preparation, union, and return.

79. Retaining the breath for a long period can result in a natural acidification of the blood. This, in turn, provokes dizzy spells and can even lead to hallucinations.

80. *Ch'ung-Lü ch'uan-Tao chi,* f. 25b. Compare the words of the Zen Master Lin-chi: "If you see the Buddha, kill him"; see Demiéville, 1972, p. 117.

81. These three phases of *ching* ("essence"), *ch'i* ("breath"), and *shen* ("godhead") mark the three principal stages towards perfection. They play an important role in the Taoist theories of modern times.

82. *Tao-te ching,* chap. 40: "*fan chih Tao chih tung.*"

83. By analogy with the sacrifice of the Real Writs (see "The Sacrifice of Writings" in chap. 5), where the signs are "sent back" to their original undifferentiated state.

84. Compare the craftsmen in the *Chuang-tzu* (see the conclusion of chapter 10).

9: The Immortals

1. The story of Lü Tung-pin is told in a famous Chinese play of the thirteenth or fourteenth century (Yüan dynasty), translated by Louis Laloy (1935).

2. This is an ancient theme: before beginning the search for immortality, one must accomplish three thousand good deeds.

3. *Lü-tsu chih,* ch. 1, f. 5a.

4. Ibid., ch. 4. f. 12a.

5. Lü Tung-pin is the great initiator in modern Taoism. Along with Ch'ung-li Ch'üan, he is considered the Master of Wang Ch'ung-yang, the founder of the Ch'üan-chen school. Today, he is still one of the most frequent characters in the mediums' revelations

6. This story is the subject of a popular novel, *Lü Tung-pin san-hsi Pai Mu-tan* [Lü Tung-pin Pokes Fun Three Times at White Peony].

7. Many modern sects worship Lü Tung-pin.

8. *Shen-hsien chuan,* ch. 2.

9. *Chuang-tzu,* chap. 12, p. 421.

10. This original meaning of *miao* is "sanctuary for the ancestors."

11. *Chuang-tzu,* chap. 1, p. 28.

12. See "The Preliminary Stage" in chapter 8.

13. See *Lieh-hsien chuan,* biographies 27 and 47 (Kaltenmark, 1953).

14. P'eng-tsu, one of the oldest characters in the mythology of the Immortals, is given the title of ku-hsien. See *T'ai-ch'ing tao-yin yang-sheng ching,* f. 6b.

15. See *Lao-chun i-pai pa-shih chieh.*

16. *Pao-p'u tzu nei-p'ien,* chap. 15, pp. 65–66.

17. One of these texts was translated into English: Read, 1939.

18. *Pao-p'u tzu nei-p'ien,* chap. 11, pp. 50–51.

19. The food taken on journeys by wandering Taoists has been studied by Stein (1972).

20. *Pao-p'u tzu nei-p'ien,* chap. 17, p. 76.

21. Ibid., p. 77.

22. Ibid., 18, p. 93. See Kaltenmark, 1974.

23. Kaltenmark, 1974, p. 159.

24. Kaltenmark, 1953, pp. 11–12.

25. *Pao-p'u tzu nei-p'ien,* chap. 17, p. 78.

26. See Granet, 1953, pp. 245–249.

27. *Pao-p'u tzu nei-p'ien,* chap. 17, p. 78.

28. That is to say, one practices embryonic breathing.

29. See Schipper, 1963, introduction.

30. See Wasson, 1968, pp. 80–92.

31. *Pao-p'u-tzu nei-p'ien,* chap. 11, p. 45.

32. See Needham, 1956–1980, vol. 5, pp. 346–355.

33. See Sivin, 1968.

34. A manuscript concerning these techniques of using minerals as food

discovered some years ago in a tomb at Ma-wang tui and was published in the journal *Wenwu*, 1975, vol. 6.

35. See Granet, 1926, chap. 3.

36. Granet, 1926, p. 489.

37. *Shih-chi*, ch. 28, "Feng-shan chih" (chapter on the Feng and Shan Sacrifices). Translated in Chavannes, 1895–1905, vol. 3, p. 465.

38. *Pao-pu tzu nei-p'ien*, chap. 4, pp. 12–13.

39. The title alludes to the legendary nine cauldrons of the great Yü.

40. *Pao-p'u tzu nei-p'ien*, chap. 4, pp. 14–15. This a paraphrase, not a direct citation.

41. See Sivin, 1980.

42. See Strickmann, 1979, p. 139.

43. "Laboratory alchemy uses rat poison as a basic ingredient. If treated with fire, it can be absorbed (in small doses); after three years, one becomes Immortal." *Ch'ih-lung tan-chüeh*, a now lost work quoted in *Li-shih chen-hsien t'i-tao t'ung chien*, ch. 45 (biography of Wang Ch'ang-yü).

44. See Wagner, 1973.

45. *Ch'i-chen yin-kuo chuan*, ch. 15.

46. See *San-tung hsiu-tao i*, f. 8a.

47. See chapter 8, note 2.

48. See Ko Hung's biography in *Chin-shu*, ch. 72.

10: Teaching without Words

1. *Shen-hsien chuan*, ch. 1.

2. See "Birth" in chapter 7.

3. The text of the *Tao-te ching* comprises about five thousand characters (current editions include exactly 5,258), and people have tried to attach to this figure the symbolics of the number five (Five Phases, five cardinal points, et cetera), so fundamental to Chinese cosmological thought. Hence the name "(Writ of) Five Thousand Words," *Wu-chen wen*, which Taoist tradition gives to this text.

4. The *Tao-te ching* is also the Chinese work most translated into Western languages. Arthur Waley's beautiful translation (1934) remains, to my mind, one of the best. It is prefaced by an excellent introduction which places the work in its religious context. Another excellent translation is by Wing-tsit Chan (1963).

5. "Watchtower" in Chinese is *kuan*. From the Han period on, the spot where legend locates the *kuan* of the Guardian Yin Hsi has been one of the sacred places of Taoism. Since that period, *kuan* has also become a general name for Taoist sanctuaries and monasteries.

6. The legend according to which Confucius is supposed to have visited Lao Tzu to ask him about the rites is very old (it is told in the *Chuang-tzu*). It

has never been challenged by the Confucianists. The *li* ("ceremonial," "rites," "etiquette") is one of the fundamental concepts of the literati's humanism. Derived from the religious ritual of feudal China (sacrifices and court ceremonial), the *li* of Confucius is meant to be the expression of proper social relations ("let each behave according to his quality"), which is a way of translating into sociological terms the identity (the *name*) of each individual.

There are several distinct versions of the legend, but its main theme is the difference between the cultural norms of classical humanism on the one hand, and the (Taoist) vision of nature and chaos (spontaneous and nonconformist)—which is enacted through the "inner ritual"—on the other. According to the historian Ssu-ma Ch'ien, Lao Tzu told Confucius that his way of practicing *li* "was not beneficial in any way to his body." The *Tao-te ching* (chap. 38) says regarding Confucianism: "*Li* is the meanest expression of integrity and the beginning of disorders," that is to say, a danger for the country.

7. Modern historiography identifies the place where the present version of the *Tao-te ching* was compiled as the academy of Ch'i, a state in North China (present-day Shantung).

8. The expression *Tao-chia,* "Taoist School," is found in Ssu-ma Ch'ien (*Shih-chi,* ch. 63) in the context of the tradition of the Immortals. Later, the bibliographer Liu Hsiang (77–6 B.C.) classified the *Lao Tzu* and the *Chuang-tzu* under the rubric *Tao-chia.* Under the later Han, we begin to find the name *Tao-chiao,* "the teaching of the Tao." In later Taoism, the two expressions, *Tao-chiao* and *Tao-chia,* are used freely one for the other. Only from modern times on have the Confucianists used the two expressions to establish an artificial distinction between "philosophical Taoism"—for which they use the term *Tao-chia*—and "religious Taoism"—for which they use the term *Tao-chiao.*

9. Confucius is supposed to have said: "My Way (Tao) is the One that links everything" (*Lun-yü* book 4, paragraph 15).

10. *Tao-te ching,* chap. 1.

11. As we have seen in chapter 1 of this book, the Mysteries of pre-imperial China were placed under the double aegis of "Lao Tzu and Huang-ti" (*Huang-lao*).

12. *Tao-te ching,* chap. 70.

13. *Tao-te ching,* chap 2.

14. *Tao-te ching,* chap. 18: "When the Great Way declines, benevolence and justice will reign; when the intellectuals appear, great artifice begins."

15. Literary subversion is a common practice in other Taoist texts as well. See Schipper, 1963, introduction.

16. *Tao-te ching,* chap. 6: "The spirit of the Valley never dies. It is called the Obscure Female. The gate to the Obscure Female is the origin of Heaven and Earth . . ." This chapter is very often quoted and discussed in connection with the Taoist Arts of Long Life.

17. *Tao-te ching,* chap. 28. This is the famous chapter that begins: "To know the male, yet keep to what is female is to become like the ravine of the world. . . . To know the white, yet keep to the black is to become the compass of the world."

18. *Tao-te ching*, chap. 20.

19. See Duyvendak, 1953, p. 131. The passage that perplexed Duyvendak was, "Close the passage, lock the door!," in *Tao-te ching*, chap. 56.

20. On Wang Pi, see below, the discussion in the section, "The Kingdom of Humpty-Dumpty."

21. See Kaltenmark, 1965. p. 45.

22. For example, *Tao-te ching*, chap. 59: "To govern men and serve Heaven, there is nothing like moderation."

23. *Tao-te ching*, chap. 17.

24. *Tao-te ching*, chap. 57.

25. *Tao-te ching*, chap. 58.

26. *Tao-te ching*, chap. 65.

27. *Tao-te ching*, chap. 38. Concerning the "knowledge about the future," see the remarks in Waley, 1934, p. 251.

28. *Tao-te ching*, chap. 19 (Here I follow Kaltenmark, 1965, pp. 61–62).

29. *Tao-te ching*, chap. 80. (I follow the translation of Duyvendak, 1953:180–181). The knotted cords, mentioned in this chapter of the *Tao-te ching*, were an ancient form of communication before the invention of writing.

30. *Tao-te ching*, chap. 21. The word *pu*, which I translate here as "beginnings," can also be translated as "soldiers."

31. *Tao-te ching*, chap. 12.

32. *Tao-te ching*, chap. 16 (I follow the translation of Kaltenmark, 1965, p. 55).

33. *Tao-te ching*, chap. 20. During the seasonal festivals, feasts and orgies were held in the towers or on the terraces. The word *hun*, meaning "stupid" or "idiot," sounds exactly like *hun* meaning Chaos. "Restless as the ocean": For this reading, I have relied on manuscript "A" of Ma-wang tui (see *Lao-tzu Ma-wang tui Han-mu po-shu*). Compare Kaltenmark, 1965, p. 85).

34. *Tao-te ching*, chap. 10. (reading *wu-wei* [non-action] instead of *wu-chih* [not-knowing]).

35. *Tao-te ching*, chap. 3.

36. *Tao-te ching, Yin-chu Ho-shang kung Lao-tzu Tao-te ching*, chap. 3, (ch. 1, ff. 2a–2b).

37. The date of the "Hisiang Erh" commentary, a fragment of which was found among the Tun-huang manuscripts, is controversial. The tradition that attributes it to the First Heavenly Master Chang Tao-ling has not really been proven. However, I do consider it to be a work of the later Han. Compare Jao, 1956, p. 6.

38. *Tao-te chen-ching chu-shu*, ch. 1, ff. 12b–13a, quoting a commentary attributed to Ku Huan.

39. This intellectual movement was mistakenly confused with the Taoism of the period. See Strickmann, 1981, p. 98.

40. On Taoist "non-knowledge," see below, "The Fast of the Heart."

41. For example, drug addiction to the "Powder of Cold Food." (The adepts of Hsüan-hsüeh and of Ch'ing-t'an (pure conversations) professed a disdain for personal hygiene, like our hippies of the 1960s.

42. *Shen-hsien chuan*, ch. 3.

43. I mean that the *Tao-te ching*, included among the "classical" writings since the Han period, was given its "official" gloss by Wang Pi. Later a great number of men of state felt called upon to write Confucian commentaries. But the ancient interpretive tradition was maintained for texts concerned with psychophysiological and liturgical practices.

44. That is, the body as a whole, uniting the physical and the social, is destroyed.

45. The *Shih-chi*, ch. 63, says that the work had more than 100,000 characters. The current text has around 70,000.

46. *Tao-te ching*, chap. 28.

47. *Chuang-tzu*, chap. 33, pp. 1093–1095 and 1098–1099. The quotation of Lao Tzu's words corresponds to chapter 28 of the *Tao-te ching*.

48. *Chuang-tzu*, chap. 12, pp. 433–438.

49. *Chuang-tzu*, chap. 23, pp. 777–790.

50. *Chuang-tzu*, chap. 22, p. 737.

51. *Chuang-tzu*, chap. 1, p. 17.

52. *Chuang-tzu*, chap. 2, p. 70.

53. *Chuang-tzu*, chap. 4, pp. 131–148.

54. *Chuang-tzu*, chap. 22, pp. 759–760.

55. *Chuang-tzu*, chap. 6, pp. 224–228. "The True Man breathes through his heels": this sentence is often quoted in the context of Embryonic Breathing practices.

56. *Chuang-tzu*, chap. 22. Compare with *Tao-te ching*, chap. 56.

57. *Chuang-tzu*, chap. 2, p. 79.

58. Chuang Tzu implies here that simple people are wary of men of great intelligence and are not interested in knowing the future.

59. Lieh-tzu is shown here to be the disciple of Master Gourd. He also appears elsewhere in the *Chuang-tzu*. The book has come down to us with the title *Lieh-tzu* in a collection of short pieces, similar to the *Chuang-tzu*. A certain number of anecdotes are found in both books, as, for example, the one translated here.

60. That is to say, he lost control of himself so that the shaman was able "to seize" his thoughts.

61. This remark enables us to understand that at that time in China, as is the case today, shamanism and Taoism, while different, were close enough so that a common person, in this case the disciple, might get them mixed up.

62. Compare with the sentence above: "The True Man breathes through his heels."

63. Water is the first of the elements and represents the number One. We find here the Nine permutations of the One. The version in the *Lieh-tzu* gives the names of the nine abysses.

64. *Chuang-tzu*, chap. 7, pp. 297–306.

65. *Chuang-tzu*, chap. 19, p. 647.

66. *Chuang-tzu*, chap. 19, p. 646.

67. *Chuang-tzu*, chap. 5, pp. 220–222. "You lean against a tree": that is, in his arguments Hui-tzu always needs "to lean on something." He does not have an independent mind. "You fall asleep on your lute": the lute is the instru-

ment of love. "The hard and the white": the relation between things and their attributes was one of the sophists' favorite subjects ("a white horse is not a horse").

68. *Chuang-tzu,* chap. 3, p. 115.
69. *Chuang-tzu,* chap. 2, pp. 55–56.
70. *Chuang-tzu,* chap. 12, p. 450.
71. *Chuang-tzu,* chap. 17, pp. 606–607.
72. *Chuang-tzu,* chap. 13, pp. 490–491.
73. *Chuang-tzu,* chap. 3, pp. 117–124.
74. *Chuang-tzu,* chap. 6, p. 256.

Bibliography

Chinese Sources (Printed and Manuscript)

Note: The *Tao-tsang* [Taoist Canon] is the repository of all Taoist scriptures. The earliest Taoist Canon was compiled in the fifth century A.D. Afterwards, all great dynasties reedited the collection and added new materials. The earlier collections are entirely lost. The only surviving Taoist Canon is the last one. It was published during the Ming dynasty, in 1445. A *Supplement* was added in 1606. The collection contains more than 1500 books. Many of these are undated and unsigned, and have not yet been properly studied. Only a very few among them have ever been translated into Western languages.

Even this last collection was nearly lost. At the beginning of this century, only a few incomplete copies of the *Tao-tsang* of the Ming dynasty still existed. Thanks to private initiative, a complete set was reconstructed from the remaining copies and reprinted in Shanghai by the Commercial Press in 1926. This reprint allowed scholars, for the first time, to study these extensive Taoist source materials.

Cheng-i fa-wen t'ien-shih chiao chieh-k'o ching [Rules of the Way of the Heavenly Master, from the Ritual Canon of the One and Orthodox]. Third century A.D. *Tao-tsang*, no. 789.

Chen-kao [Words of the True Ones]. Personal revelations by the saints of the Shang-ch'ing heaven during the years 364–375, edited, with a commentary by T'ao Hung-ching (456–536). *Tao-tsang*, no. 1016.

Ch'i-chen yin-kuo chuan [The Story of the Retribution of the Seven True Men]. Popular Taoist novel on the story of the Ch'üan-chen patriarchs. Probably fourteenth century. Woodblock edition of 1893, reprinted in *Tao-tsang ching-hua* [Selected Works from the Taoist Canon], 8th ser., vol. 10. Taipei, Tzu-yu press, 1965, (under the title: *Pei-p'ai ch'i-chen hsiu-Tao shih-chuan* [Story of the Practice of the Tao by the Seven True Men of the Northern School]). See also Endres, 1985.

Chin-lu su-ch'i k'o-i [Ritual of the Golden Register for the Overnight Prayer]. Liturgical manuscript (unpublished). Tainan, Taiwan, ca. 1890 (author's collection).

Chin-shu [History of the Chin Dynasty]. Compiled during the T'ang dynasty by Fang Hsüan-ling (578–648) and included in the Twenty-Four Dynastic Histories.

Chiu-t'ien ying-yüan lei-sheng p'u-hua t'ien-tsun yü-shu pao-ching [Precious Scripture of the Jade Pivot (spoken by) the Heavenly Worthy of Universal Transformation Whose Voice of the Thunder Responds to the Origin of the Nine Heavens]. A liturgical scripture, revealed in the thirteenth century. *Tao-tsang*, no. 99 (popularly known as *Lei-shu ching*).

Chou-i ts'an-t'ung ch'i [The Concordance of the Three from the *I-ching* of the Chou (Dynasty)]. Attributed to the legendary alchemist Wei Po-yang (second century A.D.), but in fact a text of the T'ang period (eighth century). *Tao-tsang*, no. 1001.

Chuang-tzu [The Book of Master Chuang]. The edition used for the translations in this book is the *Chuang-tzu chi-shih*, edited by Kuo Ch'ing-p'an in 1894. This edition contains the commentaries by Kuo Hsiang (third century A.D.) and by Ch'eng Hsüan-ying (seventh century A.D.), as well as many additional materials. The page numbers refer to the modern, punctuated edition, published in Peking by Chung-hua shu-chü, 1985. See also Watson, 1970, and Graham, 1981.

Ch'un-ch'iu Kung-yang chuan [The Kung-yang Tradition of the Spring and Autumn Annals]. This is one of the "thirteen classics" of Confucianism. The most commonly used edition is the reprint of the imperial version of the eleventh century, *Ch'ung-k'an Sung-pen shih-san ching chu-shu*, published in Nan-ch'ang in 1815.

Ch'ung-Lü ch'uan-Tao chi (The Transmission of the Tao from Ch'ung (-li Ch'üan) to Lü (Tung-pin)]. This work, presumably of the eleventh century, is included in the *Hsiu-chen shih-shu* [Ten Books on the Cultivation of the True Self] collection. *Tao-tsang*, no. 263, ch. 16.

Chung-shen chou [Formulas to Call on All Gods]. Handbook for the vernacular ritual. Taiwan, unpublished and undated manuscript from the author's collection.

Hai-ch'iung Pai chen-jen yü-lu [The Sayings of True Man Pai of Hai-ch'iung]. Compiled by his disciples. Thirteenth century. *Tao-tsang*, no. 1307.

Hsiao-tao lun [Dissertation Ridiculing the Tao], by Chen Luan. A polemic attack on Taoism by a Buddhist convert of the seventh century, included in the Buddhist Canon. *Taishô issai kyô* [The Complete Buddhist Canon of the Taishô Period], vol. 52, no. 2103.

Hsüan-t'an mi-chüeh [Secret Formulas for the Mysterious Altar]. Unpublished liturgical manuscript from the region of Ch'üan-chou, Fukien province, dating from the early nineteenth century (author's collection).

Hsüan-yüan pen-chi [Biography of the Yellow Emperor]. T'ang dynasty (seventh century). This official hagiography has been partially preserved in the *Yün-chi ch'i-ch'ien* [Library of the Clouds in Seven Subdivisions] encyclopedia of the eleventh century. *Tao-tsang,* no. 1032, ch. 100.

Hsün-tzu [The Book of Master Hsün]. A philosophical treatise of the fourth century B.C. *Chu-tzu chi-ch'eng* [Complete Critical Edition of the Classical Philosophers] edition. Shanghai, Shih-chieh shu-chü, 1935.

Huai-nan tzu [The Book of the Master of Huai-nan]. Second century B.C. *Chu-tzu chi-ch'eng* [Complete Critical Edition of the Classical Philosophers] edition. Shanghai, Shih-chieh shu-chü, 1935.

Huang-ti nei-ching su-wen [Simple Questions of the Yellow Emperor]. *Ssu-pu ts'ung-k'an* edition. Shanghai, Commercial Press, 1920–1922.

Huang-t'ing ching [The Book of the Yellow Court]. Second or third centuries A.D. Included in the *Yün-chi ch'i-ch'ien* [Library of the Clouds in Seven Subdivisions] encyclopedia of the eleventh century. *Tao-tsang,* no. 1032, ch. 17. See Schipper, 1975b.

Hun-yüan sheng-chi [Sacred Records About [Him Who Was] at the Origin of Chaos]. A hagiography of Lao Tzu, written by Hsieh Shou-hao (1134–1212). *Tao-tsang,* no. 770.

I-ching [The Book of Changes]. This is one of the "thirteen classics" of Confucianism. The most commonly used edition is the reprint of the imperial version of the eleventh century, *Ch'ung-k'an Sung-pen shih-san ching chu-shu,* published in Nan-ch'ang in 1815. The most current translation in English is Wilhelm, 1968.

Lao-chün shuo i-pai pa-shih chieh [The One Hundred and Eighty Commandments (for Libationers) spoken by the Old Lord]. A set of religious rules intended for the Taoist clergy and dating from the third or fourth centuries A.D. Included in the *Yün-chi ch'i-ch'ien* [Library of the Clouds in Seven Subdivisions] encyclopedia of the eleventh century. *Tao-tsang,* no. 1032, ch. 39. See also Schmidt, 1984.

Lao-tzu chung-ching [The Book of the Center of Lao-tzu]. Included in the *Yün-chi ch'i-ch'ien* [Library of the Clouds in Seven Subdivisions] encyclopedia of the eleventh century. *Tao-tsang,* no. 1032, ch. 18 and 19. See also Schipper, 1979.

Lao-tzu Hsiang-erh chu [The Hsiang-erh Commentary of the *Tao-te ching*]; see Jao, Tsung-i, 1956.

Lao-tzu: Ma-wang t'ui Han-mu po-shu [The Silk Manuscript of the *Lao-tzu* Discovered at Ma-wang t'ui]. Peking, Wen-wu chu-pan she, 1976. See also *Tao-te ching.*

Lao-tzu pien-hua ching [Book of the Transformation of Lao Tzu]. Manuscript of a Taoist work from the second century A.D., found among the scrolls discovered at Tun-huang (North-East China) at the beginning of this century. See Seidel, 1969.

Lao-tzu pien-hua wu-chi ching [Book of the Unending Transformations of Lao Tzu]. *Tao-tsang*, no. 1195.

Lieh-hsien chuan [Biographies of Famous Immortals]. Second century A.D. See Kaltenmark, 1953.

Ling-pao wu-liang tu-jen shang-p'in miao-ching [Book of the Immense Salvation of Mankind, from the Ling-pao Canon]. End of the fourth century A.D. *Tao-tsang*, no. 1, ch. 1.

Li-shih chen-hsien t'i-tao t'ung-chien [Comprehensive Mirror of the True Immortals Who Embodied the Tao]. By Chao Tao-i (Yüan dynasty, thirteenth century). *Tao-tsang*, no. 296.

Lü-tsu chih [Annals of Patriarch Lü]. Probably fourteenth century. *Tao-tsang*, no. 1484.

Lü Tung-pin san-hsi Pai Mu-tan [Lü Tung-pin Pokes Fun at White Peony]. A popular novel. Seventeenth century? Taipei, Wen-hua editions, 1951.

Lun-yü [The Analects (of Confucius)]. This is one of the "thirteen classics" of Confucianism. The most commonly used edition is the reprint of the imperial version of the eleventh century, *Ch'ung-k'an Sung-pen shih-san ching chu-shu*, published in Nan-ch'ang in 1815.

Nü chin-tan fa-yao [Essentials of Female (Interior) Alchemy]. Eighteenth century. Reprinted in *Tao-tsang ching-hua* [Selected Works from the Taoist Canon], 5th ser., vol. 5. Taipei, Tzu-yu press, 1960.

Pao-p'u tzu nei-p'ien [The Inner Chapters of the Book of the Master-Who-Embraces-Simplicity]. By Ko Hung (283–343). Critical edition by Sun Hsing-yen (1753–1818). *Chu-tzu chi-ch'eng* [Complete Critical Edition of the Classical Philosophers] edition. Shanghai, Shih-chieh shu-chü, 1935.

Pei-tou ching [The Book of the Bushel]: see *Tai-shang hsüan-ling pei-tou yen sheng miao-ching*.

Pi-tsang t'ung-hsüan pien-hua liu-yin tung-wei tun-chia chen-ching [True Book from the Secret Canon of the Hidden Periods of the Six Yin Forces Which Pervade the Invisible through Transformation and Communication with Mystery]. Early Ming (fourteenth century?). *Tao-tsang*, no. 857.

San-chiao yüan-liu sou-shen t-ch'üan [Complete Stories of the Gods of All Ages of the Three Religions]. Anonymous hagiography of the early seventeenth century, reprinted by Yeh Te-hui, private edition, Peking, 1907.

San-kuan ching [The Book of the Three Officials]: see *T'ai-shang san-yüan tz'u-fu she-tsui chieh-ê hsiao-tsai yen-sheng pao-ming miao-ching*.

San-kuo chih [Annals of the Three Kingdoms]. Compiled by Ch'en Shou (233–297) and included in the Twenty-Four Dynastic Histories.

San-t'ien nei-chieh ching [A Treatise for Initiation into the Doctrine of the Three Heavens]. Fifth century. *Tao-tsang*, no. 1205.

San-tung hsiu-tao i [Protocol for the Practice of the Tao of the Three Caverns]. Tenth century. *Tao-tsang*, no. 1237.

Shang-ch'ing huang-shu kuo-tu i [Ritual for Passing, from the Yellow Book of the Shang-ch'ing]. Rites of sexual union from the early period of the Heavenly Master movement, presumably from the third century A.D.. *Tao-tsang*, no. 1294.

Shen-hsien chuan [Biographies of Divine Immortals]. By Ko Hung (283–

343). Partially preserved in the *Yün-chi ch'i-ch'ien* [Library of the Clouds in Seven Subdivisions) encyclopedia of the eleventh century. *Tao-tsang*, no. 1032, ch. 109.

Shih-chi [Historical Records], by Ssu-ma Ch'ien (145–86 B.C.). See Chavannes, 1895–1915.

Shu-i chi [Tales of the Marvellous], by Jen Fang (sixth century). Republished in the *Han-wei ts'ung-shu* [Collected Books of the Han and Wei Dynasties] of the seventeenth century.

Sou-shen chi [Collected Stories of the Gods]. By Kan Pao (fourth century). Reprinted in the *Shuo-fu* [Repository of (Ancient) Works] of the Ming dynasty.

Su-nü ching [Book of the White Maiden]. Ancient manual of "bedroom" techniques, now lost but reconstructed from fragments and published in the *Shuang-mei ching-an ts'ung shu* [Reprinted Works from the Shuang-mei ching-an Library] of Yeh Te-hui (1903).

T'ai-ch'ing fu-ch'i k'ou-chüeh (Oral Instructions for Breathing Exercises of the T'ai-ch'ing tradition]. T'ang dynasty (seventh century?). *Tao-tsang*, no. 822.

T'ai-ch'ing tiao-ch'i ching [Book of the Harmonization of Energies of the T'ai-ch'ing Tradition]. T'ang dynasty (seventh century?). *Tao-tsang*, no. 820.

T'ai-shang ch'u-chia ch'uan-tu i [Most High Ritual of Ordination of Monks]. *Tao-tsang*, no. 1236.

Tai-shang hsüan-ling pei-tou yen-sheng miao-ching [Marvellous Book of the Mysterious Powers of the Northern Bushel (Stars) Which Prolong Life, Revealed by the Most-High (Lao-chün)]. Sung dynasty (twelfth century?). *Tao-tsang*, no. 622 (popularly known as *Pei-tou ching*, Book of the Bushel).

Tai-shang Lao-chün ching-lü [Canonical Rules by the Most High Old Lord]. Six Dynasties. *Tao-tsang*, no. 562.

T'ai-shang Lao-chün shuo T'ien-fei chiu-k'u ling-yen ching [Book of the Miracles of the Heavenly Consort Who Saves from Distress, Spoken by the Most High Lao-chün]. Ming dynasty (fourteenth century). *Tao-tsang*, no. 649.

T'ai-shang Lao-chün yang-sheng chüeh [Instructions for Nourishing Life by the Most High Old Lord]. T'ang dynasty? *Tao-tsang*, no. 821.

T'ai-shang san-yüan tz'u-fu she-tsui chieh-ê hsiao-tsai yen-sheng pao-ming miao-ching [Marvellous Book of the Most High Three Principles Which Protect and Prolong Life, Eliminate Disaster, Abolish Danger, Forgive Sins, and Confer Blessings]. Southern Sung or Yüan dynasty. *Tao-tsang*, no. 1441 (popularly known as *San-kuan ching* [The Book of the Three Officials]).

Tai-shang tao-yin yang-sheng ching [Book of the Most High for Nourishing Life by Conducting the Energies]. T'ang dynasty? *Tao-tsang*, no. 820.

Tai-shang tung-hsüan ling-pao chung-chien-wen [Texts from All the (Revealed Writings) on (Wooden) Strips, from the Most High Tung-hsüan Ling-Pao Canon]. By Lu Hsiu-ching (406-477). *Tao-tsang*, no. 411.

T'ao-hua nü t'ou-fa [The Magic Battles of the Peach Blossom Maiden]. Popular novel of unknown date, also known as *Yin-yang t'ou* [The Battle of Yin and Yang]. Tai-chung, Jui-ch'eng Book Store, 1956.

Tao-te chen-ching chu-shu [Commentary of the Book of the Way and Its

Power]. This edition comprises fragments of a commentary to the *Tao-te ching* by Ku Huan (420–483). *Tao-tsang*, no. 710.

Tao-te ching [The Book of the Way and Its Power]. I have used the Sung edition with the Ho-shang kung commentary: *Yin-chu Ho-shang kung Lao-tzu Tao-te ching*, edited by Lü Chu-ch'ien (1137–1181) and printed in Ma-sha (Fukien). Some translated passages have been amended with readings from the Ma-wang t'ui manuscripts. See also *Lao-tzu*.

Tsai-hua chi-hsi k'o [Ritual for Planting Flowers and Praying for Happy Events]. A vernacular rite in the regional (Hokkien) language of South Fukien. Liturgical manuscript (author's collection).

Tung-hsüan ling-pao sheng-hsüan pu-hsü chang hsü-shu [Glosses and Comments on the Stanzas of Walking the Void for Ascending to Mystery, from the Tung-hsüan Ling-pao Canon]. Six Dynasties. *Tao-tsang*, no. 614.

Tung-hsüan ling-pao tzu-jan chiu-t'ien sheng-shen yü-chang ching [Book of Precious Stanzas on the Spontaneous Birth of the Gods of the Nine Heavens, from the Tung-hsüan Ling-pao Canon]. End of the fourth century A.D. *Tao-tsang*, no. 318.

Tz'u-chih t'ung-chien [Comprehensive Mirror for Aid in Government]. By Ssu-ma Kuang (1019–1086). Peking, Chung-hua publishing Co., 1978.

Wu-shang pi-yao [Supreme Essentials (of the Tao)]. A Taoist encyclopedia of the sixth century A.D. *Tao-tsang*, no. 1138. See Lagerway, 1981.

Yin-fu ching [Book of the Hidden Concord]. Probably early seventh century. *Tao-tsang*, no. 31.

Yüan-yang tzu fa-yü [Teachings and Instructions of Master Yüan-yang]. By Chao I-chen (Yüan dynasty). *Tao-tsang*, no. 1071.

Yü-fang chih-yao [Essentials for the Jade (Bed) Room]. Ancient manual of "bedroom" techniques, now lost but reconstructed from fragments and published in the *Shuang-mei ching-an ts'ung shu* [Reprinted Works from the Shuang-mei ching-an Library] of Yeh Te-hui (1903).

Yü-fang pi-chüeh [Precious Instructions for the Jade (Bed) Room]. Ancient manual of "bedroom" techniques, now lost but reconstructed from fragments and published in the *Shuang-mei ching-an ts'ung shu* [Reprinted Works from the Shuang-mei ching-an Library] of Yeh Te-hui (1903).

Yü-huang pen-hsing ching [Book of the Fundamental Action of the Jade Emperor]. Sung dynasty. *Tao-tsang*, no. 11.

Yün-chi ch'i-ch'ien [Library of the Clouds in Seven Subdivisions). A Taoist encyclopedia of the eleventh century by Chang Chün-fang. *Tao-tsang*, no. 1032.

Yü-shu ching: see *Chiu-t'ien ying-yüan lei-sheng p'u-hua t'ien-tsun yü-shu pao-ching*.

Yü-yin fa-shih [Rites of Precious Sounds]. A collection of Taoist hymns, probably of the thirteenth century. *Tao-tsang*, no. 607.

Studies and Translations

Baldrian-Hussein, Farzeen. 1984. *Procédés secrets du joyeau magique: Traité d'alchimie taoïste du XIe siècle.* Paris: Les Deux Océans.

Berthier, Brigitte. 1988. *La Dame-du-Bord-de-l'Eau.* Nanterre: Société d'ethnologie.

Bokenkamp, Stephen R. 1983. "Sources of the Ling-pao Scriptures." *Tantric and Taoist Studies in Honour of R. A. Stein,* 2. *Mélanges Chinois et Bouddhiques,* vol. 21. Brussels: Institut Belge des Hautes Etudes Chinoises.

Boltz, Judith M. 1987. *A Survey of Taoist Literature: Tenth to Seventeenth Centuries.* Berkeley: Center for Chinese Studies.

Cedzich, Ursula-Angelika. 1987. *Das Ritual des Himmelmeister im Spiegel früher Quellen.* Ph.D. dissertation, University of Würzburg.

Chan, Wing-tsit. 1963. *The Way of Lao Tzu (Tao-te ching).* Indianapolis and New York: Bobbs-Merrill.

Chavannes, Edouard. 1895–1915. *Les mémoires historiques de Se-ma Ts'ien* (Partial translation of the *Shih-chi*). 5 vols. Paris: Leroux.

———. 1910. *Le T'ai-chan: Essai de monographie d'un culte chinois* (appendix: "Le dieu du Sol dans la Chine antique"). Annales du Museé Guimet. Paris: Leroux.

———. 1919. *Le Jet des dragons.* Memories concernant l'Asie Orientale publiés par l'Académie des Inscriptions et Belles-Lettres. vol 3. Paris: Leroux.

Chu, Kun-liang. 1991. *Les Aspects rituels du théâtre chinois.* Paris: Institut des Hautes Etudes Chinoises.

Demiéville, Paul. 1970. "Le Bouddhisme chinois." *Histoire des religions,* vol. 1, *Encyclopédie de la Pleiade,* 1288. Paris: Gallimard

———. 1972. *Les Entretiens de Lin-tsi.* Paris: Fayard.

Despeux, Catherine, trans. 1979. *Traîté d'alchimie et de physiologie taoíste,* by Chao Pi-chen. Paris: Les Deux Océans.

———. 1981. *Taiji quan: Art martial, technique de longue vie.* Paris: Editions de la Maisnie.

Doré, Henri. 1911–1918. *Recherches sur les superstitions chinoises,* 18 vols. T'usewei, Shanghai. Partially translated into English by M. Kennelly, D. J. Finn, and L. F. Mc Great: *Researches into Chinese Superstitions.* Shanghai: T'usewei, 1914–1938.

Dunstheimer, G. G. H. 1964. "Le Mouvement des Boxeurs: Documents et études publiés depuis la Deuxième Guerre mondiale." *La Revue historique* 470:387–416.

Duyvendak, J. J. L. 1953. *Tao Tö King: Le Livre de la voie et de la vertu* Paris: Maisonneuve.

Elliot, Alan J. 1955. *Chinese Spirit-Medium Cults in Singapore.* London: London School of Economics and Political Science.

Endres, Günther. 1985. *Die Sieben Meister der Volkommenen Verwirklichung. Würzburger Sino-Japonica,* vol. 13. Frankfurt: Peter Lang.

Franke, Herbert. 1977. "Bemerkungen zum Volkstümlichen Taoismus der Ming Zeit." *Oriens Extremus* 24:205–215.

Fung, Yu-lan. 1952. *A History of Chinese Philosophy*. Translated by Derk Bodde. 2 vols. Princeton: Princeton University Press.

Gernet, Jacques. 1956. *Les Aspects économiques du bouddhisme*. Hanoi: Ecole française d'Extrême-Orient.

Girardot, Norman J. 1983. *Myth and Meaning in Early Taoism*. Berkeley, Los Angeles, London: University of California Press.

Goodrich, Anne Swann. 1964. *The Peking Temple of the Eastern Peak*. Nagoya: Monumenta Serica.

Graham, A. C. 1970. "Chuang-tzu's Essay on Seeing Things Equal." *History of Religions* 9, no. 2/3:137–159.

———. 1981. *Chuang-tzu: The Inner Chapters*. London: George Allen and Unwin.

Granet, Marcel. 1919. *Fêtes et chansons anciennes de la Chine*. Paris: eroux.

———. 1920. *La Religion des Chinois*. 2d ed. Pairis: Presses Universitaires de France.

———. 1925. "Remarques sur le taoïsme ancien." *Asia Major* 2:146–151. Reprinted in *Etudes sociologiques sur la Chine*, 245–249. Paris: Presses Universitaires de France, 1953.

———. 1926. *Danses et légendes de la Chine ancienne*. Paris: Alcan.

———. 1934. *La Pensée chinoise*. Paris: Albin Michel.

Groot, J. J. M. de. 1886. *Les Fêtes annuellement célébrées à Emoui [Amoy] Étude concernant la religion populaire des Chinois*. Translated from Dutch into French by C. G. Chavannes. Annales du Musée Guimet, vols. 11 & 12. Paris: Leroux.

———. 1892–1910. *The Religious System of China*. 6 vols. Leiden: Brill.

Gulik, R. H. van. 1961. *Sexual Life in Ancient China*. Leiden: Brill.

Gyss-Vermande, Caroline. 1984. *La Vie et l'oeuvre de Huang Gongwang (1269–1354)*. Paris: Institut des Hautes Etudes Chinoises.

Hou, Ching-lang. 1975. *Monnaies d'offrande et la notion de trésorerie dans la religion chinoise*. Paris Institut des Hautes Etudes Chinoises.

Jao, Tsung-i. 1956. *Lao-tzu Hsiang-erh chu chiao-chien* [A Study on Chang Tao-ling's Hsiang-erh Commentary of Tao Tê Ching]. Published by the author. Hong Kong.

Johnson, David, Andrew J. Nathan, and Evelyn S. Rawski, eds. 1984. *Popular Culture in Late Imperial China*. Berkeley, Los Angeles, London: University of California Press.

Jordan, David K. 1972. *Gods, Ghosts and Ancestors: The Folk Religion of a Taiwanese Village*. Berkeley, Los Angeles, London: University of California Press.

Kaltenmark, Max. 1953. *Le Lie-sien tchouan*. Peking: Centre Sinologique Franco-Chinois.

———. 1960. "Ling-pao: Note sur un terme du taoïsme religieux." *Mélanges publiés par l'Institut des Hautes Etudes chinoises*, 2, 559–588. Paris: Institut des Hautes Etudes Chinoises.

———. 1965. *Lao-tseu et la taoïsme*. Paris: Editions du Seuil.

———. 1974. "Miroirs magiques." *Mélanges de Sinologie offerts à Paul Demiéville*. Vol. 2, 151–169. Paris: Institut des Hautes Etudes Chinoises.

———. 1979. "The Ideology of the T'ai-p'ing ching." In *Facets of Taoism*, edited by Holmes Welch and Anna Seidel, 19–52. New Haven: Yale University Press.

Kandel, Barbara. 1979. *Taiping jing: The Origin and Transmission of the "Scripture on General Welfare": The History of an Unofficial Text*. Published by the author. Hamburg.

Kao, Heng. 1933. "Lao-tzu cheng-ku ch'ien-chi," *Ku-shih p'ien* IV, 351–353. Shanghai: Commercial Press.

Kohn, Livia, ed. 1989. *Taoist Meditation and Longevity Techniques*. In cooperation with Yoshinobu Sakade. Ann Arbor: University of Michigan.

Kraatz, Martin, et al. 1980. *Religiöse Malerei aus Taiwan*. Marburg: Religionskundliche Sammlung der Philipps-Universität.

Lagerwey, John. 1981. *Wu-shang pi-yao: Somme taoïste du VIe sièecle*. Paris: Ecole Française d'Extrême-Orient.

Laloy, Louis. 1935. *Le Rêve du Millet Jaune* [The Dream of the Yellow Millet]. Paris: Desclée de Brouwer.

Le Blanc, Charles. 1985. *Huai-nan tzu: Philosophical Synthesis in Early Han Thought*. Hong Kong: Hong Kong University Press.

Loon, Piet van der. 1977. "Les Origines rituelles du théâtre chinois." *Journal Asiatique*, 141–168.

Maspero, Henri. 1971. *Le Taoïsme et les religions chinoises*. Paris: Gallimard.

———. 1981. *Taoism and Chinese Religion*. Translated by Frank A. Kierman. Amherst: The University of Massachusetts Press. (Translation of Maspero, 1971).

Mollier, Christine. 1990. *Une Apocalypse taoïste du Ve siècle: Le Livre des incantations divines des grottes abyssales*. Paris: Institut des Hautes Etudes Chinoises.

Needham, Joseph. 1956–1980. *Science and Civilization in China*. Vols. I to V, 4. Cambridge: Cambridge University Press.

Ngo, Van Xuyet. 1976. *Divination, magie et politique dans la Chine ancienne*. Paris: Ecole pratique des Hautes Etudes.

Overmeyer, Daniel. 1976. *Folk Buddhist Religion: Dissenting Sects in Late Traditional China*. Cambridge: Harvard University Press.

Porkert, Manfred. 1979. *Biographie d'un taoïste légendaire: Techeou Tseu-yang*. Paris: Institut des Hautes Etudes chinoises.

Read, B. E. 1939. *Famine Foods Listed in the Chiu Huang Pen Tsao*. Shanghai: Lester Institute.

Robinet, Isabelle. 1977. *Les Commentaires du Tao-tö king jusqu'au VIIe siècle*. Paris: Institut des Hautes Etudes chinoises.

———. 1979. *Méditation taoïste*. Paris: Dervy livres.

Saussure, Léopold de. 1909. *Les Origines de l'astronomie chinoise*. Leiden: Brill.

Schafer, Edward H. 1973. *The Divine Woman: Dragon Ladies and Rain Maidens in T'ang Literature*. Berkeley, Los Angeles, London: University of California Press.

————. 1977. *Pacing the Void: T'ang Approaches to the Stars*. Berkeley, Los Angeles, London: University of California Press.

————. 1978. "The Jade Woman of Greatest Mystery." *History of Religions* 17:387–398.

Schipper, Kristofer. 1963. *L'Empereur Wou des Han dans la légende taoïste*. Paris: Ecole Française d'Extrême-Orient.

————. 1967. "The Divine Jester: Some Remarks on the Gods of the Chinese Marionette Theater." *Bulletin of the Institute of Ethnology* 21. Taipei: Academia Sinica: 81–95.

————. 1969. "Science, magie et mystique du corps: Notes sur le taoïsme et la sexualité." In *Jeux des nuages et de la pluie*, edited by M. Benedeley, 11–42. Frieburg: Office du Livre.

————. 1971. "Démonologie chinoise." In *Génies, Anges et Démons*, Sources orientales 8:405–427. Paris: Le Seuil.

————. 1974. "The Written Memorial in Taoist Ceremonies." In *Religion and Ritual in Chinese Society*, edited by A. Wolf, 309–324. Stanford: Stanford University Press.

————. 1975a. *Le Feng-teng: Rituel taoïste*. Paris: Ecole Française d'Extrême-Orient.

————. 1975b. *Concordance du Houang-t'ing king*. Paris: Ecole Française d'Extrême-Orient.

————. 1977. "Neighborhood Cult Associations in Traditional Tainan." In *The City in Late Imperial China*, edited by G. William Skinner, 651–678. Stanford: Stanford University Press.

————. 1978a. "Messianismes et millénarismes dans la Chine ancienne." *Actes du XXVIe Congrès d'Etudes chinoises. Cina*, suppl. 2. Rome, ISMEO, 1978:31–47.

————. 1978b. "The Taoist Body." *History of Religions* (Chicago) 17, nos. 3–4:355–386.

————. 1979. "Le Livre du Centre de Lao-tseu. *Nachrichten der Gesellschaft für Natur und Völkerkunde Ostasiens* 125 (1979):75–80.

————. 1985a. "Seigneurs royaux, dieux des épidémies." *Archives des sciences sociales des religions* 59, no. 1:31–41.

————. 1985b. "Vernacular and Classical Ritual in Taoism." *The Journal of Asian Studies* 45, no. 1 (November 1985): 21–57.

————. 1985c. "Taoist Ordination Ranks in the Tun-huang Manuscripts." *Religion und Philosophie in Ostasien* (Festschrift für Hans Steininger, Würzburg, 127–149.

————. 1986a. "Chiens de paille et tigres en papier." *Extrême-Orient / Extrême-Occident* (Paris) 6:83–95.

————. 1986b. "Comment on crée un lieu-saint local: à propos de *Danses et légendes de la Chine ancienne* de Marcel GRANET." *Etudes chinoises* (Paris) 4, no. 2:41–61.

————. 1986c. "Taoist Ritual and the Local Cults of the T'ang Dynasty." In *Tantric and Taoist Studies in Honour of R. A. Stein*, edited by Michel Strickmann, 812–834. Vol. 3. Brussels: Institut Belge der Haute, Etudes Chinoises.

————. 1987. "Master Chao I-chen and the Ch'ing-wei School of Taoism." In *Dôkyô to Shûkyô Bunka,* edited by Akizuki Kan'ei, 724–715. Tokyo: Hirakawa Shuppan.

————. 1990a. "Mu-lien Plays in Taoist Liturgical Context." In *Ritual Opera, Operatic Ritual,* edited by David Johnson, 127–154. Berkeley, Los Angeles, Oxford: University of California Press.

————. 1990b. "Purifier l'autel, tracer les limites à travers les rituels taoïstes." In *Tracés de foundation,* edited by Marcel Détienne, 31–47. Louvain and Paris: Peeters.

————. 1990c. "The Cult of Pao-sheng ta-ti and Its Spreading to Taiwan: A Case Study of *Fen-hsiang.*" In *Development and Decline in Fukien Province inthe 17th and 18th Centuries,* edited by E. Vermeer, 397–416. Leiden: Brill.

————. 1990b. "A Study of *Buxu:* Taoist Liturgical Hymn and Dance." In *Studies of Taoist Rituals and Music of Today,* edited by Pen-yeh Tsao and Daniel P. L. Law, 110–120. Hong Kong: Chinese University of Hong Kong.

Schipper, Kristofer, and Hsiu-huei Wang. 1986. "Progressive and Regressive Time-Cycles in Taoist Ritual." In *Time, Science and Society in China and the West,* edited by J. T. Fraser, N. Lawrence, and F. C. Huber (*The Study of Time,* 5), 185–205. Amherst: The University of Massachusetts Press.

Schmidt, Hans-Hermann. 1984. "Die Hundertachtzig Vorschriften von Lao-chün." In *Religion und Philosophie in Ostasien* (Festschrift für Hans Steininger), edited by G. Naundorf, K.-H. Pohl, and H.-H. Schmidt. Würzburg: Köningshausen und Neumann.

Seidel, Anna. 1969. *La Divinisation de Lao-tseu sous les Han.* Paris: Ecole Française d'Extrême-Orient.

————. 1970. "The Image of the Perfect Ruler in Early Taoist Messianism: Lao-tzu and Li Hung." *History of Religions* 9, nos. 3–4:216–247.

Sivin, Nathan. 1968. *Chinese Alchemy: Preliminary Studies.* Cambridge: Harvard University Press.

————. 1978. "On the Word 'Taoist' as a Source of Perplexity." *History of Religions* 17:303–330.

————. 1980. "The Theoretical Background of Elixir Alchemy." In J. Needham, *Science and Civilization in China,* 210–324. Vol. 5, 4. Cambridge: Cambridge University Press.

Soymié, Michel. 1954. "Le Lo-feou chan: Étude de géographie religieuse." *Bulletin de L'Ecole Française d'Extrême-Orient* 48:1–139.

Stein, Rolf A. 1942. "Jardins en miniature de l'Extrême-Orient: Le Monde en petit." *Bulletin de l'Ecole française d'Extrême-Orient* 42:1–104. Hanoi.

————. 1957. "Les religions de l'Orient et de l'Extrême-Orient." *l'Encyclopédie française,* 54–55. Vol. 19. Paris.

————. 1963. "Remarques sur les mouvements politico-religieux au IIe siècle ap. J.-C." *T'oung Pao* 50:1–78.

————. 1972. "Les Fêtes de cuisine du taoïsme religieux." *Annuaire du Collège de France,* 431–440. Paris: Collège de France.

————. 1979. "Religious Taoism and Popular Religion from the Second to

Seventh Centuries." In *Facets of Taoism,* edited by Holmes Welch and Anna Seidel. 53–82. New Haven: Yale University Press.

———. 1987. *Le monde en petit: jardins en miniature et habitations dans la pensée d'Extrême-Orient.* Paris: Flammarion.

Strickmann, Michel. 1979. "On the Alchemy of T'ao Hung-ching." In *Facets of Taoism,* edited by Holmes Welch and Anna Seidel, 123–192. New Haven: Yale University Press.

———. 1981. *Le Taoïsme du Mao-chan: chronique d'une révélation.* Paris: Institut des Hautes Etudes Chinoises du Collège de France.

Sun, Ching-yang. 1950. "Pang-men wai-tao chi" [Notes on Devious Teachings and External Schools]. In *Tso-tao pang-men siao-shu chi-yao* [Essentials of the Minor Practices from Devious Teachings and Schools]. *Tao-tsang ching-hua* ed. Taipei: Tzu-yu press.

Sun, Kai-t'i. 1952. *K'uei-lei-hi k'ao-yüan* [A Study on Marionettes in China]. Shanghai: Shanghai shang-tsa press.

Tsiuen, T. H. 1962. *Written on Bamboo and Silk.* Chicago: The University of Chicago Press.

Verellen, Franciscus. 1989. *Du Guangting (850–933): Taoïste de cour à la fin de la Chine médiévale.* Paris: Institut des Hautes Etudes Chinoises.

Wagner, Rudolf. 1973. "Lebensstil und Drogen im Chinesischen Mittelalter." *T'oung Pao* 59, nos. 1–5:79–177.

Waley, Arthur. 1931. *The Travels of an Alchemist.* London: Routledge and Kegan Paul.

———. 1934. *The Way and Its Power* (a translation of the *Tao-te ching*). London: George Allen and Unwin.

———. 1939. *Three Ways of Thought in Ancient China.* London: George Allen and Unwin.

———. 1955. *The Nine Songs: A Study of Shamanism in Ancient China.* London: George Allen and Unwin.

Ware, James A. 1966. *Alchemy, Medicine, Religion in the China of A.D. 320: The Nei P'ien of Ko Hung (Pao-p'u tzu).* Cambridge: M.I.T. Press.

Wasson, R. Gordon. 1968. *Soma, the Divine Mushroom.* New York: Hartcourt Brace and World Co.

Watson, Burton. 1970. *The Complete Works of Chuang-tzu.* New York: Columbia University Press.

Watson, James L., and Evelyn S. Rawski, eds. 1988. *Death Ritual in Late Imperial and Modern China.* Berkeley, Los Angeles, London: University of California Press.

Weber, Max. 1964. *The Religion of China, Confucianism and Taoism.* Translated and edited by H. H. Gerth, with an introduction by C. K. Yang. New York: The Free Press.

Welch, Holmes H. 1957. *Taoism: The Parting of the Way.* Boston: Beacon Press.

———. 1966. *The Practice of Chinese Buddhism.* Cambridge: Harvard University Press.

Welch, Holmes H., and Anna Seidel, eds. 1979. *Facets of Taoism.* New Haven: Yale University Press.

Wilhelm, Richard. 1968. *The I Ching or Book of Changes*. The Richard Wilhelm Translation rendered into English by Cary F. Branes. Foreword by C. G. Jung. Preface to the Third Edition by Helmut Wilhelm. Bollingen Series XIX. Princeton University Press.

Wolf, Arthur P., ed. 1974. *Religion and Ritual in Chines Society*. Stanford: Stanford University Press.

Yü, Anthony. 1977. *The Journey to the West*. Chicago: University of Chicago Press.

Zürcher, Erik. 1959. *The Buddhist Conquest of China*. Leiden: Brill.

———. 1980. "Buddhist Influence on Early Taoism." *T'oung Pao* 66, nos. 1–3:84–147.

Index

Designer: U.C. Press Staff
Compositor: Maple-Vail Book Manufacturing Group
Text: 10/13 Galliard
Display: Galliard
Printer: Maple-Vail Book Manufacturing Group
Binder: Maple-Vail Book Manufacturing Group